C000139119

Sinicizing International Relations

Sinicizing International Relations

Self, Civilization, and Intellectual Politics in Subaltern East Asia

Chih-yu Shih

SINICIZING INTERNATIONAL RELATIONS
Copyright © Chih-yu Shih, 2013.

First published in 2013 by
PALGRAVE MACMILLAN®
in the United States—a division of St. Martin's Press LLC,
175 Fifth Avenue, New York, NY 10010.

Where this book is distributed in the UK, Europe and the rest of the World,
this is by Palgrave Macmillan, a division of Macmillan Publishers Limited,
registered in England, company number 785998, of Houndmills,
Basingstoke, Hampshire RG21 6XS.

Palgrave Macmillan is the global academic imprint of the above
companies and has companies and representatives throughout the world.

Palgrave® and Macmillan® are registered trademarks in the United
States, the United Kingdom, Europe and other countries.

ISBN: 978–1–137–28944–5

Chapter 2 originally appeared in *The Newsletter*, no. 60 (summer 2012). Permission
to reprint is courtesy of the International Institute for Asian Studies.
Chapter 6 originally appeared in *Millennial Asia*, vol. 1, no. 1, as "Anomaly as
a Method: Collect Chinese Micro-theories of Transition." Permission to reprint
is courtesy of the Association for Asia Scholars.
Chapter 7 originally appeared in *Asian Politics and Policy*, vol. 1, no. 2 (April/June
2009), as "A Country of No Significance? Interpreting the *Japan Times*'s Inattentive
Approach to Chinese Affairs in 1997." Permission to reprint is courtesy of John
Wiley and Sons. © 2009 Policy Studies Organization.

Library of Congress Cataloging-in-Publication Data

Shih, Chih-yu, 1958–
    Sinicizing international relations : self, civilization, and intellectual
politics in subaltern East Asia / Chih-yu Shih.
        pages   cm
    Includes bibliographical references.
    ISBN 978–1–137–28944–5 (alk. paper)
    1. China—Foreign economic relations—East Asia.   2. East Asia—Foreign
economic relations—China.   3. China—Foreign economic relations.
    I. Title.
    HF1604.Z4E18425 2013
    327.5105—dc23   2012033753

A catalogue record of the book is available from the British Library.

Design by Integra Software Services
First edition: February 2013
10 9 8 7 6 5 4 3 2 1

Contents

Part IV   Worlding East Asia through China: Multisited Perspectives

List of Tables

List of Figures

Preface

Civilizational history and individualized intellectual possibilities lie at the two extremes on the dimension of identity, with endless sites in between. The political nature of identity exists in the impossibility of a stable identity. Identity is always about strategic choice. Fluidity in identity across time and place can be instantaneous and strong under globalization. Fluidity of this sort generates the wish for a permanent solution but unavailability of any stable solution often leads to frustration that requires and produces mechanisms of projection onto a scapegoat. Traveling to multiple sites, with each either suffering or enjoying its own identity matrix, resembles an in-depth tourist activity that provides opportunities for one to appreciate politics of possibilities and broaden one's mind.

For this reason, this book brings forth reflections based upon personal encounters in Korea, Japan, China, Vietnam, Mongolia, India, Russia, Czech Republic, Poland, Thailand, Malaysia, and Singapore. The research project of this book aims at opening and sharing. Travelling physically to different communities, in combination with travelling intellectually to different discursive constructions, is at the same time practicing self-criticism. Colleagues from all over the world who have generously supported my self-criticism with their own self-criticisms contribute to and provoke thinking and changes of thinking that have come together in this project's reflections on civilizations, nations, and (sub)ethnic groups.

Due to limited space and fading memory, I cannot thank all of my colleagues in any exhaustive manner. The list is too long. They include Jamesran Bayasakh, David Blaney, late Vladimir Ganshin, Gustaaf Geeraerts, Valentin Golovachev, Svetlana Gorbunova, Peizhong He, Fu Hu, Marcin Jacoby, Peter Katzenstein, Hirano Kenichiro, Doohee Kim, Suryadinata Leo, Lily H. M. Ling, Olga Lomova, Colin Mackerras, Prapin Manomaivibool, Reena Marwah, Jeanne Miasnikova, Yujiro Murata, Chow

Bing Negow, Shigeo Nishimura, Hajime Osawa, Thi Hue Phung, Swaran Singh, Gunter Schubert, Jae-hoon Song, Sharad Soni, Bang Anh Tuan, Zbigniew Wesolowski, Sin Kiong Wong, Hongmei Yao, K. K. Yeoh, and many momentarily unnamed others who have been equally significant in their enriching lessons to the research of this book.

Over a span of 12 years, grants that have enabled all the meetings and reunion come from Taiwan's National Science Council, Ministry of Education, National Taiwan University, National Sun Yat-sen University, National Cheng Kung University, Mongolian and Tibetan Affairs Commission, Chiang Ching-kuo Foundation, Taiwan Democracy Foundation, National Taiwan University's Political Science Foundation, Center for China Studies Abroad of Chinese Academy of Social Sciences, and many younger colleagues who have generously supported either the civilizational studies or the studies of intellectual history with hard-saved surplus of their own research accounts.

Rongjen Hsu and Guizhi Li have been two most careful and diligent executive secretaries. It was they who had effectively managed an impossible array of agendas and receipts of various languages to comply with bureaucratic procedures of all sorts and all over the world. Their travelling in the world's accounting systems is more extensive than anyone else that I have known.

Introduction: Transcending National Identities

The purpose of this book is to question the notion of a rising Chinese nation by deconstructing the possibility of looking at China in its entirety. China rising has attracted an enormous amount of scholarly attention in the twenty-first century. However, influenced by their own historical and philosophical backgrounds, and the mundane political and economic conditions in which they live and work, writers actually treat China in a variety of ways. How one reads meanings out of the image of China rising intrinsically reflects one's own encountering and choice. The resulting vast epistemological and civilizational difference between Asian, European, and American approaches to China is no longer a secret.[1] Even those seemingly sharing overlapping research agendas in any particular community nevertheless contrive to make contrasting strategic choices of theoretical and ideological perspectives. That said, most China scholars decide not to tackle or even acknowledge the embarrassing reality that different scholars study different notions of what China is. Adding to the textbook list of theoretical positions, one could present a geographically impressive array of views on China rising, coming out of South and Southeast Asia, Russia, Tibet, Australia, postsocialist Europe, and so on. In all these national and civilizational communities, political considerations and memories of historical relationships with premodern China intertwine with each other to produce distinctive opinions about the way China rising should be studied today. In a nutshell, no writing on China rising can avoid the self-involvement of either the writers or their readers.

Studying the rise of China in international relations in a global age involves almost immediately interactions between two sets of identities—consisting of the observers' identities and the identities of "their" China. Each set comprises choices at least at three levels: civilizational, national, and (sub)ethnic. Take, for instance, Mongolia. Mongolia is representative of a nomadic and prairie civilization as opposed to a maritime, agricultural, or industrial civilization. It is simultaneously a sovereign nation seeking a potential alliance with Japan or the United States in order to balance its two powerful neighbors, namely, China and Russia. Furthermore, Mongolia denotes an ethnic group in the Chinese autonomous region of Inner Mongolia, with a population larger than that of the Republic of Mongolia. Needless to say, reference to China evokes similar images of civilizations, nations, and ethnic groups. When a self-regarding Mongolian scholar does research on China, or inversely, a self-regarding Chinese scholar does research on Mongolia, the scholar (subject) should know from which and on which identity he or she writes. Accordingly, the intellectual choice of identity becomes intrinsic to international relations scholarship. Any choice or change of choice designates an institutional identity that bears upon the distribution of rights and duties, public as well as private. In addition, the choice affects the balance of social relationships. Thus, the scholarship treating such choices is by necessity multisited, political, and global.

Due to widespread perceptions that China is on the rise, designating China's identity has become essentially a political matter. It could be a coagulatory decision that reinforces a specific identity and relationship for China. Or, alternatively, it could be a transformational decision that ushers in a new, different identity for China. However, the meaning of such a decision or choice is rarely unilaterally determined by the scholar, nor is it invariable over time. The possibility of what such choice signifies constitutes a discursive site of constant contestation. Such contestation centers on whether or not China should be viewed as a threat and to whom this threat is posed. Moreover, the contestation implies how one should treat those agents who carry the identity of China, willingly or reluctantly. This is why studying China is a political as well as personal engagement, not to mention studying the international relations of China. This political engagement speaks to both China's identity and the researcher's self-identity and could therefore be highly controversial and volatile over time.

Between any civilizational and individual identities, there could be an unlimited number of cultural sites where one can acquire perspectives through learning, practicing, or simulating particular identity strategies that make sense to the sites that home the available alternatives for the time being. Not only could the choice of identity at a particular site be unstable over time, but the choice of site in itself could be unstable, reducing the choice of identity to no more than an act of role-playing, except that the latter usually requires a conscious, context-specific, and immediate decision. Globalization obscures the distinction between identity and role due to its increasingly destabilizing effects on self-other relations. Intellectual paths that come through the transformation—overthrowing, lingering on, disappearing, reproducing, fading, or backfiring—of the party-state leadership in China as well as its foreign relations are compelled to encounter such dislocation of self-other relations, which generates frustration, hope, emptiness, fear, opportunity and other types of anxiety. Sites are accordingly as much intellectual, psychological, and social as they are physical.

Reflections on the choice of site from which one has written different things on or about China could begin more easily with recollections of one's traveling experiences—as an immigrant, a student abroad, a conference participant, a visiting scholar, a field researcher, a tourist, or any of those other roles noted or unnoted on one's curriculum vitae—in which encountering that incurs the constant making of choices is pervasive. Similar pressures to make a different choice are likewise experienced when hosting, willingly or not, arriving travelers in various forms—when surrendering to their colonial rule, hiring their services, reading their writings, subscribing to their religion, consuming their products, marrying them, and so on. Travel is intrinsically a method of China studies and also a methodology of Sinicization.

This book respects the authors and readers of all the distinctive academic traditions as well as their traveling experiences, but it bypasses them to a certain extent. On the one hand, each of them deserves an entire book just to touch on the intellectual background that has prepared them to approach China rising in their own particular way. Their national and civilizational distinctiveness is typical and normal in their own context. On the other hand, and in comparison, there are others who write from a less noticeable or established national distinctiveness in terms of epistemological disposition toward China. These are subaltern writers who can demonstrate an even more powerful agency for the deconstruction of China, intended or otherwise, because they are more flexible in combining and recombining cultural resources at the individual level. In fact, the borders of China, within as well as without, including Hong Kong, Taiwan, Korea, Mongolia, and Tibet, are probably the least noted sites of original and yet silenced thinking on China and China rising.[2] Those contesting the meanings of China rising brought forth by globalization, together with the phenomenon of China rising itself, should also include at least two additional groups, namely, diasporic Chinese and Asian scholars writing on China from outside the land of their birth, and migrant and indigenous residents reflecting upon their association and identification with national China from within its territories. A further group could be composed of a particular kind of diasporic Western male scholars who have married Chinese women and established their careers in China.

In other words, the individualized intellectual tracks of scholars and the Chinese people they study show empirically how China as it is normally understood in the international relations literature is both possible and impossible. This multisited approach to China rising at the individual level is, in itself, a response to the popular belief in China rising, albeit constantly reinterpreted.³ China rising, as it has been written, read, and practiced everywhere, compels individuals who, frequently as well as sporadically, have to cope with the symbols and narratives of China in their daily activities and apply different meanings to it on different occasions. Chinese leaders usually react negatively toward any politicization of such multisited possibilities and are used to connecting it with what they see as a Western conspiracy to divide China. They could be right to some extent. Accordingly, national epistemological traditions and international relations, where Chinese leaders hope to secure China's national identity, collude in reproducing the entirety of the Chinese nationality. This is why multisited reflections on how the symbols of China are appropriated and reappropriated in various individualized conditions are so different, full of surprises, and worthy of recording.

To set up the epistemological conditions for a multisited reinterpretation of what China and China rising represent, this book begins with the historical trajectory of China's painstaking reconciliation of its innate civilizational identity with an acquired national identity. From their beginning, international relations have been a European and North American engagement, and the rest of the world used to struggle between joining and resisting. At the beginning of the twenty-first century, resistance seemed to be a long forgotten option. In fact, throughout the twentieth century, people once outside international relations were left with, at best, two ungenerous alternatives: striving either to win recognition and equality for their nation-state or to reform the international relations of the time. Among the latecomers, Chinese leaders and intellectuals have been no exception and have shifted indecisively between the two strategies.⁴ The May Fourth Movement of 1919, which took place during the Paris Conference and led to China's abstention from signing the Treaty of Versailles and which occurred less than eight years after Republican China was declared a sovereign nation-state, attempted both recognition and resistance at the same time. It called for all the world's weak and vulnerable nationalities to unite in opposition to the imperialist West and strove to achieve integrity and equality for each of them. This hesitant attitude toward existing international relations has lingered on, plaguing contemporary Chinese foreign policy to the extent that the purpose of international relations remains unclear to Chinese leaders.

Faced with the nascent image of China rising, Chinese intellectuals cannot help but seriously consider and articulately assert China's role in international relations. A shared appeal to civilizational identity comes to their rescue as they seek meaning in international relations for the future as well as the past. The two most noteworthy attempts to find this meaning that have attracted widespread curiosity and provoked enormous anxiety among the international relations (IR; thereafter, as an academic discipline) communities of Europe and North America are those of Yan Xuetong and Zhao Tingyang.[5] Recognition is still a purpose of their endeavors but the mood is one of resistance. Yan represents a kind of scientific antagonism when he contends that, historically, IR reality has always been hierarchical; thus, the principle of balance of power among equals that has prevailed over two centuries is no more than a myth. He uses Chinese historical records to demonstrate such a realist hierarchy, relying specifically on the Chinese legalist tradition. In comparison, Zhao tries to prescribe for the world a romantic philosophy of *tianxia,* one that is embedded in Taoist and Confucian teachings and that requires no more than a change of cognitive perspective—albeit an unrealistic one—in order for international relations to be characterized by peace and harmony.

Given that both writers are extensively studied and cited elsewhere, it is only necessary to point out the civilizational ironies in their works before moving away from the ontology of the nation-state. First of all, their IR theorization is, at the same time, counter-IR. For example, appropriating Chinese cultural resources for use in contemporary international relations testifies to the persistence of civilizational, hence nonrational, components in Chinese nation-building. Nonetheless, they intellectually Sinicize IR theorization in contrasting manners. Yan relies on the alleged normalcy of hierarchy to explain away the image of the China threat conjured up by China's rapidly expanding influence in international relations. The balance of power among alleged equals is a disguised conspiracy to legitimate American hierarchy, whereas Chinese hierarchy is epistemologically a hidden plea for China's equality. Thus, Yan uses civilizational resources to negotiate for China's equal status as a nation. His hierarchy appears polemical in terms of how many hierarchies there are or whose hierarchy is negotiable. Zhao's *tianxia,* in contrast, transcends the dichotomy of hierarchy versus equality, but nevertheless philosophizes everyone into a self-content worldview, which is presumably all-encompassing, nonnegotiable, and even disciplinary. What is missing in the *tianxia* philosophy, however, is something that can make sense of the prevailing violence, historically as well as practically, in Chinese international relations.

This book will begin by depicting Chinese foreign policy as a response to the arrival of modern IR, a response that eventually recombined Chinese cultural resources into a single harmonious realism in the spirit of recognition and resistance. Harmony is an echo of Zhao's *tianxia* philosophy, whereas realism embodies Yan's quest for recognition of China's status. Hierarchical realism answers to the Chinese pursuit of equality between China and the United States; the harmonious worldview preserves Chinese supremacy in a lofty gesture of welcoming the coexistence of all differences. On the one hand, realist discourses that recombine Chinese civilizational identities are never realist, because power and security are neither absolute nor tangible. On the other hand, Chinese harmony is hardly harmonious, but is rather highly sensitive to and disciplinary toward breaches of ritual or role expectation, lest these should invite challenges on the periphery that would have the effect of destroying order. Symbolic shows of determination to rectify improper role performance are essential for dramatizing symbolic concessions at other times, as well as for enhancing the appeal of the *tianxia* system. A Sinicized IR is defined by harmonious realism, and it reflects high politics among those who act, think, and write on behalf of national China. This Sinicized IR abandons the Chinese practices of the past, for example those used under the tribute system, which are entirely incompatible with modern IR. It also transforms IR theorization and practice to bring IR more in line with the self-content Chinese worldview.

Given the abundant literature on the advantages and disadvantages of having an IR theory with Chinese characteristics at the national and international level, a much broader range of reflections on Sinicized IR in practice has been largely ignored. The main part of this book, therefore, deals with a few subaltern perspectives that come from those who do not act, think, or write on behalf of national China, but nonetheless reconcile and recombine different identity resources embedded in divergent civilizational trajectories with respect to IR theorization. Specifically, the book deals with Sinophone intellectuals who write China from outside China proper, especially Taiwanese and American Chinese. It also reports from the lower echelons inside China proper, such as rank-and-file urban dwellers as well as mountain villagers, none of whom can afford the luxury of writing for an abstract national China. Finally, this work reports on a few selected perspectives that arise from surrounding communities and trans-communities, including Japanese, Korean, and Asian diasporic intellectuals. Each of these multisited voices reflects an individualized kind of encountering, in combination with a choice of one identity strategy out of many that coexist in an available repertoire of civilizational discourses. This way, Sinicized IR is more a process of breaking the monopoly of European and North American IR and Chinese counter-IR. On the bases of IR and Chinese civilization, as well as other cultural resources, the process of bringing China into IR opens up endless opportunities for civilizational learning as well as individualized self-searching.

Part I analyzes two discourses of Chinese foreign policy that have emerged in the twenty-first century. Both are responses to the image of a Chinese threat that accompanies the impression of China rising and Sinicization. Chapter 1 introduces the dialectic style of harmonious realism. The purpose of Chinese foreign policy analysis that recommends concession is different from analysis that asserts national interests. Making concessions breeds an atmosphere of trust in the development of a harmonious relationship, whereas asserting national interests copes with immediate threats and opportunities. Threat usually refers to de jure and de facto territorial integrity, whereas opportunity refers to economic gains. Thus, the failure to decide the purpose of Chinese foreign policy analysis creates China's self-role conflict. Should China be only an ego state capable of defending its own national borders, protecting sovereign rights, maintaining regional order, accruing economic prosperity, and enhancing its international prestige? Or should China be a role state ready to make a concession by hedging a threat or foregoing an opportunity? Avoiding the horns of this dilemma, Beijing can now take advantage of the increase in its national capacity to create ambiguity in a confrontational situation. It can either painstakingly yield without clearly yielding or confront without clearly confronting. Ambiguity preserves flexibility for Beijing in contriving its subsequent response as the situation develops. Indeed, in this case, indecisiveness is the essence of Beijing's harmonious realism.

Chapter 2 further develops the notion of harmonious realism introduced in Chapter 1 and argues that China's Africa policy is one of "harmonious racism." Officially, the call for peaceful coexistence of different political systems symbolizes China's normative foreign policy and constitutes its soft power in the developing world in general, and in Africa in particular. Socially as well as culturally, however, the Chinese display a racist attitude toward the darker skinned Africans, although racism does not lead to practical policy discrimination nor does it constrain China from treating African nations as ideological, strategic, and global governance allies. On the one hand, China's Africa policy is characterized by classic realism in that China does what most other major powers do in Africa: they seek economic opportunities in terms of resources, markets, and labor. On the other hand, China manifests a contrast in its pursuit of a harmonious world with due respect to cultural differences. As a result of China's preoccupation with harmony and aid, its concessions to African nations are made at the state level, even if racism influences practices from time to time at the individual and corporate levels. The rise of China as an advocate of harmony has caught the world's attention. However, with the seeming Sinicization in Africa, the question remains as to the kind of soft power China needs to achieve its goal without causing anxiety among observers. The concern is more pronounced in the case of realists who do not believe a word the Chinese say about harmony.

Part II discusses how other Chinese with their own identity conditions respond to China rising. Chapter 3 proposes that China scholarship in Taiwan is constituted by the choices scholars make between encountered and constantly reinterpreted imaginations of how China's names, identities, and images are contextualized. Due to Taiwan's colonial history, its Civil War and Cold War legacies, and its internal cleavages, China scholarship in Taiwan consists of strategic shifting among the Japanese, American, and Chinese approaches to China as well as their combination and recombination. The mechanism of choice, including travel that orients, reorients, and disorients existing views on China, thereby produces conjunctive scholarship. The rich repertoire of views on China, together with the politics of identity, challenges the objectivist stance of the social sciences to the extent that no view on China is free of political implications and politicized social scrutiny. Concerns over exigent propriety in a social setting are internal to knowledge production. Therefore, understanding the process by which all the historically derived approaches inform China scholarship in Taiwan through the mechanism of encountering, reveals both the uncertain nature of knowledge in general and the uncertain meanings associated with China anywhere in the world in particular.

Chapter 4 compares the different approaches toward Chinese IR of Sinophone scholars outside China. Although China-centered studies are dominated by European or North American writers critical of mainstream China studies, the China-centered approach in China studies is not self-evident. Possible responses from overseas Chinese writers reveal at least two kinds of China-centrism: one based upon China's rise and development need, to which pre-1949 history is irrelevant, and the other embedded in Chinese history and cultural tradition, whose historiography trivializes the span of 60 years after 1949. In effect, both approaches defend China from becoming just another case of general propositions derived from the mainstream agenda and its critics. However, they have yet to give birth to an epistemic community based on nascent China-centric consciousness. Chapter 4 shows that China studies among overseas Chinese scholars are political and value laden, with each being embedded in an epistemological context. In the future, China studies in China could serve as a possible point of integration, although remaining political in nature.

In Part III, the process of Sinicization refers to China under the pressure of deconstruction. Chapter 5 gathers evidence of this deconstruction in urban life, with respect to political stability. China's *wei wen* (maintaining stability) policy, however resolute or scaled, does not unilaterally determine its results. It can cause displeasure, alienation, and even resistance in some cases. The international media attends specifically to these psychological possibilities. A study of how *wei wen* can succeed necessitates an examination of the thought processes through which people who are not directly involved in *wei wen* respond. These processes prompt people to choose sides based on the assumption that structural factors, including economic growth, ideological justification, organizational capacity, and income disparity, do not create immediate choices. Multisited observation serves as a method for examining how ordinary people can embrace a national perspective that allows them to sympathize with the Chinese Communist Party's (CCP's) *wei wen* attempt. This chapter reports on self-Sinicization, which is a common mechanism that can trigger the collectivist mindset of members of a society, thus leading them to favor stability. When people from different sites share a similar mechanism of self-Sinicization, their choice to side with the CCP is likely to be maintained as long as a trigger is present.

Chapter 6 further reads the deconstructive potential in a kind of Sinicized modernity in village China. The teleology of transition to capitalism in general, and China's turn to capitalism in particular, prescribes for observers an academic agenda preoccupied with the conditions for the growth of capitalism. Thus far, studies of transition in China have lacked bottom–up, past-oriented, and inside–out perspectives that would allow the formation of discourse among the masses, presumably driven by the force of transition to respond from their indigenous positions. Hence, the purpose of this chapter is to find the possible stories that could emerge if such perspectives— typically not intelligible from the transition point of view—were transformed into transition narratives. Epistemologically speaking, interpreting the case at hand as an anomaly could be a useful methodology that would ameliorate the deterministic and teleological proclivity in the current literature on transition. In this way, agents of transition become more than agents; they gain subjectivity by acquiring microperspectives on transition that are not allowed in the teleology toward liberalism. Agents of transition could participate in transition research by articulating, consciously as well as subconsciously, how they have strategically practiced transition, turning researchers of macrotransition into equal partners in transition.

Part IV illustrates how China's rise and its Sinicizing effects are bringing about a variety of adaptations in multiple sites. Chapter 7 uses the case of how, and seeks to explain why, *The Japan Times* takes a backseat approach to events in China. Specifically, the Japanese English-language newspaper demonstrated a lack of interest in events that took place in China in 1997, and by doing so it seems to be actualizing a familiar identity strategy of withdrawal. For such modern Japanese thinkers as Nishida Kitaro, Takeuchi Yoshimi, and Mizoguchi Yuzo, withdrawal is a common strategy in dealing with the issue of universality. This is a surprising observation, given the vast differences in their approaches when narrating Japanese identities. Accordingly, China has defined the condition from which withdrawal seems imperative for Japan to achieve modernity. *The Japan Times'* apparent lack of attention to China may serve as the contemporary example of "withdrawing for universality," thus pitting different narrators against one another to show the indecisive condition *The Japan Times* has created for all of them.

Contemporary East Asian IR as depicted in Chapter 8 began with the collapse of the Sinic hierarchy, but the image of China at the top has continued to haunt the pursuit of independent and equal status undertaken by China's neighbors. For over a century, authors writing about East Asia have creatively appropriated cultural and historical resources to downplay Chinese components in their modern identity. In practical terms, this led to Japan's imperialist civilizing undertaking in China. Against this backdrop, Mizoguchi Yuzo's notion of Sinic *kitai* (i.e., the basic substance, body history, underlying concepts, and essential being of China), whereby China's path is exclusively Chinese, becomes an epistemological prescription for Japan's obsessive–compulsive drive for Asian modernity. Many other past participants in the Sinic order cannot allow themselves to appreciate the self-neutralizing *kitai* discourse lest their historical paths should be reduced to a Chinese derivative. Their otherwise insignificant choices—unnoticeable to colonial and imperialist forces—nevertheless constitute a variety of creative "worlding" and "reworlding" possibilities. In response to Mizoguchi's call for a *kitai* method to preempt any possible return of imperialism in Japan, this chapter glances through the Korean, Mongolian, Vietnamese, and Southeast Asian literatures on China. These represent China, each in accordance with its distinctive trajectory, in a way that is opposed to the Kitai method. These still evolving narratives suggest that recognition of the enhanced relevance of the old Sinic order amidst the atmosphere of China's rise has never been the prerogative of any one major power.

In an effort to understand the mechanism of cultural Sinicization, the discursive analysis presented in Chapter 9 shows that the four selected academics consciously manage their liminal positions through scholarship—as illustrated in Kim's synthetic analysis, Iriye's centrist mediation, Tan's geocivilizational critique, and Wong's scientific Chineseness. In their work on China, there are at least two common puzzles that call for solutions. First, how do they place themselves in the Sinic world: does China belong to an identical order or a different ontological order? Second, how do they want China to be evaluated: should China conform to a Western standard expressed in values that are claimed to be universal? The professional affiliations of both Kim and Iriye in the United States seem to push them toward a universalist prescription for China's place in the world. The peripheral relationship between Kim's and Wong's homes, on the one hand, and China, on the other, pushes them, instead, toward a shared ontological identity. By contrast, freed from both American affiliation and a sense of belonging to the periphery, Tan has a different and more innocent sense of China. Given the constraining civilizational positions in which they are situated as well as the empowering cultural resources at their disposal, all four scholars have to decide, discursively, professionally, and personally, how they should formulate their own identity strategies and styles.

A brief note on methodology would be helpful before embarking upon the wild search for possibilities in the following pages. The book adopts a utilitarian approach to the selection of research methods that are functional to the gathering and deriving of philosophical intelligence from less-heard sources. They are generally interpretive methods. Personal interviews, on-site observation, textual analysis, deductive and inductive categorization, literature review, and multisited comparison are all legitimate in this book. In addition to English, data come in different tongues, including Korean, Vietnamese, Japanese, Mongolian, and Chinese, which often involves local dialects and ethnic languages other than *putonghua*. Over-reading at times is deliberate to some extent in order to retrieve, recombine, and reformulate possibilities that are not immediately apparent. There is not much positivist hypothesis testing or formal modeling, though. That does not mean that these methods are necessarily bad. In fact, the author has applied positivist methods in his other work for various purposes. These positivist methods are not appropriate in the current study because they are used to examine a reality that is believed to be just out there, reachable through parsimonious relationships between operationalized variables and/or samples that presumably represent a fixed population. In contrast, methods used in this book must be ones that allow the people under study to become part of knowledge production/coproduction. The assumption is that they learn and adapt, while the research question of this book is how different the meaning of their lives can be in the face of an inessentially sited China.

PART I
———————

A World Sinicized into Harmony:
Centralized Perspectives

CHAPTER 1

Harmonious Realism: Undecidable Responses to the China Threat

Chinese foreign policy practices contribute to international relations (IR) theory and the conduct of foreign policy analysis (FPA) in a peculiar way—they do so not necessarily by transforming IR/FPA theory but by refocusing IR theorization on the civilizational aspect.[1] From the imperial times through the Republican and socialist eras in China, the purpose of achieving modernity from the point of view of Chinese leaders and intellectuals has been to transform a civilizational gathering in pervasive space, which could be practical, customary, or spiritual, into a rational construct in territorial space in order to exclude imperialist intrusion. Ironically, in the twenty-first century, China's successful emergence as a nation-state resulted in the Chinese people's spilling over their territorial boundary. However, from time to time, Chinese people from all over the world respond to the call of the Chinese foreign policy of national consciousness, making civilizational politics noteworthy again.[2] Ambivalence among Chinese people toward China's civilizational image causes a division in Chinese foreign policy between those motivated to reaffirm the civilizational pride of being Chinese and those who desire to transcend civilizational incapacity and act rationally on behalf of territorial China.[3] Together, the two approaches create a self-role conflict within Chinese foreign policy and its analysis. This conflict further complicates and at the same time transforms the external analysis of Chinese foreign policy. In the past, FPA was not focused on ontological issues. However, as China's unsettled situation between a civilizational and a territorial state gives it an increasingly uncertain identity, the self-role conceptions that sustain Chinese FPA become ambiguous. This ambiguity is a challenge to both Chinese foreign policy practitioners and internal as well as external narrators of Chinese FPA.

Two major leitmotifs have begun simultaneously to inform the self-roles of Chinese foreign policy at the beginning of the twenty-first century, namely, the "harmonious world," which is a classic Confucian ideal that came into the spotlight in 2005 to indicate the coming of a non-threatening international relationship even between powerful countries, and "core national interest," which became significant at roughly the same time to enable mutual respect among nation states.[4] Both can be taken as responses to the "China threat" image , which is part of the nascent notion of "China rising" against a background of reflections over the past two decades concerning the "clash of civilizations" and the "end of history" in the literature of international relations and offensive realism.[5] The fact that China has been undergoing liberalization under one-party rule provides optimistic hints of the imminent end of history as well as pessimistic ones concerning the inevitability of Sino-US confrontation.[6] Beijing authorities desire neither an end of history that implies the end of Chinese Communist Party (CCP) rule nor a head-on hegemonic confrontation with the United States. The official line has always been that China is not becoming another or the next superpower.[7] However, based on enthusiastic discussions in contemporary academic literature and the media, China's rise is agreeable to most Chinese IR and FPA thinkers who are now writing on China's proper place in the world for the second decade of the twenty-first century. Nowadays, the harmonious world refuses to believe that China's rise could lead to hegemonic war; and the core national interest is a plea for minimal living space within the existing IR parameters for everyone. The former sets the ideal condition of IR, whereas the latter alludes to the method of achieving that condition.

Both concepts have philosophical roots, and have been appropriated by Chinese foreign policy makers. The "harmonious world" is a classic Confucian value that constrains the antagonistic socialist revolution to the extent that the party continues to denounce self-interest, so the group and its internal harmony can be cherished. In contrast, "core national interest" is a modernist, realist belief, albeit defensive, that reflects the uncompromised volition of each national actor to protect its own national security. Despite the notion that core national interest is defensive in the realist analysis, Beijing sometimes uses the concept in an assertive way intended to reclaim or consolidate a sphere of influence lost to Western imperialism in premodern times, most notably in Tibet, Xinjiang, Taiwan, and, before their return, Hong Kong and Macau. In practice, Beijing does not hesitate to reach tentative compromises whenever the notion of a harmonious world is invoked. However, the world, including anxious Chinese critics, still thinks that Beijing has become arrogant in the way it appropriates China's own cultural resources/models vis-à-vis the liberalistic norms.[8] Invoking the harmonious world involves civilizational politics with reference to premodern China proper while sticking to the core national interest subscribed to in the statist discourse centers on mutually exclusive territorial sovereignty that defends an enlarged China proper. Consequently, role-playing that asserts the harmonious world can defeat harmony in the following hypothetic sequence:

1. Beijing unilaterally compromises on a certain or even a core national interest in favor of another country's national interest to demonstrate harmony in a bilateral relationship. However, this implicitly imposes a duty on the other party not to push further on the issue.
2. The other party, recognizing Beijing's short-term compromise, does not refuse, accept, or even understand its own reciprocal duty, which is implicit in Beijing's role-playing.
3. Beijing unilaterally declares that the two sides have achieved a harmonious partnership, adapts accordingly, and from time to time seeks reconfirmation from the other side.
4. The external and internal politics of the other party compel it to show that it is not complying with China's unilateral role expectation.
5. Beijing loses face, reacts negatively and strongly, and enlists its self-perceived restraint as justification for imposing sanctions, often symbolic at first.
6. In the other party's view, Beijing's symbolic sanctions act as confirmation of Beijing's malicious intentions, thus fulfilling the prophecy that it will be betrayed. The same view is echoed in China, resulting in a vicious circle for both sides.

Harmonious World and Self-role Conception

China as a civilization is almost a curse on China as a territorial state. As Lucien Pye proclaimed, China is only a civilization pretending to be a nation-state.[9] Chinese foreign policy is incomprehensible unless we first penetrate this pretense. Let us conceive civilization as a way of life that can be taught and learned without a shared meaning between the giver and the taker. Civilizational foreign policy is not rational because it does not serve a tangible national actor with a definite (institutional) purpose. Rather, it comes out of one's motivation to preach a way of life practiced by those sharing the same civilizational rather than national identity or to acquire it for them.[10] Constrained by civilizational imagination, China, as a nation-state that institutionally frames the creation of foreign policy, is neither entirely territorially oriented nor entirely security driven. Whenever Beijing authorities act as the representatives of Chinese civilization, their preaching, and even learning, easily arouses suspicion because civilizational expansion trespasses on territorial security.[11] Therefore, it is critical for Chinese FPA to attend to how civilizational imagination prescribes the national self-role concept of the Beijing authorities in terms of communities teaching and learning alternative ways of life.

Teaching and learning are typical and spontaneous mechanisms of interaction that are used by the civilizations involved to understand each other's unfamiliar phenomena. Unfortunately, cultural meanings associated with any specific way of life are not easy to pass on, as they can create mutual misunderstanding. Thus, national role conceptions mediate between civilizational imagination and FPA. For many premodern latecomers, acquiring a national role conception is a confusing process. Watchers in Europe hardly appreciate that the latecomers' acceptance of the institution of the territorial state may rest upon antagonism toward European imperialism, rather than upon their national interest calculus.[12] FPA is the expedient vehicle for the postcolonial government to make use of the perceived opportunities, and deal with the threats, arising out of misunderstanding. These postcolonial nations have suffered from unfinished nation-building or even witnessed civil wars, and have thus been the targets of continuous intervention by the old colonial power or a hegemonic United States. Their national role conceptions are uncertain and changeable. China may appear to have successfully emerged from its postcolonial condition to become a leading nation-state, but confusion still exists and is increasing.

One result of this success is the spillover of influence in a pervasive process of Sinicization to which the world has to adapt. Chinese foreign policy assumes the additional mission of demonstrating China's civilizational attraction, representing regional politics along the civilizational fault line and yet attempting to present alternative principles of international relations. One important cultural resource appropriated by contemporary Chinese leaders to help them cope with the rise of China is the Confucian notion of a harmonious world. In China's return to civilizational politics, the harmonious world has both an ontological and an epistemological theme. The harmonious world is an imagined world in which its member states must play mutually congruent roles. Self-centrism is anathema to role-playing. National interest premised upon multipolarity is a typical example of such self-centrism because it exists on the presumption of the irreducible ontology of differing individual territorial states.[13] Protecting national interest involves assuming an irreconcilable conflict of interest, whereas a harmonious relationship requires transcendence of territorial divisions.

If Chinese leaders subscribe to harmony as the foundational norm of interaction, compromising Chinese national interests from time to time allows it to demonstrate that harmony is the supreme rule of human gathering. However, any compromise by China carries with it the expectation that others should also compromise. As long as no individual is deliberately taken advantage of, everyone will be comfortable with his or her role of reciprocating harmony. In this way, in one domestic example, when the reform policy of enriching a portion of society to provide sufficient incentives for production was announced in the early 1980s, those who benefitted from it were expected to help enrich the latecomers. Externally, the occasional concession of territorial gains—for example, China's unilateral withdrawal from captured territory during the Korean War, the Sino-Indian border war, and the "punitive" war with Vietnam—are classic invitations to reciprocal self-restraint and efforts to preempt the territorial ambitions of the other side.[14]

The reform-socialist style of sequential egalitarianism connects the image of rising China to premodern Confucianism and modern socialism. Briefly, no individual should be left out of a social engagement. Although they are two millennia apart, the two ideologies share the motto that food and security for the people should be the first rule of government. Both internal reform and openness to the outside world over the past three decades have been committed to emancipating individual productivity for the sake of collective welfare. The reality that not everyone has benefited equally is detrimental to the reputation of socialism. The same is true in FPA if Chinese leaders cannot avoid the impression that China is rising at others' expense. To ensure that all are confident in their social roles, the most powerful player has a duty to perform occasional self-sacrifice to prepare the rest of the society in the spirit of the commonwealth. This duty is not as easy in FPA as it is in domestic politics, where the Communist Party is in charge. In fact, during the Cold War, neither superpower took note of its responsibility to make concessions to weaker nations. Nevertheless, as China rises, Chinese leaders are beginning to see the possibility of preaching the harmonious world.[15] Finally, in the twenty-first century, Confucianism and socialism are officially intertwined.

The nascent quest for a harmonious world justifies and demands concessions on extant foreign policy stances. From the harmonious world point of view, short-term concessions are conducive to long-term harmony. When China achieves a reciprocal role relationship with every nation in the world through such concessions, it will have achieved the harmonious world. Granted that concession is critical to achieving harmony, China's role of facilitating reciprocal harmony can be broken down logically into three modes. First, China could resort to a unilateral compromise to demonstrate the value of a harmonious partnership. In territorial settlements with North Korea, Burma, and Bhutan, for example, the Chinese people generally perceive that China yielded more land to the smaller parties.[16] Second, China could push for a mutual compromise to ensure that the other side will not take advantage of bilateral relations or abuse China's consent to retreat from a previous stance. One notable example is the negotiation with Britain over the return of Hong Kong, especially on how democratic elections were to be installed. Beijing backed out of a scheme to which it had already consented in response to what it perceived as insatiable demands from London. Third, when China is not a direct party in any conflict, it believes it should serve as a platform for mutual compromise. This is particularly the case in conflicts involving so-called failed states, such as the attempted international intervention in North Korea and Myanmar.

Harmony is not easily measured. Notably, both premodern Confucianism and contemporary socialism stress a positive attitude toward teaching and learning more than the results of learning and thus testify to the critical relevance of face-saving in Chinese FPA. A compromise is an act of face-giving that invites reciprocal face-giving from the other side. In this regard, unilateral compromise is not only a symbolic act of role enactment but also an indicator of harmony for the rising nation, allowing it to discover how willing the world is to accept Sinicization as a way of life rather than as a threat. This compromise explains why the notion of the China threat is shameful. In fact, the entire Chinese FPA community is devoted to its repudiation, giving rise to a variety of themes, including those in seeming defiance of harmony such as "national interest." The idea of a harmonious world is a nascent response to the fear of a China threat.

The China threat, as a derivative of realism, is a quintessential point of poignancy. Unimpressed with the pervasive space of a harmonious world, the China threat locks China back into its territorial boundaries. This situation generates anxiety with regard to national security among writers of Chinese FPA and ironically poses an increasing threat to the rest of the world.[17] The question for Beijing is how far China should compromise to establish a friendly image of Chinese civilization on the reciprocal rise. Similarly, Beijing has to decide whether this compromise will succeed in luring the other party to reciprocate. If the image of a China threat is strongly felt by Chinese leaders, it is possible that these leaders will compromise unilaterally in the hope that they will be reciprocated, and then assume that the other party consents to tabling their dispute in order to secure an immediate resolution, regardless of what the other party actually thinks.[18]

Core National Interest and Self-role Conception

In light of the practical difficulty of the harmonious world being too symbolic to enforce beyond those closely acquainted with Chinese civilization, policy makers need to create another role for China to present it to states that are strangers to Chinese civilization. Accordingly, the notion of core national interest has become fashionable since the turn of the century. Initially, the term was defensive, aimed at warning Washington not to interfere with China's territorial integrity, referring specifically to Taiwan and Tibet. Logically, if leaders of all countries felt that their core national interests were secure, relations between them would remain harmonious. However, such logic presumes a methodological statism that should be abhorred by leaders of the harmonious world who strive to demonstrate that territorial states have a duty to reciprocate harmonious relations. As one core national interest is that national leaders should never compromise for whatever reason, harmonious relations among them can only be transient and coincidental. Instead, protected mutual estrangement among territorial states threatens to negatively affect everyone's core national interests. This situation is the familiar security dilemma in which territorial security is taken to be the ultimate reason for the state, thus attracting suspicion and threat.

The idea of a core national interest resonates with China's long-held principle of peaceful coexistence,[19] which states that peace is possible only when no one interferes with the internal affairs of others and when territorial integrity is respected unconditionally. Peaceful coexistence of this type does not promise harmony though, as harmony proceeds from the willingness to teach, learn, and adapt rather than the capability to refuse teaching, learning, or adapting. In the discourse of national interest, Chinese FPA comprises exclusion rather than mingling or exchange. The focus on core national interest reduces harmony to a by-product of foreign policy, which is no longer the ontological, initial condition that enables national leaders to appreciate their duty to reciprocate harmonious role-playing. This situation explains to some degree why, through their plea for a core national interest, Chinese leaders intend to be defensive but give the impression of refusing to assume international responsibility, hence the China threat.

Historically, the replacement of the self-image of a civilizational state with that of a territorial state in Chinese FPA is a result of civilizational learning. For over a century, Chinese FPA has gradually moved from concern about face-saving on behalf of the emperor to issues such as military security, diplomatic alliance, and legal equality. Indeed, obsession with core national interests and peaceful coexistence is the result of a historical learning process throughout China's modern history all the way back to the Opium War and the consciousness of inferiority it engendered. The memory of a century of imperialist invasions marked by territorial concessions still makes contemporary Chinese FPA extremely sensitive about absolute territorial integrity.[20] Territorial issues are ever present, and the aftermath of imperialism has witnessed territorial disputes of all kinds everywhere. Against this background, Beijing's firm adherence to the principle of sovereignty dominates Chinese FPA. Note that sovereignty, a legal concept invented in the aftermath of the Peace of Westphalia in the Christian West, is the enemy of Confucian harmony. Thus, the adoption of sovereign integrity as the highest principle of Chinese FPA is evidence of both civilizational learning and civilizational retreat.

The FPA of national interest emerged in the Chinese diplomatic literature in the late 1970s. Initially, it was called nationality (*minzu*) interest, but it was later changed to national (*guojia*) interest. Academic literature on Chinese national interest expanded in response to Deng Xiaoping's call for a more statist reading of world affairs rather than an ideological interpretation. However, national interest and core national interest did not become the dominant policy themes in China until the turn of the century. The first official definition of national interest, contained in the White Paper on National Defense 2002, includes territorial integrity, economic development, social stability, the socialist system, and regional order.[21] The notion of core national interest had appeared in the academic literature in the mid-1990s, but the active use of it by narrators of FPA began only after 2010. For example, the White Paper on Peaceful Development lists Tibet, Xinjiang, and Taiwan as core national interests, indicating territorial integrity as their definitive reference.[22]

Notably, Chinese FPA and world politics have evolved in a scissors-like fashion, with the former moving from worldism to statism and the latter from statism to globalism. Before the 1980s, international exchange was insignificant in China under the bipolar system. Whereas national security issues dominated FPA agendas, the narratives were transnational. In actuality, China's transnational role was contradictorily coupled with territorial conflicts. All China's military confrontations since the establishment of the PRC took place before 1980. Although these wars—the Korean War, the shelling of Quemoy, the Sino-Indian border war, the Sino-Soviet border clash, and the "punitive" Sino-Vietnamese War—were all practically territorial, they took place in the years when FPA relied primarily on Marxist worldism, which is transnational. "The world people," "the working class," and "the revolutionary" were the most familiar roles highly praised in Chinese FPA. Themes of war and peace in the world as a whole prevailed on the agenda (Figure 1.1).

Today, in contrast, as China becomes increasingly involved in globalization and its state capacity is enhanced, there is increasing reference to national interest. China's territorial security should be much less under threat in the twenty-first century than it was in the early days of the PRC. However, territorial integrity has gained prominence on the FPA agenda because transnational exchanges have made Tibet and Taiwan more complicated

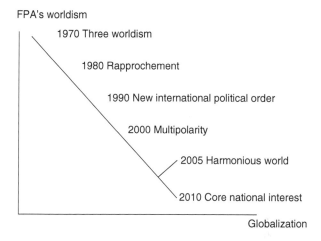

Figure 1.1 Chinese FPA and world politics.

issues of sovereignty. Civilizational awareness and civilizational discourse return to FPA when the literature on Taiwan and Tibet attains civilizational dimensions that preach trans-local immigration, human rights, religious beliefs, electoral politics, ethnic identities, and environmental resources. In relation to China's global presence, accordingly, nascent challenges to Chinese FPA should be transnational in essence. However, the inability to enforce territorial sovereignty in Tibet, Xinjiang, and Taiwan tarnishes Beijing's image and reduces its confidence as the representative of Chinese civilization. All these compel Chinese FPA to stress territorial sovereignty as a core national interest, on the one hand, while encouraging it to explore and appropriate the alternative theme of a harmonious world, on the other, as this can provide China's leaders with a national role in which they may confidently participate globally. Although Beijing may see no contradiction between advocacy of core national interests and belief in a harmonious world, implicit ontological incongruence between the two themes makes them less credible in the eyes of the rest of the world.

China's reference to core national interests will not necessarily have a negative effect on harmony if adoption of the concept by Chinese foreign policy practitioners is intended to reduce the fear of China threat by appearing defensive instead of trying to protect an absolute entity that subsists ultimately and exclusively by itself. In fact, reference to national interests on one occasion may be conducive to the reinforcement of harmony on another. This situation could occur when Chinese FPA shows Beijing's sincere adherence to a mutually constituted relationship by softening its national interest stance.

Beijing, as a credible advocate of harmony, could compromise a core national interest that has been previously clearly conveyed and invested in. The retreat from a core national interest can provide dramatic testimony to Beijing's dedication to a harmonious relationship. In the negotiation of a border settlement with smaller neighbors, for example, Beijing usually resorts to concessions in order to establish trust. Concessions of this kind include giving up a seaport to North Korea and the compromise on the McMahon line with Burma (now Myanmar).[23] In summary, a core national interest is core not because Chinese FPA recognizes its absolute nature but rather because the FPA of any equal and respectful state should treat it as absolute. In other words, the notion of "core" is about civilizational learning.

Consequently, there are two sets of national self-role conceptions: that informed by the civilizational value embedded in the Confucian ideal of harmony and that of the core national interest that echoes realist FPA. According to the former, Beijing should make short-term concessions to maintain harmonious relationships in the long run, whereas the latter indicates that national interests should always be protected even at the cost of harmony. As the world does not appreciate the simultaneous subtle playing of these two roles, Beijing has to find ways to preach the idea and style of harmony. To dispel the confusion of others, including Washington, Chinese FPA employs the familiar realist discourse as a shortcut to suggest the method of harmony. However, Chinese FPA is always prepared to make a compromise even on core national interests, resulting in the reconciliation of two seemingly contradictory national self-role conceptions. It is difficult to discern a pattern in China's alternate use of the two role conceptions, probably because of their ontological contradiction. This contradiction attests to the importance of human judgment in Chinese FPA and China's self-role conception, which results in a necessary fluidity in the purpose of Chinese FPA.[24]

Harmonious Realism in Practice

The purpose of an FPA that recommends concessions is different from one that asserts national interests. Making concessions breeds an atmosphere of trust that facilitates the development of a harmonious relationship, whereas asserting national interests is a way of coping with immediate threats and opportunities. These threats usually involve de jure and de facto territorial integrity, opportunity, and economic gains. Thus, the undecided purpose of Chinese FPA creates China's self-role conflict. Should China be only an ego state capable of defending its own national borders, protecting sovereign rights, maintaining regional order, accruing economic prosperity, and enhancing its international prestige? Alternatively, should China be a role state ready to make a concession by hedging a threat or foregoing an opportunity? Walking between the two horns, Beijing can now take advantage of the increase in its national capacity to create ambiguity in a confrontational situation. Beijing could either painstakingly yield without clearly yielding or confront without clearly confronting. Ambiguity preserves flexibility for Beijing in contriving the subsequent response as the situation develops. Undecidability is the essence of Beijing's harmonious realism.

Conforming to the Chinese assessment, core national interests focus on territorial security and domestic stability. Territorial security is serious if the challenge is direct and strong. Domestic stability is in danger when the legitimacy of territorial integrity is questioned. Accordingly, harmonious realism yields five kinds of self-role dilemmas and policy styles depending on whether the other party in the dispute has global or local power (the strength dimension) and whether the dispute directly challenges China's territorial integrity (the directness dimension). If the party challenging China has local (i.e., weaker) power, Beijing can opt for either disciplining or conceding, depending on which is conducive to maintaining harmony. However, if the party challenging China has global (i.e., stronger) power, Beijing's choice is between defending and conceding. If the party has local power that poses no challenge to China's territorial integrity (i.e., indirect), Beijing can most easily preserve harmony by making short-term concessions. Similarly, if the party has global power, is involved in a local situation, and does not directly challenge China's territorial integrity, Beijing avoids involving itself in a direct confrontation with the global power and helps coach the local power in how to make concessions to restore harmony in the short run. Finally, a fifth situation exists where Beijing enjoys total control of the disputed area (the legitimacy dimension). Immediate suppression with the promise to grant benefits is not unusual anywhere in the world. It is a convenient combination of harmony and realism that does away with the acquired inconsistency (Table 1.1).

When coping with defiance within territory under its control, Beijing adopts "harmonious suppression." This involves control by real force followed by the granting of privileges. Tibet and Xinjiang are areas that have

Table 1.1 Harmonious realism in areas not directly controlled by China*

Conditions of harmonious realism	Local initiative	Global initiative
China as target	Harmonious sanctions e.g., South China Sea and Taipei	Harmonious balancing e.g., Washington
China not as target	Harmonious racism e.g., Africa	Harmonious intervention e.g., Naypyitaw and Pyongyang

*Xinjiang and Tibet belong to a different category.

experienced this kind of suppression. Suppression supposedly buys time for achieving harmony. FPA deals with areas not directly under China's control. In a situation where Beijing perceives China to be a high stakeholder, it resorts to "harmonious disciplining," which employs both the carrot and the stick to compel target individuals to accept Beijing's unilateral concession. The South China Sea and Taiwan belong to this category, in which the purpose of harmonious disciplining is the concealment of disharmony.[25] When a superpower is believed to target China, Beijing responds with "harmonious balancing," alternately asserting and compromising its core national interests to discourage antagonism. Washington is the pertinent actor in this category. Harmonious balancing controls the level of disharmony in the Sino-US relationship. When a remote country only is involved in an event, Beijing resorts to "harmonious racism" aimed at exercising benevolence while exploiting the other country with a posture of innocence, as in the case of Africa. Harmonious racism is the basis for positive discrimination. When a neighboring country becomes the target of major international powers, Beijing's approach is "harmonious intervention," which has the immediate purpose of persuading the target country into conceding rapidly to the intervention in exchange for enhanced autonomy in the long run. Myanmar and North Korea are good examples of countries where harmony is reproduced in the process of intervention.

Harmonious Disciplining in the South China Sea

The territorial dispute over the South China Sea vividly testifies to Beijing's self-role conflict. The current policy stance was initially expressed by Deng Xiaoping when he met with the vice president of the Philippines in June 1986, and it was reiterated to President Corazon Aquino of the Philippines in April 1988. Deng raised two policy principles, namely, "setting aside disputes and pursuing joint development" and "keeping our sovereignty."[26] The first principle seeks to avoid escalation to allow room for mutual benefit. It is in accordance with the pursuit of peaceful development and an ideal harmonious world, reducing Washington's leverage in the region. Beijing stayed with the first principle and distanced itself from the identified disputed waters with the expectation that the other parties involved would also refrain from the unilateral exploitation of the area's abundant natural resources. Accordingly, bilateral and multilateral efforts should focus on joint development.

As regards the second principle of "keeping our sovereignty," Deng's reference to "our sovereignty" appears to involve a statement of national interest. However, this position presumably demonstrates that China is making a concession by deemphasizing sovereignty and welcoming joint development.

With the assumption of no outright challenge, Beijing can comfortably shelve the sovereignty issue. The same principle was presented to Washington in the hope that the latter would learn how to avoid disrupting harmony by acquiescing on the sovereignty issue. However, the opposite result was achieved. On one occasion in 2010, a Chinese official stated that the South China Sea was one of China's core national interests, which caused agitation in Washington. Throughout the twenty-first century, Beijing and the other parties to the dispute have alternately resorted to unilateral action either to reiterate or to respond to others' attempts to declare sovereign ownership.

To promote the "harmonious relationship," a term specifically mentioned in the Declaration on the Conduct of Parties in the South China Sea of 2002 (DoC), Beijing seemingly compromises its national interests. Beijing specifically rules out the non-peaceful resolution of the dispute and virtually neutralizes its predominant military power that forced Vietnam out of the Paracel Islands in 1974. The term unprecedentedly acknowledges the disputed rather than the nonnegotiable nature of China's sovereign borders. Beijing additionally concedes to a quasi-multilateral format that incorporates the Association of Southeast Asian Nations (ASEAN) as a negotiating party, at the expense of its long-held insistence on a bilateral framework. Finally, Beijing allows and even encourages joint development in its claimed territorial waters around the Spratly Islands.[27]

Nevertheless, the self-proclaimed concession is at best a unilateral kind of reciprocity, generating positive as well as negative feedback.[28] The principle of "setting aside disputes, pursuing joint development" received a lukewarm welcome in Hanoi. From the Vietnamese perspective, Beijing's exclusion of the Paracel Islands from the dispute list is particularly unfair.[29] Vietnam believes that Beijing considers only those areas not controlled by China as being under dispute or suitable for joint development. As a result, Beijing's self-proclaimed restraint has met with refusal to conform from the other parties. Hanoi, for example, held elections for members of its National Assembly and local people's delegates in the disputed territory in May 2011. On one occasion, China's maritime patrols escorted Chinese fishing boats to destroy the drilling facility of a state-owned Vietnamese firm on the pretext of Vietnam's failure to commit to joint development. Beijing also keeps an eye on Washington's expressed interest in returning to East Asia through Hanoi. Nevertheless, the harmony approach continues to prevail in high politics. Hard negotiation between Beijing and Hanoi continues without Vietnam's explicit consent to the principle of putting aside disputes. Facing the danger of escalation, Beijing consistently registers futile protests.[30]

Manila does not comply either. The Philippines' maritime patrols regularly detain and fine Chinese fishermen allegedly in Philippine sovereign waters. Drilling for oil continues without any joint arrangement with the Beijing authorities. Naval patrols from both sides take turns in making gestures of sovereignty. Indeed, President Benigno Aquino of the Philippines evaded any commitment to the first principle in a public declaration issued jointly with his Chinese counterpart, Hu Jintao. In his unenthusiastic contribution to the declaration, Aquino states that "the South China Sea issue does not constitute all Philippines–China relations" and that "the issue should not affect the development of bilateral ties and friendly cooperation in various fields."[31] Aquino's statement is tantamount to declaring that the dispute must not be shelved, as it is not that important to a good relationship anyway. China's principle of reciprocity is at best unilateral in actuality, as both Vietnam and the Philippines have signed contracts with international oil firms to explore/drill in the controlled area.

The Chinese FPA communtiy should be discussing the issue of how far or how much further should China yield. China's unavailing concession breeds a shared sense of bitterness, candidly revealed in this popular FPA quote:

> For many years, we have followed the principle of "setting aside disputes." We prefer to shelve the disputes. We do not want to rush a resolution because we hope these issues will not hinder the development of our friendly relationship with these countries. Peaceful and calm negotiation could lead to [something that is] mutually acceptable. However, some countries do not take our sincerity seriously. They insist either that "there has never been a dispute" or that we keep creating problems. This trend has to be stopped. Let it be known that "setting aside disputes" is not only done by one side nor is it the same as one side yielding endlessly. It requires all sides to place their priority on the greater goal of development, to persevere and obey together. China will never swallow the bitter fruit of unilateral "putting aside disputes" while other parties are encroaching step-by-step.[32]

As other major powers do in their respective spheres of influence, Beijing uses carrots and sticks in its approach to the South China Sea, where global interference is not direct. However, there is a prospect of disharmony at the expense of China's alleged national interests. Destroying drilling facilities, pressing for high-level negotiations, and promising economic benefits are among the most frequent responses that Beijing makes.[33] Once the other side's claim is effectively challenged, Beijing does not even push for tacit acknowledgment of its sovereign claim by other parties to the dispute even if violation of its terms is clear and present. Instead, by inflicting minor pain and immediately providing comfort, Beijing manages to assert its sovereignty in an abrupt but controlled way. Resorting immediately to offering economic benefits before the other side can respond strongly,[34] presumably with the support of a superpower ally, allows Beijing to muddle through with ambiguous statements designed to stifle the issue for the time being. In brief, restoring harmony is a higher goal than clarifying sovereign status, which in turn is higher than stimulating economic returns.

The same style can be seen in Beijing's Taiwan policy. This issue is another one over which China has no real control, which is faced primarily with a local challenge, and which carries the threat of disharmony. Similarly, positive sanctions to lure the Taiwanese away from immediately seeking independent statehood after abrupt disciplining suggest no desire for an immediate solution other than a face-saving state of avoiding further discussion. Thus, harmonious disciplining is abrupt, ambiguous, and frustrating.

Other Forms of Harmonious Realism: Balance, Racism, and Intervention

In harmonious balancing, both balancing and giving up balancing are done for the sake of harmony. Harmonious balancing fits China's relationship with Washington, where a global force challenges China's territorial security. For over a decade, Beijing has coped with the anticipation of threat as well as offensive realism, which predicts a final unavoidable confrontation between Beijing and Washington.[35] Beijing appeals to a number of role conceptions, including Sino-US strategic partnership, China as the stakeholder, China's peaceful rise, the harmonious world, and so on, in the hope of portraying a nonconfrontational future for China and the United States. Sporadic disruptions over human rights, Taiwan, and exchange rates as well as trade issues expose the volatile nature of the bilateral relationship. To avoid escalation, Beijing has decided to draw a line between core national interests and other interests to drive Washington away from what Beijing cannot ostensibly afford to lose. Implicitly, there is the threat that China could act uncooperatively where US core interests are concerned. Unlike its South China Sea agenda where Beijing does not seek a clear acknowledgment, Beijing asks for silence or ambiguity in its arrangements with the United States. By highlighting Taiwan as a core interest, where the United States arguably has an extended core interest in selling arms, Beijing hopes that the balance of core national interests will facilitate self-restraint in a reciprocal way, enabling both sides to avoid the traps of escalation and to remain in harmony in the long run.

The rhetoric of harmony that alleviates fears of imminent confrontation in the rest of the world is inevitably symbolic. Harmony addresses Beijing's anxiety over whether Washington accepts China's role as a territorial state. Therefore, Beijing's list of core interests comprises those that a territorial state should nominally consider to be its core interests. Such nominal core interests are not necessarily Beijing's real core interests. The list includes Taiwan, for example, which is an issue whose significance has ironically never been predicable in the past. However, given that Taiwan is nominally a current core interest, the selling of arms to Taiwan by the United States has to be understood as an intrusion. How serious the issue could become cannot be ascertained from past experience.[36] Over the years, US arms sales to Taiwan have increased. In China's eyes, this is a blunt violation of a previous bilateral communiqué.[37] As Taiwan has previously been listed as a core national interest, Beijing has no alternative but to protest vehemently, going as far as unilaterally halting bilateral military exchanges to show its disapproval of the continued arms sales. Ironically, Beijing resumed military exchanges in an effort to generate goodwill on the eve of Hu Jintao's state visit to Washington, though there had been no change in the US policy on arms sales to Taiwan. The so-called core interest of Taiwan is apparently dispensable, as Hu's state visit demanded a friendly atmosphere between the two sides. In short, the balancing of core interests is not done for the sake of balance but for the sake of harmony. If harmony is in prospect, balance is dispensable.

Harmonious racism reflects China's hierarchical sensibility. In Africa, in particular, no direct global or local challenge to China's quest for a harmonious world is present. Beijing preaches Chinese ways of development along with positive discrimination, in contrast to the heavy interference typically associated with Western aid. Beijing unilaterally determines what is good for its African allies as an indication of brotherhood or comradeship. Nevertheless, the Chinese people remain socially and culturally racist, although with good intentions.[38] Harmony and racism usually coexist. Although the government provides fellowships to attract African students, society still cannot accept black-skinned males having Chinese girlfriends. Although Chinese FPA embraces equality and friendship, the Chinese venture in Africa dispatches managers who are ignorant about local customs, languages, religions, and cultures.[39] Even though in terms of policy, the rationale is to offer benefits and assistance, their style of administration can feel impertinent. Africa may be a site of proud civilizations, but to the business world it is predominantly about natural resources. One bloody incident in Zambia, in which two frightened Chinese managers wounded 12 local workers during a demonstration, is quintessential proof of the lack of mutual appreciation. Chinese culture should be able to accommodate African cultures, but Chinese individuals dread contacts with African strangers. In this contrarian logic, racism actually dramatizes China's self-perceived role of a friend versus the (often Western) exploiter. In short, true friendship balances powerful racism.

Harmonious intervention describes how Beijing, under global pressure to intervene in specific neighboring nations such as North Korea, Myanmar, or East Timor for humanitarian or security reasons, decides to exercise its expected role as a global stakeholder and becomes a responsible nation and self-proclaimed defender of the sovereign order.[40] The latter role is antagonistic and poignant because of contemporary Chinese historiography, which takes note of repeated imperialist interventions in China by the Western powers throughout the country's modern history. Beijing is inclined to apply private persuasion to convey the seriousness of the global pressure.[41] Beijing can also suggest acceptable adjustments to the global power. The target country can maintain minimal trust in Beijing. Beijing's purpose is to coach the target country on how to avoid direct global intervention. Intervention of this sort is counter-intervention in the long run, as it assures the supremacy of sovereignty over the concerns of global governance by stopping the latter from becoming a source of disharmony.

Finally, when Beijing deals with areas under its firm control, harmonious realism emerges as harmonious suppression, in the form of suppression of the external connection of the land in question, usually in Buddhist Tibet and Islamic Xinjiang. Externality is territorially defined, whereas internality is substantiated by specially arranged policy privileges and subsidies,[42] which are the reward for civilizational fusion and the imperative of territorial security.[43] In particular, subsidies are evidence of harmony,[44] but they also justify harsh suppression of those who refuse to comply with Beijing's role as the central government. Similarly, continued local resistance that challenges harmony usually incurs further subsidies to demonstrate that the fault is not that of the central government.

These various modes of harmonious realism have one thing in common: actors interacting with Beijing do not always appreciate the claim of harmony or the reciprocal duty that Beijing's self-proclaimed concession imposes upon them. For example, on harmonious balance, one US observer keenly points out that Beijing's softening on the arms sales issue before Hu's state visit indicated that China needed the United States.[45] In other words, it was evidence of weakness rather than a desire for harmony. The implication is that Washington should keep pushing Beijing. In another example, in Myanmar, the authorities who have now decided to accommodate the forces of democracy in order to avoid US intervention also agreed to a US request that they pull out of a joint dam project in which China had invested heavily. Harmonious intervention has seemingly failed to sustain China's immediate interests in Myanmar. Rather, it obliges Beijing to comply with harmony and adapt to the evolving situation. Similarly, when the opposition in Zambia campaigned for election on an anti-China platform, the tens of thousands of job opportunities created by Chinese investment in the country could not stop the accused Chinese managers from being taken into custody. Both Tibet and Xinjiang have witnessed revolts on various scales with and without international support. The subsidy policy implants only limited reciprocal consciousness in the minds of local minorities.

Conclusion

Role conceptions mediate civilizations and policy. The notion of national interest embedded in the system of a nation-state does not resonate with the premodern Chinese world order characterized by a Confucian preoccupation with harmony. The sudden arrival of the territorial state, which replaced all-under-heaven, transformed China's identity. Learning by practice suggests that the territorial state should only be a role acted out by the Chinese leaders. Watching how the audience, especially in the West, evaluates China's role performance deprives Chinese leaders of their familiar self-role conception of all-under-heaven. China's rise has led to a recombination of cultural resources informed by both Western and Chinese civilizations. The harmonious world is by itself a system of role-playing, and the national interest, which has been an acquired role right from the beginning, coincides with the FPA agenda of reconciling competition between China and the United States. The formula is that when neither challenges the other's core national interests, a harmonious world will emerge. However, this formula does not work in either theory or practice.

In theory, national interests are premised upon an irreconcilable ontology that easily exposes the conflict of interest between the rising power and the reigning superpower. In practice, the role-playing nature of China's emphasis on national interests makes it difficult for it to remain consistent across different scenarios, where different actors have different policy preferences. As a result, in Chinese FPA, core national interests are never really core, and the harmonious world is never harmonious. Sacrifice of one is necessary to achieve the other. There are four ways in which the concept of core national interests can, ironically, be a method of achieving harmony. First, the pronouncement of a core national interest is a way of warning how harmony can be destroyed. Second, the renouncement of a core national interest in the short run or under certain circumstances demonstrates sincerity toward the harmonious relationship. Third, reference to a core national interest justifies disciplining the violators. Finally, core national interest tests how seriously the other actors value harmony. In short, harmonious realism is neither a harmonious nor a realist idea. It is the acting out of a self-role conflict rooted in a civilizational encounter.

CHAPTER 2

Harmonious Racism: China's Civilizational Soft Power in Africa

According to one Chinese analyst, international observers evaluate the expanding Chinese presence in Africa according to their own countries' past involvement in the continent.[1] Thus, China is accused of practicing a new form of the colonialism practiced by Europeans.[2] The charge of new colonialism has two aspects, which are not completely compatible with each other. Hillary Clinton articulates one of them when she criticizes Chinese investment in Africa as investment in the elite, which undermines good governance. She compares it unfavorably with US investment in Africa, which, she claims, is long term and focused on people. A second view of the new Chinese involvement in Africa includes a suspicion that there is a long-term plan behind China's Africa policy.[3]

The colonialists of the past systematically exploited Africa, and this fact has given rise to the convenient analysis that China is exploiting Africa in a similar, well-planned manner. The term *new colonialism* implies, likely correctly, that the new colonialism mimics the old one.[4] Hence, it is a sort of Anglicization of Chinese foreign policy. From this angle, the aim of Chinese new colonialism should be economic gain (i.e., capitalism) and political influence, as well as strategic security (i.e., realism). Even the critical reflections are Anglicized.[5] Few, however, have detected the irony that the spirit of colonialism may have been lost in translation. What critics of China fail to address are views and values arising out of a non-Christian historical trajectory. If China's new colonialism, so to speak, is the result of the Anglicization of China's Africa policy, the Sinicization aspect is also worth exploring.[6]

This chapter continues the analysis of harmonious realism and elaborates on China's Africa policy as a typical case of "harmonious racism." Officially, China's normative foreign policy calls for the peaceful coexistence of different political systems, and this constitutes China's soft power in the developing world in general, and in Africa in particular. Socially as well as culturally, however, the Chinese display a racist attitude toward the darker skinned Africans,[7] although that racism does not lead to policy discrimination in a practical sense nor does racism constrain China from treating African nations as ideological, strategic, and global governance allies. On the one hand, China's Africa policy is characterized by classic realism in that China does what most other major powers do in Africa; that is, it seeks economic opportunities in terms of resources, markets, and labor.[8] On the other hand, this contrasts with China's pursuit of a harmonious world with due respect to cultural differences. As a result of China's preoccupation with harmony and aid, its concessions to African nations are made at the state level, even if racism influences practices from time to time at the individual and corporate levels. The rise of China as an advocate of harmony has caught the world's attention. Meanwhile, with the seeming Sinicization in Africa, the question of what kind of soft power is needed by China to achieve its goal without causing anxiety among observers remains unanswered. The concern is more pronounced in the case of realists who do not believe a word the Chinese say about harmony.

Sinicization and Realism

Foreign and Chinese observers regard 2006—dubbed by the Chinese as the "Year of Africa"—as a milestone in China's return to the continent.[9] The rapid growth in Chinese investment, trade, immigration, and aid testifies to the expansion of Chinese influence there. At the same time, the African presence in China is also on the increase. By and large, the Chinese believe that China and Africa are in a win–win economic situation. In addition, China has been able to gain significant new sources of energy in Africa while continuing to provide aid to needy African nations. China's position in multilateral organizations is usually in line with that of the African countries, while the distance between them rules out the kind of territorial disputes that still poison contemporary international relations in Asia.[10]

Chinese enthusiasm for its opportunities in Africa is met with suspicion, if not hostility, in some parts of the world.[11] The debate over the nature of the seeming Sinicization of Africa centers on concerns about the China threat. In the United States, critics conceive the threat both in terms of the substitution of US supremacy and as an impediment to the spread of liberal democracy in Africa. For local African writers, the threat is seen against the background of the alleged exploitative consequences, both environmental and economic, of Chinese investment. That said, African governments predominantly see China in a positive light despite localized incidents, which sometimes generate a negative attitude among Africans. China supports and enjoys the support of African nations on most global governance issues. Accordingly, the multiple and varied results of Sinicization do not permit any easy assessment.[12]

Sinicization is, in part, Anglicization to the extent that the institutional setting of the growing Chinese presence in Africa represents and embraces market capitalism, which reproduces globalization and the liberalistic values undergirding it. The feeling of threat inspired by China's growing influence in Africa reinforces, rather than undermines, certain American values and is therefore premised upon China's assimilation of globalization through its own variety of Anglicization, namely, marketization and privatization. Chinese corporations in Africa are driven by profitability, which parallels nineteenth-century European mercantilism and blinds them to any socialist spirit of sharing their gains with local labor. The environmental consequences of Chinese ventures are also similar to those of their Western predecessors, despite consistent reminders by the Chinese authorities to behave otherwise. Most noteworthy to Western observers is China's quest for energy. They believe that concerns about energy security explain China's acquiescence in the suppression of human rights in Africa's failed states. In response to the accusation that China supports African dictators, the Chinese official rebuttal points to Hosni Mubarak of Egypt and Zine El Abidine Ben Ali of Tunisia, both of whom used to be "staunch allies of the West," and Muammar Gaddafi of Libya, who was never China's ally but "a guest of many Western leaders."[13] In short, China is insinuating its Anglicized national interests into the Sinicization process in Africa, except that it is China instead of the United States that appears ready to take the lead in the coming decades.

Harmony

Another aspect of Sinicization, which, to a certain degree, justifies the charge of a China threat, is China's consistent rejection of global intervention on the grounds of human rights violations. However, China's insistence on the principle of sovereign autonomy that questions the legitimacy of intervention has much deeper cultural roots than its critics are willing to acknowledge.[14] Long-held cultural values in China, embedded in Confucianism, Taoism, and even modern Maoism, share the wisdom of rule by modeling, which is all about preaching and learning.[15] Intervention would be a sign of moral decay on the part of the intervening party as it would signal the loss of its civilizational attraction. Much stronger early Chinese dynasties did not value intervention of any sort either. Therefore, China's relative weakness in recent decades cannot fully explain its dislike of intervention.

Nonetheless, China does intervene, but in a peculiar way. Specifically, it intervenes privately through persuasion, instead of by means of punitive sanctions. Thus, Chinese intervention depends heavily on the personal faculty of its diplomats. Chinese diplomats mediate behind the scenes for solutions that are acceptable both to the forces of global intervention and to the target local government. The purpose is by no means global governance. It is about avoiding having to choose sides, hence preserving harmony.[16] Harmonious intervention ensures that the local government understands its own precarious situation under both external and internal pressures. Harmonious intervention reassures African nations of China's continued support for their autonomy, and prepares a platform that could meet the demands of global forces at least half-way. In this manner, the local government can give in without granting recognition to the norms proclaimed by the global forces, and by doing so it reduces the legitimacy of the proposed intervention. China has painstakingly applied harmonious intervention to North Korea, Myanmar, and the former Sudan.[17] Also, honoring its non-interventionist stance, China was the last to recognize the new regime in Libya in 2011, although it paid a high price for its slow response. China's non-intervention philosophy carried it to the point of yielding to France the right to exploit Libyan oil—concern for which is suspected by critics to dominate China's Africa policy.

In effect, the process of Sinicization that yields enhanced relationships between China and the African nations, in particular, demonstrates a style of realism unheard of in Western international relations textbooks.[18] China is ready to pay for the preservation of the autonomy of an African nation plagued by whatever institutional failure. In the case of pre-divided Sudan in 2008, for example, China adamantly opposed the proposed unilateral intervention without the prior consent of the local authorities.[19] China took this stance at the risk of provoking an international campaign against the Beijing Olympics.[20] Furthermore, since the 1960s, China has characteristically financed large projects in Africa that had no prospect of making a profit, such as the Tanzania–Zambia railroad and, more recently, the conference center for the African Union in Addis Ababa. Beijing refrained from voting on a UN resolution to launch air strikes against Gaddafi's troops because, according to one official source, the wording indicated the possibility that the resolution might be abused. However, the Chinese did not vote against it because it was widely supported by the Arab League.[21]

The practice of cajoling states into harmony was part of China's Africa policy long before critics began to suspect that China favored African dictators for the sake of convenience. Chinese foreign ministers have toured Africa annually, much more frequently than their counterparts outside the African continent have ever done. The Chinese style of realism carries the belief that outsiders cannot solve domestic conflicts, least of all by applying an arrogant universal standard of human rights. As long as a legal government is installed in a country, the Chinese principle of harmony demands that China cope with it as far as it is able. When there is a need to do even slightly otherwise, the Chinese government relies heavily on regional organizations to take the lead. The involvement of regional organizations was apparent in the cases of Myanmar (ASEAN), the former Sudan (the African Union), and Libya (the Arab League).

Soft Power

The Chinese have their particular style of realism, which underlies the Chinese understanding of soft power. This understanding is dramatically incompatible with the US viewpoint. US realism would draw others to voluntarily practice American values and adapt to American institutions regardless of their apparent indifference to the US government.[22] In contrast, Chinese soft power lies in the intellectual capacity to appreciate diversity in harmony. This concept earned the appreciation of the late Lucian Pye, who noted the Chinese tolerance for cognitive dissonance as well as the mystery of China as a civilization pretending to be a nation-state.[23] In other words, whereas the US version of soft power compels even its rivals to practice American values, the aim of Chinese soft power is to make its rivals believe that China does not contest any value, and therefore never to see China as an adversary. If China's advocacy of non-intervention fails on any of the numerous global governance issues on the current agenda, developing countries all over the world may anticipate the unrestrained application of liberalistic universalism coming their way shortly. It is no wonder, therefore, that most of them support the Chinese position that resonates with their quest for national autonomy.

The rise of China has been accompanied by a peculiar style of harmonious diplomacy that comes into play whenever China detects a hint of confrontation. One form of this harmonious diplomacy is the ambiguous disciplining that is part of China's policy toward its smaller neighbors. Occasionally, smaller developing countries in the Asian region challenge China. In response, China resorts to an ambiguous hit-and-run disciplining that demonstrates its resolute strength, but since it is closely followed by concessions, it is almost undetectable. This kind of harmonious discipline is most apparent in the South China Sea dispute. Similarly, harmonious diplomacy may lead to a style of ambiguous balancing as regards global powers. When faced with confrontation with a global power, China tends to put forward a set of core national interests, just so that it can sacrifice them in the short run in order to indicate its readiness to compromise. China's on and off opposition to US arms sales to Taiwan is a quintessential example of this kind of behavior. The purpose of ambiguous balancing is the opposite of that of harmonious disciplining, namely, to compromise without the appearance of compromising. Both are in line with the aforementioned style of harmonious intervention whereby China intervenes on behalf of the global forces for the sake of restraining them from really intervening. China does this by persuading the target nation to accept a symbolic short-term compromise.[24]

The other form of harmonious diplomacy is harmonious racism, which is relevant in Africa. For the Chinese, learning Chinese institutions, practicing Chinese medicine, and receiving Chinese investment pose no threat to existing African value systems or lifestyles.[25] Unlike encounters with Western capitalism, none of these involves a transformation of values. However, the lack of any motivation to move from civilizational learning to cultural assimilation sometimes hinders social mingling and breeds racism in daily life. Liking China yet disliking the Chinese way of life is a form of soft power that contrasts with the combination of liking the American way of life but disliking the United States. If it is true that China cares more about its public image in the global arena than it does about putting the world to rights, then preaching specific civilizational devices without any implications of cultural transformation would be the appropriate style.

Racism

Lofty policy concessions and aid, as well as normative support for autonomy, are not sufficient to reconcile Africans to Chinese racism toward black people.[26] Sinicization brings more extensive engagement between the two continents. Ironically, the longer African students stay in China, the more negative are their feelings toward the country.[27] One major impression among African students in China is the racism they experience,[28] and confrontation is reportedly common when male African students flirt with their female Chinese peers. Not surprisingly, the increasing number of African workers in Guangzhou has led to racially motivated complaints from local residents.[29] One Chinese migrant to Africa was quoted as saying that she had come to Africa because in Europe both yellow and black people had equally low status.[30] Larger corporations tend to send their less-talented personnel to Africa as the best employees avoid African assignments.[31]

However, racism of this sort never translates to the public policy arena.[32] Chinese racism toward Africans is a classic case of "old-fashioned racism" from a foreign policy point of view. In its old-fashioned sense, racism is an atavistic attitude functioning only to sustain a pretentiously higher self-image, presumably of a previously privileged class or group, but it has no behavioral implications in daily interaction. To that extent, high-ranking Chinese officials have little difficulty liking, befriending, or cooperating with their African counterparts. At a lower level, however, diplomats dispatched to Africa do not enjoy their social contacts much. Lower down the hierarchy, managers of Chinese corporations in Africa may be afraid of their workers. They sometimes overreact to situations in their workplaces. The shooting of the protesting Zambian workers by Chinese managers and the opposition this provoked in Zambia is a case in point.[33]

Civilizational Soft Power

Whereas China's rapidly growing investment in Africa carries the same realist logic of national interests as it does elsewhere in the world, the conscious provision of aid and privileges to African states will most likely give China's Africa policy a much longer and steadier future. Africa is distant from China, and the Chinese have no immediate stake in the continent. This absence of an immediate stake is the reason why Africa used to be the moral theater where China played out its dramas of anti-imperialism, anti-hegemonism, the Three Worlds Theory, and so on. For almost half a century, Africa has been boosting China's foreign policy morale, thus helping it cope with the West in general, and the United States in particular.[34] In an age of global governance where universal values and multiculturalism compete with each other, Chinese civilization, which values variety and modeling, can be heuristic in Africa. Both harmony and racism are external to the realist logic of national interest, but they are effective in combination with calculated national interest. How these ways of thinking combine/recombine, impede, or bypass each other will depend on the choices of actual individuals at all levels.

PART II

China International and Intellectual:
Perspectives Beyond

CHAPTER 3

Taiwan Chinese: Encountering and Choice in Postcolonial Scholarship

Sinicization takes place in people's minds, and the intellectual Sinicization of IR scholarship does so consciously and to an even greater extent than other forms of Sinicization. One intellectual aspect of Sinicization is how IR theory can be made more suitable for China. The other side of the coin is how to make China more suitable for IR theory. In chapters 1 and 2, I show how Chinese leaders and writers who consider these questions exclusively on behalf of China have come up with strategies of harmonious realism. They differ from those other Chinese who ponder China's changing role in world politics, those who possess an identity that is simultaneously Chinese and non-Chinese and yet come from lower echelons or outside territorial China. They include Chinese in Taiwan, Southeast Asia, North America, and elsewhere. They have acquired a dimension of identity in addition to just being Chinese, largely because of the local political conditions in which they find themselves as they consider the issue of China rising. Their Chinas are illustrative of the endless number of Chinas that serve different life purposes that watchers of the national China could not care less about. Part II of this book looks at a few of these liminal Chinese communities and the unlimited intellectual possibilities of their writing of China. The present chapter is concerned with the approaches of Taiwanese Chinese.

The following discussion records individual intellectual trajectories that necessarily reflect both conscious and subconscious choices between the epistemological possibilities allowed by social conditions over which individuals have no choice. The two mechanisms that facilitate intellectual growth are encounters with the existing epistemological perspectives beyond one's own volition, and the choice that strategically selects, recombines, and renovates perceived (im)possibilities. The mechanism of encountering constrains the range of intellectual puzzles,[1] and the mechanism of choice reflects the strength of volition.[2] Whereas encountering is largely socially prepared and yet unavoidably mediated by coincidence, choice depends on the existence of alternatives that the differing decisions and narratives of others either preserve or create. Between one's choice and encountering, the latter being beyond one's own choice, there is the second-order mechanism of traveling, conceived in terms of both physical movement and career path. Traveling always involves choices that facilitate subsequent encountering; hence, it is a second-order mechanism that fosters individual intellectual growth.

In the present chapter, on the basis of in-depth interviews with senior Taiwan scholars and activists,[3] I will discuss how China is accessed through knowledge of China in Taiwan. Given Taiwan's ambiguous Chinese identity, self-understanding is an essential ingredient of Taiwan scholars' understanding of China. Decisions taken in ever evolving individual biographies challenge the objectivity of knowledge.[4] The knowledge of China and the practices associated with the name of China constitute each other in China as well as elsewhere.[5] The evolution of knowledge on China follows trajectories of intellectual growth, each of which is embedded in its own social practices. The historical bearings of Taiwan's society and culture comprise the epistemological foundation of Taiwanese writings on China. They incorporate various biographies that have given rise to unusually rich and often mutually incompatible intellectual resources and inspirations, including, at the very least, the collective memory of all those groups with which one has sequentially identified throughout one's life. These historical bearings refer particularly to political and social movements launched and wars fought in the name of, or targeted at, China, and the associated political upheavals that caused social cleavages, political disarray, ideological confusion, and, at times, antiforeign nationalism.

China scholarship in Taiwan is composed of the choices scholars make between encountered and constantly reinterpreted imaginations of how China's names, identities, and images are incurred. Thanks to the legacies of colonialism, the Chinese Civil War, the Cold War, and the island's internal cleavages, China scholarship in Taiwan consists of strategic shifting between and combinations of the Japanese, American, and Chinese approaches to China. The mechanism of choice, including traveling, that orients, reorients, and disorients existing views on China produces conjunctive scholarship. The rich repertoire of views on China, together with the politics of identity, challenges the objectivist stance of the social sciences to the extent that no view on China can be exempted from political implications and politicized social scrutiny.[6] Concerns over exigent propriety in a social setting are internal to knowledge production. Therefore, understanding the process by which all the historically derived approaches inform China scholarship in Taiwan through the mechanism of encountering reveals both the uncertain nature of knowledge in general and the uncertain meanings associated with China anywhere in the world in particular.

Historical Bearings: Anti-Japan, Anticommunist, and Japanese Colonialism

World War II concluded with Japan's defeat and the termination of its five decades of colonial rule in Taiwan, which was then returned to China. Four years later, the Chinese Civil War ended with the defeat of the Kuomintang, which withdrew to Taiwan in order to prepare for retaking the mainland, but which gradually came to accept that it would remain in Taiwan. The defeat of the Kuomintang coincided with the beginning of the Cold War in East Asia, and Taiwan became a US base for the containment of communism. Both the Civil War and the Cold War compelled the ruling Kuomintang to portray Taiwan as Free China, an entity distinct from Communist China on the mainland. Initially, the regime appealed to anticommunist ideologues, but later, in response to Mao Zedong's Cultural Revolution, it came to rely on Confucianism and the alleged legitimacy of its claim to govern the whole of China. In the aftermath of the Vietnam War, the regime relied for its legitimacy on its adherence to modernization. After the Ford Foundation created the concept of the Pacific Rim, Taiwan became known as one of the capitalist newly industrialized countries (NICs).[7] Political and economic modeling was then substituted for military recovery of the mainland in the Kuomintang's narratives on China. More recently (specifically after the suppression of the 1989 prodemocracy movement in China), the Kuomintang and its pro-Taiwan independence competitor/successor, the Democratic Progressive Party (DPP), have enlisted the plea for democracy and human rights as components of Taiwan's identity. The Kuomintang and the DPP hoped to win the United States back to Taiwan's side following a ten-year interlude after the normalization of Washington-Beijing relations in 1979. They have also resorted to highlighting the value of peace and international security in the face of a threat from a China that they agree no longer includes Taiwan.[8]

This array of adaptations gives scholars in Taiwan a rich repertoire of perspectives to choose from when writing about China. The choice of any one scholar at any particular time and in any particular context also reflects which kind of China he or she believes in, and what combination of historical legacies he or she has inherited. Indirectly, all have been caught up in a century-long civilizational encounter imposed by European imperialism with all its ideological underpinnings and social changes. These social changes motivated a considerable number of Taiwanese activists and intellectuals of the early twentieth century, some of whom are still living today, to travel to China during the Japanese colonial period. These trips engendered among them a sympathetic attitude, the alienated feelings of the outsider, or ambivalence toward Chinese problems, depending on their actual experiences and interpretations.

Shih Ming (born 1918), the author of the first book to theorize the evolution of a distinctively non-Chinese Taiwan nationality, fought against Japanese imperialism in China under the leadership of the Chinese Communist Party. While the idealistic notion of nationality is incompatible with materialistic socialism, he painstakingly attempted to prove that the proletarian class in Taiwan had a much stronger pro-Taiwan consciousness than the bourgeoisie. He did this in order to demonstrate that Taiwanese nationalism composed of proletarian consciousness had a materialist foundation. China left him with a negative impression of its feudal legacy, which convinced him that Taiwan should divest itself of its Chineseness after the war. The defeat of Japan resolved his ambivalence toward the Japanese and reservations about the end of Japanese imperialism. He was able to support his research and writing due to the success of his business in Japan. There, Shih Ming accorded modernity referential significance. He accused the Kuomintang of being the representatives of a feudal and colonial China in Taiwan, exploiting the island but unable to bring it modernity.[9]

Liao Wenkui (1905–1952), another writer of note who was dubbed the "Father of Taiwan Independence," studied at Nanjing College before enrolling at the University of Chicago. Liao started out as a disciple of Sun Yat-sen's Chinese nationalism and an opponent of Japanese imperialism. Unlike Shih Ming, though, he was always a liberal, thanks to American influence. Liao embarked on a teaching career in China after receiving his PhD from Chicago. After witnessing the February 28 incident of 1947, the bloody clash between the Kuomintang and the semi-decolonized society, Liao became a supporter of Taiwanese nationalism based upon an emerging self-awareness embedded in strategic adaptation to changing social conditions.[10] The constructed style of Liao's Taiwanese nationalism makes China less of an enemy to him than Shih Ming's class enemy is to him. Compared with other Taiwanese writers of the time, Shih and Liao were neither unique nor typical; experiences of China produced in other people a variety of feelings over time, reinforcing the Chinese identity of some and producing ambivalence toward China among others.

The retreat of the Kuomintang regime to Taiwan expedited clashes of interests between the newly arrived and the indigenous populations. It also caused a clash of identities among the indigenous Taiwanese themselves.

In contrast with the distinct self-identification of those who relied on either classic Chinese or modern American intellectual resources, local intellectuals, informed by Japanese perspectives on China, could instead engage with the postcolonial pursuit of a modern Asia that transcended Taiwan's return to China.[11] The latter strategy epistemologically relegates China's culture to the unworthy bondage of the past. The February 28 incident, which had contributed to anti-Chinese sentiment among locals and anti-Japanese sentiment among the newly arrived mainlanders, reproduced this impression of mutual aversion. After all, the Kuomintang brought with it memories of the Nanjing Massacre and was primordially anti-Japan. Chen Li-shen (born 1931), a veteran China hand, spoke of China as being "our acquired concept—a concept of race, a concept of nation, and a concept of family . . . as [engrossed] in the most difficult time of the War of Resistance before 1945 . . . "[12] In fact, Yu Tzong-shian (born 1930), a former head of the Chinese Institute of Economics and Business, still refers to the Japanese by the pejorative term "ghosts" (*guizi*) throughout his interviews.[13] The transition to Taiwan was further complicated in Yu's case by his double orientation of anticommunism (due to the political alignment of his home village) and anti-Japanese (due to his personal experience during the war) before both became politically obsolete, if not politically incorrect at all, much later in Taiwan's proindependence atmosphere. The post–Civil War generations could not escape the challenge of choosing between these perspectives if they ultimately went into public life. Li Kuo-chi (born 1922), a German-trained historian, wrote his dissertation on the ceding of Taiwan to Japan in 1895, after spending his entire youth on the run from the Japanese invaders.[14] Ironically, his historiography has become increasingly unpopular among younger generation colleagues.

Migrant scholars who were born before or during the Sino-Japanese war share a deep distrust of Japan. They all refer to the suffering they experienced during childhood or youth as a result of the Japanese invasion. They carried these memories with them when they came to Taiwan around 1949 with their families or the Kuomintang troops. Many of them see China as a victim of imperialism. It is difficult for them to conceive of the defeated Kuomintang, who led the war against Japan, as an alien regime, as they believe Taiwan would not have been liberated from Japanese rule without the suffering of the Chinese people. Their scholarship is deliberately aimed at serving China whenever such an opportunity arises. Notably, Chang Huan-ching (born 1935), another old China hand, relinquished his academic career in the United States in 1980, after Washington established diplomatic ties with Beijing and abandoned his beloved Republic of China. Chang returned to Taiwan to support the cause of anticommunism.[15] Yeh Chi-cheng (born 1943), a leading proindependence scholar of indigenous sociology, empathizes with the hostility of his migrant colleagues toward the Taiwan independence movement and how they were treated as aliens by the proindependence force in return:

> . . . so, the local Taiwanese and the migrant residents each carry their own sorrow. When sitting next to each other, they are pathetically unable to share each other's feelings. On the contrary, they may even become confrontational and hostile to each other. It is understandable that ordinary people may act this way, but when intellectuals likewise meet head-on, that is a really big problem. Especially when this [mutual animosity] alludes to relations with China, the problem is increasingly complicated. Allow me to say that, from here, the ultimate challenge is, in fact, that the Taiwanese and the migrant people have had different life experiences and have followed two historical trajectories.[16]

The colonial trajectory does indeed contrast sharply with the migrant one. As the culmination of their five decades of colonial rule (1895–1945), the Japanese initiated the *kōminka* movement, through which they generated emotional loyalty to the Japanese emperor, mostly among the educated, landed, and professional echelons of Taiwan society. Soldiers recruited to serve in the ranks of the imperial army in Southeast Asia later proved to be another group of loyal supporters. *Kōminka* convinced the colonial subjects that they were no longer "slaves of the Manchus," as they had been labeled during the earlier period of colonial rule, giving them a status that was below even that of the barbarian non-Han intruders from the North. This elevation from the status of a slave to that of an equal subject shaped the attitude of the postcolonial society toward the Kuomintang and the China it symbolized. However, Chen Peng-jen (born 1930), a veteran native Taiwanese historian affiliated with the Kuomintang, attests to a largely Chinese society in the countryside that remained untouched by *kōminka*. This prepared him to empathize readily with both his Japanese-influenced acquaintances and migrant Chinese colleagues, although the former tended to view China from a modernist perspective whereas the latter saw it through the lens of the Civil War.[17]

Post–World War II Developments:
Between Civil War Scholarship, Scientism, and Proindependence

The February 28 incident, in which people on both sides were killed, started with rioting among Taiwanese, many of whom were disillusioned with the Kuomintang takeover after World War II. The riots were supported both by the colonially educated youth and by soldiers returning from service in the Japanese imperial army in Southeast Asia. The violence was directed at recent migrants from China, and it provoked retaliation by Kuomintang reinforcements sent from China. This was the point at which the Kuomintang gained the image of an alien regime, and China, symbolized in Taiwan by the Kuomintang, began to be viewed from time to time as just another country. The subsequent land reform, which the Kuomintang, haunted by the peasant revolution that had toppled their regime in China, enforced so successfully, was depicted by Taiwanese anti-China campaigners in the 1990s as Chinese beggars robbing their Taiwanese hosts of their land. Parris Chang Hsu-cheng (born 1936), an expert in Chinese factionalism and later a proindependence legislator, confirms this impression. It was only after he reached adulthood that he was able to understand what he saw as the absurdity of the Kuomintang's land reform policy. Agricultural workers were given their own land, and landowners were compensated with stocks that proved to be of little worth.[18]

Shih Ming and Liao Wen-kui are not alone in believing that it took the February 28 incident to make the Taiwanese realize the alien nature of the Kuomintang regime. Chen Peng-jen recalls his experience of the incident as a failed takeover attempt, whereas Yeh Chi-cheng maintains that it was a matter of a clash of cultures. Putting aside the causes, the February 28 incident has shaped the way China is understood in Taiwan by subsequent generations. However, it would be an oversimplification to divide the two sides into pro-Japan and pro-China. Both Chen Peng-jen and Hsu Chieh-lin (born 1935), the retired dean of social sciences at National Taiwan University, were trained in Japan but were unenthusiastic about the idea of independence. Chen was vehemently against it as his career benefitted from his early acquaintance with a senior migrant Kuomintang (or the Nationalist Party, thereafter KMT) official. Both specifically mention that their political attitude toward China was unaffected by their Japanese mentors.[19] In parallel, Shih Chian-sheng (born 1917), the migrant author of the first college-level economics textbook in Chinese and a dedicated Keynesian, declares his deep love for Taiwan even though he was never involved with the political campaign for independence. He concludes his interview with an expression of his love for both China and Taiwan:

> I have been suffering my entire life [because of the historical victimization of China]. In 1979, Deng Xiaoping was about to establish diplomatic relations with the United States. I was in the States when TV reporters asked him during his visit why he advocated communism. He replied that the communists were simple; they only hoped for freedom and equal status in the world so that the Chinese people could live and work peacefully. This was unimpressive, but it touched me deeply. Now, thirty years have passed. Thirty years is a short span

in history. Whether we like it or not, China has risen. With its huge territory and population, it has many problems, but the trend is undeniable. I think I love Taiwan because I love China, because loving Taiwan is [a way of] loving China, and because loving Taiwan requires loving China. Taiwan will be fine when China is fine. Taiwan would be the first to suffer if China were chaotic. So, I am satisfied. Two years ago, I went to China every year for a conference, but I would also visit the new construction sites, so many of them. I never went there as a tourist. In Taiwan, I am a prounification hardliner, but I think I love Taiwan dearly.[20]

The larger context was the Cold War. In the midst of the "who lost China" debate and the subsequent McCarthyism, the Kuomintang was deemed by Washington to be its only viable ally in its containment circle. The political and economic support of the United States brought the Kuomintang through all the diplomatic setbacks of later decades, even after it renounced its claim to be the legitimate ruler of China and its plans to return to the mainland. Students from Taiwan have been going to the United States for higher education since the 1960s. Today, the Taiwanese cabinet and legislature is full of graduates of US universities. The social sciences in Taiwan are dominated by American methodologies, and as a consequence, the better schools in Taiwan discriminate against holders of degrees from non-English-speaking countries. In a peculiar way, the anti-Chinese and the anticommunist forces have converged in an epistemological choice that promotes theoretical approaches that place China at a lower stage of development. This epistemological proclivity constructs an image of a successful Taiwan that appears closer to its Western supporters than its rival, Communist China.

Scientism was the general choice of later generations who either sought to generate a distinct professionalism to make up for their lack of the direct experience of China that privileged the Civil War generation or were trying to move away from the historical and philosophical China in preparation for Taiwan assuming an independent identity. Both of these attitudes find comfort in scientism, which renders the Kuomintang's older Chinese identities, along with the unresolved issue of the Chinese Civil War, seemingly irrelevant, although the identities that replace them are very different from each other. Even Taiwanese scholars in Hong Kong were able to benefit from scientism. Peter Li Nan-shong (born 1940) adopts a comparative approach at a macro-level, enabling him to be conversant with the English-language literature of public policy and management. This presumably provides Li with an objectivist position that transcends Hong Kong's return to China.[21] Scientism is so strong that only a few people in Taiwan are able to escape its effects, but how it should be used is uncertain. For example, realism in international politics could be used to support an anti-China policy by treating

China's rise as a threat that should be balanced. However, it could likewise support a pro-China policy that sees China as a plausible ally in balancing the overwhelming influence of the United States. Nevertheless, China studies have moved from being problem oriented (Civil War, political security, legitimacy) to being theory and method oriented, as exemplified by such topics as civil society, agency, political efficacy, and the like.[22] China is reduced to one case in a comparative frame embedded in methodological individualism. Members of the now retiring generation of academics from all disciplines have been anxiously watching the younger generation of researchers who embrace the American research agenda, some reflecting methodologically, others practically.

Interest in indigenous methodology dates from the early 1980s. Scholars are unsure if there is ultimately only one system of knowledge that can transcend cultural and national differences. Nevertheless, the call for Chinese methods to be used to discover Chinese reality seems to be shared by all. In short, while there is no consensus regarding an ontologically distinct China, an epistemology specifically for studying China is agreed upon. One group of social scientists, the majority of them migrant scholars, began to promote the Sinicization of the social sciences. While Hu Fu (born 1929) and Li Yi-yuan (born 1931) worked on the indigenous research agenda in political science and anthropology, respectively, it was Yang Kuo-shu (born 1932), a leading social psychologist, now retired, who officially launched the indigenous psychology movement in 1991, which led to the successful establishment of a new subdiscipline in Taiwan.[23] In sociology, the local proindependence scholar Yeh Chi-cheng has been the most vocal advocate of an indigenous methodology as he reflects upon sociology in the Chinese context, something that is basically all about the expansion of Western influence. He is attempting what he calls the anthropology of philosophy, in an effort to de-Westernize his academic training.[24] His late colleague, Lucie Cheng (1939–2010), coming from a socialist, feminist, and Chinese consciousness, was more straightforward in her criticism of Western social science's championing of democracy, although she acknowledged that at present, criticisms of this kind were appropriate only in private:

> I don't agree that democracy is essentially a universal value. The form of democracy we know now, voting for example, should not be a universal value. We could say democracy emerges in certain conditions. So, Chinese conditions may produce a kind of democracy that is not the Western form. It would be wrong to take the Western form of democracy and compare it with China to determine whether there is democracy [in China]. However, when I say this, Western scholars think that I am only trying to justify China's lack of democracy.[25]

Practical concerns and policy issues may likewise sensitize a veteran scholar to the limitations of imported social science theory. Hsieh Jiann (born 1934) relies on his ethnology to alert him to the perceived misconceptions of Marxism, Western anthropology, and the application of Western psychology to China. In particular, he notes the way China's multiple ethnic components have come together to form a common Chinese identity. He accuses the Kuomintang of colluding with imperialism in the exploitation of Chinese ethnic minorities. He is particularly concerned with prejudice among Western academics concerning Tibet and China's Tibet policy.[26] Yu Tzong-shian, in the same pragmatic tone, questions the fashion for econometrics, which he believes has led to useless engagement with the Western research agenda. As a consequence, knowledge that is useful to Taiwanese manufacturing and other industries appears inferior, if not entirely dispensable. This specifically refers to Taiwan's economic opportunities in China. In opposition to the mainstream view, Yu maintains that economics should be local, not general:

> . . . so many economists fail to attend to economic reality or past economic practice. They are obsessed with refining mathematical models almost unrelated to the economics of the real world. This is because Taiwan is too small a sample for its research to attract the attention of international academics . . . Studies of technology are not geographically bonded. Research of this sort, for example, mathematics, physics, biology, and chemistry, is international, but the humanities and social sciences are not international. They are local in nature.[27]

At Academic Conjunctures: Institutions and Personal Career Tracks in Transition

Most contemporary scholars are indebted to migrant scholars of earlier generations in a variety of ways, and this urges tolerance and respect toward members of the older generation, although they have, to some extent, been ghettoized because of their Chinese identities in the drive for a separate Taiwanese statehood. Migrant scholars typically left their families or their hometowns during the war and eventually followed the Kuomintang into exile in Taiwan. Some became China scholars by accident, but for others, it was something to which they were assigned. Early on, the migrant Kuomintang recruited China scholars from this group because they were typically young, single, and independent of any postcolonial social and political networks.

Rui He-chen (born 1921) is one example. He was constantly given instructions by his Kuomintang guardian as he moved from one academic post to another, even when he finally took charge of Taiwan's first and most renowned China studies institution—the Institute of East Asian Studies. The institute was affiliated to National Chengchi University (NCCU), but was under the tight control of the Kuomintang regime, especially the regime's intelligence sectors. Rui was instructed by his superiors to teach at NCCU as an adjunct professor, and was soon appointed head of the Department of Political Science. He was reassigned to manage student affairs at the university during a time of political change, and he was then moved to the Institute of East Asian Studies. He was taken by surprise each time he was called upon to move. His nonpolitical career, willingness to cooperate, and disciplined personality were the criteria for selecting him for promotion each time.[28] Similarly, Wang Chang-ling (born 1927), a Bureau of Investigation researcher who taught at National Taiwan University as an adjunct professor for 17 years, obediently studied what he was told to study and taught the courses he was advised to teach.[29] In comparison, a younger scholar, Chang Huan-ching, thanks to an unexpected encounter with a US-based Chinese scholar who took him under his wing, embarked on a study trip to the United States, which prepared him for a career in China studies. Eventually, he acquired the position of the head of the Institute of East Asian Studies.[30] Most interestingly, Li Kuo-chi came to Taiwan after refusing to take over the management of his family's business. He came to a coastal city to help the Kuomintang with cargo shipments.[31]

The Institute of East Asian Studies was supported by the national security sector of the regime, which also financed a variety of other research institutions devoted to the study of Communist China in the first few decades after 1949. According to Chang Huan-ching, those recruited by the Institute of East Asian Studies predominantly came from three sources: political cadres in the military, students in exile, and members of the intelligence sector. The last group was also in charge of internal security.[32] Any competition between them was purely factional because they shared an anticommunist ideology, aversion to Japan, and anxiety about Taiwan independence. Given that China studies at that time was seen as part of the Civil War, as Chen Li-shen (born 1931) recalls, real power belonged to the intelligence sectors, the most significant of which were the Bureau of Military Intelligence (BMI) under the Ministry of Defense and the Kuomintang's Mainland Affairs Department (MAD).[33] The latter's huge budget supported intelligence work in mainland China and overseas. Hsiao Hsing-yi (born 1939), a latecomer to the organization, confirms that the climax of its work was during the Cultural Revolution when internal documents were leaked en masse and gathered by Kuomintang agents. In addition to the BMI and the MAD, the Bureau of Investigation also had its own research branch that collected information regarding China.[34] Chiang Hsin-li (born 1941), a prolific writer on political ideology, began his career in the Bureau and recalls how he was able to develop expertise in Marxism, something that no longer interests the younger generation.[35] It was when the Institute of East Asian Studies was established in 1970 that China studies was given the chance to attain an academic identity. As the Civil War lost its momentum and democratization appeared on the horizon, MAD gradually lost its function.

New think tanks staffed by university faculty were established and funded out of the government's national security budget. One prominent participant in these is Chen (Philip) Ming (born 1935). Once considered for the position of deputy secretary of the National Security Bureau, Chen took over as deputy director of MAD instead. He was deeply involved in the operation of the powerful Asia and World Institute in the early 1990s and, after its demise, in the launch of the Prospect Foundation in 1997.[36] His contemporary Chang King-yuh (born 1937), former chairman of the Mainland Affairs Council and a former president of NCCU, seems to have followed exactly the same track as Chen Ming. Having been active in organizing academic gatherings, he was recruited by the Kuomintang for consultancy positions at first and subsequently for policy-making positions. Both Chen and Chang were in the younger age bracket and mentally prepared for public office. Chang decided early in his childhood that he wanted to strengthen his nation and he picked Bismarck as his role model.[37] Chen regrets that he was not able to serve the public sector more after his retirement. Their participation in the new think-tanks is a product of their time as well as of their personalities.

Since the 1990s, establishing think tanks has become fashionable among politicians-in-waiting, or those who have just left public office. China studies are always one of the most popular subjects. Think tanks are an important feature of contemporary China studies in Taiwan. They rise and fall as their sponsors come and go, following in the entourage of certain politicians. Think tanks are an investment in power for local businesses. The National Security Bureau establishes the most stable and resourceful think tanks. The researchers connected with these have the additional responsibility of carrying out second-track diplomacy. Affiliation with think tanks can be full- or part-time, and the research scholars carry out for the think tank is focused on either policy orientation or current affairs. Most think tanks have either an established policy tendency or a preferred political candidate. Thus, think tank research has to toe the political line.

Discursive Politics of China Studies

The common feature shared by China scholars in Taiwan is an ability to constantly adapt and change. Most have the intellectual capacity to look at China from both an external and an indigenous standpoint. Many are bilingual in terms of the academic literature with which they engage, and many of them have switched politically from a Chinese perspective to a consciously Taiwanese one. Writing for a Chinese audience, an international audience, and a Taiwanese audience poses different challenges. Many are able to respond to all conditions, but all of them have to decide whether or not to shift to a different perspective under particular conditions. Some who have taught about China in the United States typically felt awkward as they attempted to make sense of the Chinese situation. In the eyes of their audience, they could appear to be trying to justify China and they might on occasion actually wish to do this. Lee (Leo) Ou-fan[38] (born 1942), an expert in Chinese literature, once experienced the embarrassment of seemingly speaking on behalf of China. He recalls his teaching career in the United States as one of being consciously interdisciplinary, peripheral, and, occasionally, revolutionary. While he chose to challenge the mainstream, he also had to adapt because the mainstream was different at different times or at different sites. Weng (Byron) Sung-jan (born 1934), an expert in international law, is more straightforward with regard to his political color, considering that he has also traveled widely in the United States, Hong Kong, and Taiwan. He acknowledges that he "may have some color." In his interview, he says that his "color was once pink," owing to his ability to expound on China's position during the Vietnam War. He knows that others see him as "green" today because he appears to be sympathetic to the proindependence DPP. However, he admits that he was once "blue"—the representative color of the Kuomintang. His answer to his own question "what am I?" is "neither fish nor fowl."[39]

Epistemologically, one can imagine watching from a number of combinations of temporal and spatial positions. One could, for example, watch from somewhere outside of China, in a position that is defined territorially, culturally, or socially in contrast to a position somewhere inside of China. The Civil War generation typically positions its scholars to watch from the inside. To that extent, studying China resembles self-examination, relies on one's own experiences, and involves ideological polemics, fault-finding, political forecasting, and even international propaganda. Specifically, this particular kind of China scholarship sees Taiwan as a base for the cultural and national revival of China. In comparison, "containment" is an external position that does not have as its goal the toppling of the Communist regime. On the contrary, stability is a major issue for these scholars, China's domestic stability as well as the stability of the entire East Asian region. In security narratives, China's otherness is accepted as given, and it is seen as an undesired opponent. The contemporary literature on the China threat belongs to this school of thought. Finally, the scope of China is territorially defined from both the internal and the external point of view.

One could also choose to watch from a Western, qua universal, position as opposed to a non-Western position. Accordingly, one's scholarship would be limited to an imagined Euro-American audience although due to the language of the scholarship, one's main audience would remain in Taiwan. The Western identity of scholarship is clearer when it is juxtaposed with Civil War scholarship, for example. This identity is apparent in its method, theoretical perspective, and the literature from which scholars draw their academic puzzles heuristically. The state-society approach and the institutionalist approach are among the most popular examples. Another example, the game theory model, dominates the study of international relations. In contrast, it is cultural sensibility that gives rise to the non-Western position. It could lead to a binary or relativist worldview insinuating some uniqueness into the Chinese phenomenon. It may not be a bad view, in the postcolonial sense, if one celebrates cultural hybridity and appreciates the discursive appropriation of Chinese legacies and Western influences in an undecidable and mixed way suited to the needs of the time and the occasion. Studies of Chinese ethnic issues or Chinese overseas belong to this strand of thought.

The Western perspective is particularly popular. If being Western means adopting methodological individualism in social science, being Western also means liberalism, philosophically speaking. Interestingly, two senior scholars from Taiwan with completely different approaches with regard to China— one liberal, the other cultural—begin with a similar observation: that the Chinese Communist Party has not really transcended traditional Chinese culture. Huang (Mab) Mou (born 1935), a determined human rights advocate, wants to separate political identity from discussion of human rights, so that the promotion of human rights in the Chinese context will not be hindered by political confrontation between proindependence and antiindependence forces in Taiwan or between communism and anticommunism over the Taiwan Strait. He is also suspicious of Confucianism, which he believes has unnecessarily complicated and obscured the human rights issue.[40] Hsiung (James) Chieh (born 1935), a professor at New York University and by no means a liberal or a Western theorist, has been particularly keen on maintaining a balance between China studies and international relations, between left and right, and between China and Taiwan. In his research on China, he takes a pragmatic view that incorporates Chinese and Confucian practices and worldviews. To be pragmatic, one has to rely on international law and knowledge of the world. Hsiung has thus been deeply involved in policy consultation and negotiation between Taipei and Beijing.[41]

Another mode of positioning that is temporal and usually implicit involves deciding on a linear, pluralist, or cyclical perspective. From a linear perspective, Taiwan and China are the same except that they are at different historical stages. Part of China is possibly more advanced than another part, but it is the watcher in Taiwan who is in the more advanced position. Taiwan represents China's future. Its economic development provides a lesson for Beijing to learn. Its political democratization is a harbinger of what China will be like in the generations to come. Even Taiwan's problems anticipate China's future problems, and as such, Beijing can learn from them.[42] From a pluralist perspective, Taiwan and China have their own separate historical trajectories, and other parts of China may have their own distinctive trajectories also. The indigenous practices of Chinese localities are the focus of pluralist historiography. Each study is a representation of an exotic site or practice. According to the cyclical perspective, Taiwan and China are both different and the same depending on the stage of history they have reached. The two entities are involved in a competition to decide which will prove dominant when they once again merge together. The criterion could be modernist or Confucianist; therefore, the function of scholarship is to justify one's choice of criterion for evaluating the performance of Taiwan in comparison with China.

Anticommunism has declined since the 1980s, but the anticommunist orientation has lingered on in that agenda in the humanities that reconnects China with the Confucianism of China's East Asian neighbors and sees communism as merely a brief interruption in the Chinese historical trajectory, which has its deepest origins in Confucianism. There has been a revival of various aspects of Confucianism in the twenty-first century. Both the aforementioned indigenous psychology and the nascent transnational project of East Asian Confucianism have begun to explore a social science and humanities agenda that incorporates Confucian epistemology.[43] This approach divides Confucianism and Christianity into a binary world. Liu Shu-hsien (born 1937), a neo-Confucianist scholar of Chinese political thought who taught in the United States, Hong Kong, and Taiwan, is anticommunist in his belief that Confucianism and Western liberalism share a common epistemology. For him, the study of China is accordingly premised upon the problem of how to cope with Chinese tradition as a continuing legacy, a transcended irrelevance, or a modernized culture.[44]

Few Taiwanese study in Korea, India, Singapore, Eastern Europe, or Russia. Some study in China, Australia, or Canada, and more study in Japan and Western Europe. However, most of those who study abroad do so in the United States. These countries all provide different contexts for the study of China. Once trained, Taiwanese scholars may return home straight away, stay on for a while, stay permanently, or return home only after retiring.

How Can Taiwan's China Scholarship Create Multiple Chinas?

Is there a core concept that is China-unique or Communist-unique? Can a Chinese become someone else or vice versa through learning and teaching? How can China change through practice? Is there a core China that is static, incapable of adapting to external changes, and inaccessible to outsiders? There are many answers to these questions, and Taiwanese scholarship is familiar with almost all of them. China experts in Taiwan encounter all kinds of historical trajectories and their concomitant ideological and political contexts. The encountering, both physical and psychological, allows and compels them to choose among a variety of theoretical possibilities, each with certain political implications. Ignorance of alternatives is at best a decision not to act upon them, rather than being innocently unavoidable. Scholars of China, or any other conceptual actors, are responsible for their choice, in terms of its consequences in the real world, in a way that most social scientists are afraid to contemplate.

Initially, one may conclude that China can be approximated only by looking at samples of Chinese people and Chinese sites at various levels, for example, the village, township, county, or province, and seeing in each an aspect of the Chinese whole. Taiwanese scholars are better equipped than others for this, in terms of their proficiency in the social sciences and the Chinese language. Alternatively, China can be seen as a combination of separate yet overlapping parts, consisting of different civilizations, ecological conditions, forms of political economy, and human conventions, each characterized with subjectivity. Taiwanese scholars are culturally and linguistically sensitive to the nuanced meanings that are not expressed in official documents but are representative of local uniqueness.

For others, China is practically unique. It has faced various problems associated with central planning, the threats posed by US imperialism and Soviet hegemonism, the Cultural Revolution, ownership reform, and global governance, all of which require solutions but give rise to future problems that cannot be theoretically anticipated. Taiwanese scholars have better access to documents and people, and have the degree of political sensibility necessary to appreciate the problems faced by contemporary Chinese society. One could also decide that China has an "Oriental" identity that motivates it to reproduce or transcend differences between the East and the West. Taiwanese scholars are well versed in the Western and Chinese narratives on China in which both Orientalizing and Occidentalizing are viable solutions.

However, most scholars have begun with the assumption that China is a piece of territory marked by sovereign borders protected and reproduced through national defense and political control. Taiwanese scholars are familiar with both the Civil War and the Cold War, while Chinese military exercises in the Taiwan Strait keep them alert to the international security issues that reduce China to a geopolitical unit.

For many Sinologists in Taiwan and elsewhere, China is a source of wisdom and lessons, and a continuing tradition drawn from the classic literature. Most Taiwanese scholars were schooled in the Chinese classics, and they creatively apply these values to their interpretation of how contemporary Chinese cope with mundane issues. As Francis Hsu noted, Han Chinese live under the shadow of their ancestors, and China is where their ancestors' graves are located. Taiwanese scholars, who are undoubtedly Han Chinese, are constantly forced to decide whether their ancestors represent an irrelevant past or a lineage that they can reconnect with for cultural as well as economic reasons.

Postmodern writers growing up with the clichés of multiculturalism are now promoting the idea that China is a drama in which the players are constantly reinterpreting their roles, thereby creating different Chinas; hence, there is a dramaturgical script, a constructed subject of knowledge, and a text serving the authors' purpose. Taiwanese scholars are either the initiators or the potential allies of an Asianism that promotes multiple Chinas. Postcolonial writers could further construct a self-concept from nuanced multicultural sensibilities, concluding that China is culturally defiant of Confucianism, racially Han, and ideologically authoritarian and socialist—this is categorically different from one's self-identity. Taiwanese identities, informed culturally by modern capitalism as well as Confucianism, racially by aboriginal nativism, and politically by liberal democracy, enable scholars to assert a mutual estrangement in the relationship between Taiwan and China.

CHAPTER 4

Global Chinese: Contending Approaches to Defending Chineseness

W hy it is difficult to form a China-centric methodology? Although China-centered studies are called for by European or North American writers critical of mainstream China studies, the China-centered approach is not particularly evident in published work. Responses from overseas Chinese writers reveal at least two kinds of China-centrism: one based on the country's development needs, to which pre-1949 history is irrelevant, and another embedded in Chinese history and cultural tradition, the historiography of which sees the span of 60 decades since 1949 as trivial. Both approaches, in effect, are opposed to relegating China to another case of general propositions derived from the mainstream agenda and its critics. They have yet to give birth to an epistemic community based on a nascent China-centric consciousness. This chapter demonstrates that China studies as practiced by overseas Chinese scholars is political and value laden, each scholar embedded in an epistemological context. In the future, China studies in China can serve as a possible point of integration, albeit remaining political in nature.

Whose Centrism?

Recent disputes in the Korean literature over "ownership" of the dragon boat festival, as well as the Goguryeo relics located in Chinese Manchuria, challenge the long-established myth of mainland China as the center in East Asian history. There is a rumor in China that even soy milk, one of the most popular Chinese breakfast beverages, could be claimed as a Korean invention. While most Chinese may laugh with disbelief on hearing about the Korean origins of "their" cultural legacy, we should remember that this is not the first time such arguments have been made. Huang Chun-chieh, a leading Confucian scholar at National Taiwan University, is interested in how and why premodern Japanese intellectuals in the seventeenth century advocated the view that Japan is the real China.[1] It has not occurred to him that, to the puzzlement of bystanders, his home country of Taiwan had—for over four decades—also insisted that Taipei was the real capital of China.

How should and can China and its rise be represented? The answer depends on who wants to do the representing. That is why the arguments that China studies should be China centered, instead of Euro-, US-, or Japan centered, still exist separately. The scholars making these arguments are not Chinese writers, but Anglophone and Japanese ones.[2] In Taiwan, for example, there was a call for the establishment of "Chinese social science" in the 1980s. These efforts sought to correct the bias in the universal claims of "Western" behavioral patterns by supplying a "Chinese" perspective that is epistemologically different. Applying a Chinese perspective allegedly enhances the universality of knowledge.[3] However, no China-centrism can be fully China centered if its primary purpose is to improve the universality of social science, which is dear to Western academics. It is the recent Korean challenges to China's centrality that have finally shifted people's attention to a different, contending representation of China that aims to do something other than improve social science.

Accordingly, the thinking process of China-centrism involves a decision between identity and image. An individual's choice of identity is about achieving a perspective on "China" that establishes his or her difference from either "China" or the "West," hence Korea-centrism, Singapore-centrism, Vietnam-centrism, India-centrism, and so on. The choice of image, in contrast, is about how well this added perspective on China contributes to a reflexive "Western" social science, so it is an image of being universal in the eyes of American colleagues rather than being different. To have a better image, one must therefore evaluate China-centrism as a kind of self-criticism of "Western" social science, which is aimed at enhancing Western universality and, ultimately, epistemological Euro-centrism. For most Chinese social scientists,[4] the image problem is of utmost importance, while the identity problem takes a back seat. This is because paradigms in contemporary Sinophone China studies are generally copies of Western paradigms. In the study of Chinese foreign policy, for example, one sees the familiar (or copied) divisions between realism, idealism, and constructivism. Sinophone international relations scholars simulate the debate by providing either the Chinese "case" (when confirming a theory) or the Chinese "anomaly" (when denying one).

While more and more Chinese social scientists develop their careers in Anglophone academia (and therefore need to take care of their image), most Chinese obviously do not appreciate the Korean re-presentation of "their" cultural heritage. The Korean challenge creates an identity dimension for Chinese social scientists, predominantly also China experts, because the China they want to present to their Korean colleagues is not the same as the one they want to present to the Anglophone world. The Korean challenge, or, along the same lines, the Vietnamese, Indian, Singaporean, or perhaps simply the Asian challenges, all provide an incentive for Chinese intellectuals to look away from the Anglophone world and redirect their attention toward a self-knowledge that comes from within. Only then is an epistemic community embedded in Chinese China-centrism possible. The excitement surrounding the way that *tianxia* (literally "all under heaven") rhetoric has gained momentum in the past few years is a clear indicator of this trend.

With the exception of the once predominant debate on the Sinicization of Marxism in China,[5] signs of China-centrism in the non-Marxian social sciences in China can be traced back to the mid-1990s.[6] However, there is as yet no awareness of the need for a transnational China-centric epistemic community. These domestic traces were largely responses to the challenge of re-presenting China in the Anglophone world. Note that before the new Asian challenges, the China threat and the clash of civilizations discourses in the aftermath of Tiananmen Square incident in 1989 took center stage. There was also the unresolved Chinese Civil War; as the rivalry developed into peaceful competition, the intellectual representation of China became a point of contention between the two sides—as well as for forces within Taiwan. These occurrences prompted self-reflection among Chinese social scientists. This chapter will look at how these early traces may or may not serve as the foundation for a China-centric epistemic community in the future. Without such a foundation, it would be difficult for Chinese social scientists to effectively adjust to the Asian challenges or to the China threat discourse. Put differently, this chapter will examine how an image problem for Chinese social scientists, that of how to become universal in compliance with Western criteria, has the opportunity of evolving into a quest for an entirely different identity.

Nonaligned Sinophone Experts on China

Unlike their Indian, Latin American, or African colleagues, Chinese scholars rarely join forces to challenge Euro-centrism in social science. Most other non-European academics likewise imported social science disciplines from their former colonial masters. Dominated by a consciousness best described as "resisting," this later led to the rise of dependency theory, the assertion of Asian values, and the crusade associated with the principles of postcolonialism/Orientalism. In contrast to other parts of the world, China was never completely colonized, and neither did a single colonial power manage to conquer the entire country. The difference felt by China in relation to its invaders was understood as one against a diffusive, inconsistent (but often attractive) West. Chinese intellectuals were not enthusiastic about treating the social sciences as a battleground for resistance, as they did not have a specific colonial master to resist.[7] This provides a partial explanation as to why Chinese social scientists have yet to become an integral part of Western scholarship. The same probably applies to Japanese, Korean, and Taiwanese academics. Compared with the confidence that dependency theorists and postcolonial/Orientalist critics exhibit when faced with mainstream scholarship, the intellectual task for Northeast Asian academics remains one of mimicking rather than resisting.[8] Their style of scholarship is one of image, rather than one of identity.

Even today, overseas Chinese social scientists typically go about their social science debates in the same fashion as American academics would.[9] The ability to keep up to date with developments in the field distinguishes their scholarship from that of their domestic counterparts. An anomaly that prompts a shift of paradigm in social science in the West could lead to a similar shift in the world of overseas Chinese academics. In other words, there is no indigenous Chinese "anomaly" that contributes to the evolution of universal social science disciplines. Harry Harding once wished that a new generation of China experts could detect a certain origin of theorization in their Chinese "anomaly."[10] This is a wish originating within the circle of Western academics, but is nevertheless simultaneously an assignment that overseas Chinese social scientists are usually given and expected to carry out. This further reinforces a particular mindset among overseas Chinese scholars, making them see themselves as informants to social scientists. The quest for a different identity for Chinese China studies is simply out of the question. Alignment among Chinese scholars has thus been avoided, lest it should obstruct their quest for recognition by Western academics.

It was 45 years ago that writers in English first called for the integration of China studies and the social science disciplines,[11] but the process is still far from complete. American and British China experts have a conscious choice to make when applying for professional promotion; they need to decide whether they should arrange to have their work reviewed by China experts or disciplinary scholars. Interestingly, few overseas Chinese scholars feel the tension between area identity and disciplinary identity, since they are usually ready to be reviewed by both sides. As an area expert, one is expected to use literature written in Chinese and field studies conducted in China, as well as historical analysis. In contrast, to be a disciplinary scholar, one has to employ generalized theory and operational methods that use China as a case to confirm or revise selected universal behavioral patterns. Chinese China experts are skillful in enlisting both original materials and scientific methods.[12]

Most of the time, their Chinese origin is enough to convince Anglophone area experts to accept overseas Chinese China scholars as China experts. They are well trained in the social sciences, too. Many of them collect Chinese material with ease, allowing them to confirm or revise general theories according to their theoretical position at the time. This is no different from the way their counterparts within China use one theory or another to justify a policy platform. Although the theoretical identity of most Sinophone China experts is far from determined and usually open to change, few of them have experienced the kind of struggle that once tormented the late Ray Huang, the author of such bestsellers as *1587, a Year of No Significance: The Ming Dynasty in Decline*,[13] *China: A Macro History*,[14] and *Broadening the Horizons of Chinese History: Discourses, Syntheses, and Comparisons*.[15] Huang lacked methodological training and was infused with a sense of resistance, which are factors rarely present among contemporary overseas Chinese scholars.

Huang engaged in two kinds of defense at the same time. The first kind was his defense of Chiang Kai-shek's leadership and his rule through the Kuomintang, which made him appear to his colleagues as though he spoke on behalf of the regime.[16] Indeed, his scholarly findings suggested that the familiar criticisms of Chiang's rule showed insufficient understanding of the conditions in China at the time when Chiang came to power. For example, on the issue of corruption, Huang was able to show why public and private finance often had to mingle under the circumstances of the time by choosing an indigenous approach to China's financial system. This argument actually led to his making a theoretical contribution toward the explanation of Chinese economic history.[17] Unfortunately, each time he submitted a manuscript, Huang invariably faced overwhelming criticism from disciplinary reviewers in economics. Later in his career he was laid off by his college, along with other historians who taught classes on areas other than Europe or America.[18] This caused him to feel an enormous sense of shame.

Huang consciously chose not to subscribe to disciplinary methods, which he denounced as the cause of US scholars' inability to gain an overview of China.[19] He was heavily involved in defending his association with the defeated Kuomintang even as he developed his academic career. This distanced him from his mentors and colleagues both academically and socially, including John King Fairbank and William Theodore de Bary.[20]

Contemporary overseas Chinese scholars, born mostly in China, do not share the same Kuomintang background or the stance of resistance against American scholarship. In contrast, there has been a shared tendency for the new generation of scholars to shake off the legacy of the Cultural Revolution by embracing "Western" methodology. The fact that some of them have given thought to issues such as their position in the US academic establishment and their expertise in disciplinary methods indicates that they will find it easier than Huang did adapting to academic politics.

It is their familiarity with disciplinary methodology and intellectual capacity to adapt that sets contemporary overseas Chinese scholars apart from their predecessor. However, the same facility also reduces their need to form alliances: they are always concerned about accommodating various seemingly contradictory theories over the long haul of their careers, some even simultaneously. Here again is an example of the aforementioned image approach that allows them to maintain a good image in the eyes of their colleagues. In other words, decisions concerning the choice of theoretical position are not purely academic. They are also social decisions since they will affect their relationships with their mentors. Though many of them have acquired tenure, they do not feel comfortable with refuting the opinions of their teachers, even though they may disagree with them. After all, theories are short lived and limited, while relationships with teachers might last a lifetime. Since academic and social decisions are inseparable, they do not feel justified in adhering to a specific disciplinary method or theory. All these factors contribute to their flexible and ever changing academic positioning.

Individual efforts that revise (or even overturn) mainstream theories do not always win respect from colleagues, especially when scholars are not careful to adopt the disciplinary discourse. Huang decided to turn to high school students and college freshmen as a way of shunning tedious peer reviews that usually pay homage to disciplinary methodology. Huang likewise sought alliances back in Taiwan, but only received a lukewarm response.[21] He had more general readers buying his books than he had colleagues conversing with him in the ivory tower. For contemporary overseas Chinese scholars, their occasional critical reflections do not cause them serious career problems because they have, at the same time, published work that is well within the permitted parameters of academic dialogue. As long as one can survive, it makes no sense to form alliances with other Chinese scholars that reveal one's nonscientific identification. Collusion between overseas Chinese China experts and mainstream English-language writers when they theorize about China does not mean that the Chinese do not engage in critical reflection; it is only that such reflection is highly individualized and private, contingent upon the choice of a survival strategy, other personalized conditions, and their relationship with China.

National Conditions as China-centrism

Their adoption of highly individualized survival strategies explains why nonaligned overseas Sinophone China experts have yet to respond to the call for a China-centrism that is critical of the mainstream discipline. Ironically, this lack of response is a sign that they are not interested in improving universalism. To the extent that their concern is not about improving universalism, theirs is not a Euro-centric position, either. Their ability to adapt to and reconcile different theoretical propositions further suggests that these people are more interested in good social relationships than they are in judging theories. This lack of interest in theoretical identity is not uniquely Chinese; the Japanese scholar Akira Iriye describes his own scholarship as "centrist," and the Korean academic Samuel Kim characterizes his as "synthetic"[22] (see Chapter 9). To find merits in each of those contending theories and take advantage of their strengths reflects a kind of research style that is foreign to the majority of their American colleagues.[23] The implicit image approach in their writings on China is similarly incompatible with Euro-centrism. As a result, while many of them are neither consciously reserved about Euro-centrism nor oriented toward China-centrism, there are still indicators in their scholarship that show a promise of developing China-centrism.

Perhaps it was in 1997 that the first attempt was made at alignment among Sinophone scholars. Sponsored by the Taiwanese Current Foundation and under the leadership of Hu Fu, who is both a long-time student of behavioral political science and an admirer of the legendary Chinese liberal Hu Shih, overseas Chinese political scientists met with scholars from China, Taiwan, and Hong Kong at College Park, Maryland. A clear division of consciousness separated the Chinese visitors from their brethren in the United States, with the former pushing for some kind of China-centrism and the latter, with their mission to discover universal behavioral patterns, offering only a lukewarm response.[24] A subsequent meeting was held in Hong Kong two years later, followed by workshops on a smaller scale in Tokyo. The result was a seeming reduction in attempts at alignment coupled with a paradoxical rise in China-centric consciousness.

One scholar from China who has managed to establish a successful career in the United States since 1990 is Zhao Quansheng. It is hardly surprising that Zhao does not appreciate being engaged in debates among pundits. He is able to group together various theoretical perspectives with the intention of forming a unique explanation of Chinese foreign policy. One conversation between Zhao and a French colleague at the American Political Science Association in San Francisco in 1990 characterizes the different styles of scholarship.[25] After Zhao had explained that the context of "principle" in Chinese foreign policy was something not changed by situations, someone in the audience challenged him for presenting a circular argument. Indeed, his argument might have appeared circular as he advised the audience to look at the foreign policy behavior of the Chinese government in order to judge if a particular matter involved an issue of principle. Zhao's argument would not have been circular if he had been able to move away from social science discourse.

Zheng Yongnian, a long-time scholar of Chinese politics in Singapore, has encountered the same problem. Zheng gave Chinese political reform the label of "incrementalism." This suggests both the necessity to engage in reform to ensure the survival of the regime and the need to control the pace of reform to maintain domestic stability.[26] He was challenged by Hsu Su-Chien, a Taiwanese political scientist, for being a "minimalist"—someone only willing to accept as little reform as possible.[27] Zheng explained that the situation facing the Chinese leaders was very complicated. Since they had to balance different forces at once, it was unlikely that they could establish an objective platform for reform. This explanation echoes Zhao's understanding of "principle." For Zhao, the Chinese leaders had to judge the intentions of their opponent in order to decide if there was a matter of principle involved. For example, if the opponent was willing to subscribe openly to antihegemonism, there would be no need to test his or her intentions in later encounters. It would be a matter of principle that could block ongoing processes if a malicious intention to violate that principle had been detected. How much is needed for the Chinese to declare malicious intentions of the other side depends on individual judgment.

A phenomenon that neither Zhao Quansheng's French critic nor Hsu Su-chien understood was how the factor of "judgment" has fared in social science theorization. Judgment—in accordance with the national goals and conditions of the time—sabotages universalism because real judgment is premised upon the inability to make a prediction on choice; hence, no pattern is sufficiently predictive. An analyst is vulnerable to coincidence, to the extent that the incurrence of a diplomatic principle or nationalism remains stuck in a state of undecidability. Chinese leaders have to balance all the goals and conditions they perceive to be relevant. Among all those goals and conditions, priority in the age of reform, in Zheng's view, is accorded to economic development, given the constraint imposed by the various institutional legacies of socialism and the lure of market opportunities. The decline in belief in socialism demands the use of nationalistic appeals, yet the preservation of stability requires controls on nationalism. Zheng Yongnian explains the rise and fall of nationalist cycles in China by treating nationalism first as a response to Western imperialism[28] (which even Wang Feiling, a disciple of scientism, would agree with[29]) and then as a tool of the grand strategy of development.

In fact, Zheng should have used the same appreciation of China's national conditions to support his "incrementalism" explanation of political reform. According to incrementalism, political reform is necessary to facilitate socialist reform, but again, stability is also necessary if socialist reform is to succeed. There is no "rule" other than human judgment that a Chinese leader can follow when torn between the need for stability and the need to use nationalism for the sake of legitimacy (or to use political reform for the sake of socialist transformation). While most political scientists see the Chinese Communist Party's (CCP's) political judgments as a reflection of the regime's interest in maintaining political control, Zheng Yongnian argues that the ultimate policy concern is actually the quest for development. The development-driven interest suggests a kind of thinking beyond universalism because whatever explanations are given for the pace of reform must also factor in the element of judgment. One might argue that Chinese leaders should actually give priority to political stability, thereby challenging Zheng to produce evidence to back up his theory that development is the ultimate motivation. However, this is precisely the kind of challenge that indicates a common research agenda that looks first at the problems Chinese political leaders believe are most urgent in China. Since political reform could still be useful to development, incrementalism should not necessarily provoke a criticism of minimalism. Following the same mindset, few people can generalize as to how much nationalism is good for development.

Yang Dali, another leading political scientist who falls into the "overseas Chinese" category and whom few would regard as a believer in China-centrism, similarly subscribes to the methodology of national condition (albeit implicitly) when revising Douglas North's famous theory of path dependency. In his earlier work, Yang finds that the most successful reform in China took place in the areas hardest hit by the commune movement in 1958—hence path rupture. While he appears to have revised North's theory of path dependency by using China as a case example, his revisionism is based on a peculiar mode of historiography. Note that the rupture he witnessed at the beginning of reform is actually a return to pre-1949 practices. A longer historical perspective would suggest that the rupture came about in 1949, when the socialist experiment began. The experiment finally failed in 1978, and its demise confirms North's theory. The year 1978 should accordingly be regarded as a case of path dependence. Zheng's historiography reflects that of Yang, since Zheng also roots China's special development needs in the socialist legacy that has no pre-1949 presence.

The historiography that assumes history began in 1949 is usually called "revolutionary historiography" in the English-language literature. However, neither Yang nor Zheng shows active interest in justifying the socialist revolution of 1949. Their agenda points to the future and is preoccupied with the national strategy of development that departs from rather than celebrates the socialist revolution. This departure from socialism has received few mentions in the English-language literature; it is likewise difficult for non-socialist China experts to appreciate that for Zheng and Yang, post-1949 national conditions are more important than the pre-1949 historical context. Leadership serves this national condition of diminishing socialism; it does not seek to control the nation for its own political benefit. Yang's work shows how the party did not have total control; Zheng's analysis goes a step further by showing how the party retains sufficient control for the nation to carry on anyway.

In addition, sensitivity toward post-1949 national conditions does not require one to adhere strictly to revolutionary historiography. Rather, attention to Chinese national conditions can be represented horizontally. Zhao Suisheng, for example, skillfully juxtaposes contentions concerning Chinese nationalism and political reform. It is skillfully done, in a way that makes all related parties appear to have a justifiable rationale.[30] Acknowledging that his scholarship is not one of position-taking,[31] Zhao Suisheng is able to introduce argumentation that either echoes the official CCP position or defends it in a way that is not completely compatible with the official line by enlisting writings by Chinese critics of Western social science. Zhao Suisheng invites or quotes liberal critics at the beginning of many of his books, and he never forgets to simultaneously incorporate rebuttals on behalf of China or the CCP. By providing balanced and well-rounded views from all possible sides, his treatment is by far the kindest those speaking in favor of China receive in English-language publications. Needless to say, Zhao Suisheng's engagement in Euro-liberalism and ahistorical scientific theory likewise leads to a research agenda oriented toward a forward-looking perspective on contemporary national conditions.

Acceptance of development and a move away from using either revolutionary or command socialism as the starting point seem to be the values shared by all overseas Sinophone China experts, despite differences of discipline or theoretical proposition. This particular agenda coincides with that of the CCP. Therefore, they are heavily inclined to a standpoint that enables them to appreciate the challenges of undecidability faced by Chinese leaders. Their Anglophone counterparts often lack the sympathy that is essential for reaching such a standpoint. Granted that the two Zhaos (Quansheng and Suisheng), Zheng, and Yang conduct their research in an English-language environment, show little hostility toward Euro-centrism or concern over China-centric epistemology, and are versed in the disciplinary literature, they do nevertheless carry traces of China-centrism.

Culture and History as China-centrism

Knowledge that transcends revolutionary or socialist historiography began to emerge in the twenty-first century. One example is the case of the domestic Chinese scholar Zhao Tingyang's philosophy of "all under heaven," or *tianxia*, which reconnects China with its Confucian legacy dating back 2,500 years.[32] Even China's president, Hu Jintao, has enlisted the notion of "harmony" against the post-1949 platform of class struggle.[33] Harmony, one of the conceptual components of the *tianxia* system, is also a key term in the psychoanalysis of Chinese political culture conducted by Lucian Pye and his disciples.[34] The significance of this reconnection with the pre-1949 cultural legacy is that it acknowledges that those perspectives are not the result of contemporary national conditions. Moreover, this alternative approach toward historiography reconnects Chinese scholarship with China experts from Hong Kong and Taiwan.

Michael Ng-quinn and Victoria Hui, both Hong Kong natives teaching in the United States, adopt a similar epistemological strategy when they painstakingly demonstrate that behavioral patterns considered to be universal today in accordance with modern European history existed in traditional China.[35] The implication is that China belonged to the universal long before Europe came on the scene. Alastair Iain Johnston concurs with this historiography when he discovers European realism in the culture of parabellum in the Ming Dynasty.[36] This is not unlike modern Japanese intellectuals of the Meiji period who tried to show why Japan could be truly universal through reinterpretation of its cultural past.[37] Even if China could not beat Europe in terms of the extent of universalism, the slumbering giant regains its reputation nonetheless since China entered the universal behavioral pattern earlier than Europe.

It is not a coincidence that Johnston, Ng-quinn, and Hui rely on presocialist historiography since none of them grew up in socialist China nor do they politically identify with the nation. It would be hypocrisy on their part if their China complied with the national conditions in which the socialist reformist party wields the authority to make judgment calls. If being outside of post-socialist conditions is conducive to sensitivity toward cultural and historical legacy, then their lingering sense of loss and continued involvement in the context of the Chinese Civil War should have enabled the Kuomintang and its people to root their knowledge of China in presocialist history. China studies conducted in Taiwan demonstrate that these characteristics did indeed guide the Taiwan establishment's self-knowledge before the Taiwan independence mentality replaced that of China's Civil War.

Shih, for example, has found that in almost all social science disciplines,[38] Chinese culture is far removed from the intellectual spectrum of contemporary social science epistemology, thus producing dramatically different senses of Chinese behavior when compared to those introduced by social science. His conscious China-centrism is a radical way of defending China, when compared to the aforementioned strategy of emphasizing that China was universal long before the West discovered the concept. In short, under this mode of analysis, European behavioral patterns should never be legitimate criteria for either explaining or evaluating behavior based on Chinese cultural rationality. Zhao Tingyang's cultural sensibility is the Chinese (mainland) counterpart of the Chinese Civil War epistemology in Taiwan. Emerging from cultural and historical perspectives, both endeavors seek to defend China from social science's universalistic appropriation. In the English-language literature, Zhao Tingyang has won the reputation of being an engineer of soft power,[39] while his theory is actually an attempt to move away from the logic of realist power calculation. In contrast, few readers are aware that the cultural sensibility in Shih's work has any *realpolitik* implications for the Kuomintang during the Civil War.

It is the sharp contrast with post-1949 historiography embedded in the concern over national conditions—something shared by overseas Sinophone China experts—that exposes the hidden Civil War epistemology within Shih's work. To him, Chinese history seemingly ended in 1949, the year the Kuomintang left mainland China; to him, none of the national conditions after 1949 was of any epistemological significance if it did not conform to a rationale derived from cultural contexts (primarily Confucian). Against the background of the Great Leap Forward in 1958 and the Cultural Revolution of 1966, the Kuomintang dexterously returned to its role as the representative of Chinese culture, hoping to compensate for the loss of its position as the political representative of China in the aftermath of the Civil War. As a result, internal migration, the reform of state enterprises, village democracy, and even war behavior are all matters of Confucianism for Shih. Despite Hong Kong–based social psychologist Yang Chung-fang's warning against the use of collectivism to explain China due to the notion's notorious association with Fascism and authoritarianism,[40] Shih deliberately labels Confucianism as cultural collectivism. He does so for the purpose of denying the relevance of socialist collectivism and provoking anxiety in the liberal West. In this regard, one can sense the shadow of Ray Huang between Shih's lines.

Although the Kuomintang's (KMT's) claim to represent Chinese culture may not seem to be any different from the Korean claim to cultural ownership of soy milk, it does go much deeper, psychologically speaking. In Taiwan, "bandit studies" (the name given to China studies right after the Civil War) assumed that the CCP would eventually cease to exist because it was destroying Chinese culture. These scholars were particularly wary of the Kuomintang's legacy and baggage regarding the reclamation of the mainland. Although collecting intelligence was their thrust, scholars of bandit studies were different from Anglophone Pekinologist in the sense that the latter were interested only in establishing a convenient method of differentiating between radicals, moderates, and conservatives[41]—as in Third World studies during the Cold War when Western observers were focused on the expedient divisions between the pro-Western, pro-Soviet, and middle camps for the sake of policy makers. The Civil-War-oriented China experts in Taiwan were experts in detecting networking among Communist leaders at all levels. Being epistemologically illiterate in Anglophone China studies and determined to represent China culturally, the Civil War generation in Taiwan and their descendents may have been the most conscious China-centrists ever.

Reappropriation of Euro-centrism

Like overseas Sinophone China experts who improve social science theory by confirming or revising the laws on universal behavioral patterns, contemporary Taiwanese China experts have also devoted themselves to a similar mission. Wu Yu-shan, the former director of the National Science Council and current head of the Institute of Political Science at Academia Sinica, has defined the mission of China experts exactly in terms of their contribution to social science.[42] This awareness did not come out of nowhere. Wu's father, Wu Chun-tsai, who was head of the Institute of East Asian Studies at National Chengchi University when it was the only institution dedicated to China studies in Taiwan and director of the Cultural Affairs Department of the Kuomintang, represented a completely different generation of China studies scholars, although most of its original members have now been replaced.

Wu Chun-tsai represented a generation with personal experience of the Civil War; these people were capable of and confident in empathizing with their Communist counterparts to an extent very few people today would claim to do.[43] China scholarship narrated in English was of little use or significance to their mission to reclaim the mainland. This mission called for an understanding of China that was useful for evaluating the military capability of the People's Liberation Army, factional realignments within the close circle of the CCP Central Committee, the degree of legitimacy the CCP enjoyed among the rank-and-file in general, and the personal characteristics of leaders relevant in determining their judgment and policy choices. With personal knowledge and intellectual sensitivity acquired earlier on in their political careers, their analysis relied largely on hunches that—notwithstanding the lack of a clear methodology—often predicted events with a precision that would make contemporary social scientists jealous. This obvious ignorance regarding theorization appears in extremely sharp contrast to the generation that the younger Wu has led since the early 1990s.

What concerns us here is that the alienation from Euro-centric theorization that was typical of the earlier generation of Taiwanese China experts no longer exists in Taiwan. Not surprisingly, the members of the older generation were interested in sustaining the Chineseness of Taiwan to support the validity of the Kuomintang's claim to represent the whole of China. Faint shadows of China-centrism were noticeable in their response to the series of campaigns beginning with the Great Leap Forward in 1958, through the Cultural Revolution of 1966, and continuing through the conclusion of the Vietnam War in 1975. Vietnam existed in the distant background at best for China scholarship in Taiwan, yet it proved to be critical in 1975. It was the end of the Vietnam War that prompted changes in Washington's global strategy and a shift in the East–West divide into one that stressed the Pacific Rim,[44] where Taiwan was no longer a base from which the United States could contain China but was a showcase for economic success. This was a denial of dependency theory and provided Taiwan with a separate identity, outside of China, as one of the newly industrialized countries (NICs). Communist Vietnam's victory became a failure when it was compared with the NICs. For the Kuomintang, whose claim to represent China was running out of steam, a new identity as a development model for China was appealing.

Playing the Soviet card was only meaningful when Taiwan was seen as a separate entity instead of as a part of China. During the Cold War era, an alliance with the Soviet Union was political anathema. Tsai Cheng-wen was the first to mention this possibility at the beginning of the 1980s, indicating an intellectual shift that enabled the emergence of standpoints based on orientations outside of China.[45] He is intellectually indebted to Raymond Aron's thesis of a loose bipolar system in which smaller powers are able to find space to maneuver.[46] Additionally, it was no coincidence that neo-Marxism quickly became fashionable in Taiwan during the 1980s. A certain sense of distance from China was created as a result of curiosity toward an emerging Chinese "other." It is only in this context that one can appreciate the subsequent turn toward quantitative political science in the 1990s.

The first serious debate took place in the Political Science Department of Soochow University when proindependence professors pushed for the abolition of history and philosophy courses.[47] In the place of these subjects, they proposed new requirements for political science majors to take courses in intermediate and advanced statistics. The Kuomintang's self-therapy of enlisting scholarship on the NICs to sustain its role as China's best possible future underwent reappropriation. Consequently, the NICs discourse enabled the epistemological reconstruction of a Taiwan that was ready to take a universal position observing an underdeveloped and yet objective Chinese other. This presumed universal position reinforced the proindependence turn in politics. On the political front, the proindependence president, Lee Teng-hui, began his 12-year rule in 1988 and pushed forward with the reform/abandonment of the constitutional framework created in China.

While the proindependence turn reappropriated the scientific study of China, it also foreshadowed its further reappropriation by those who wanted to resolve the confrontation caused by the rising feeling against China. Proindependence scholarship evaluates China in the light of its difference from universal/Euro-centric perspectives.[48] To defend the study of China from political harassment, calls for truly objective scholarship began to emerge. This explains why the methodological procedure has become the dominant mode of communication. Many leading contemporary social scientists who study China are actually the children of the Civil War generation, who presumably feel the pressure exerted by the proindependence forces most strongly. Under their leadership, new anonymous review procedures have been introduced to avoid the politicization of scholarship and publication. Scholarship is judged on its merits, rather than according to the identity of the individual who has produced it, a proposition well rooted in Karl Popper's adherence to the epistemology of falsification and opposition to totalitarianism.

From the politically motivated adoption of the scientific study of China to a scientism that shields individual scholars with Euro-centric universalism, China scholarship in Taiwan has experienced epistemological disarray. It may look as if Euro-centric theorization has increased its domination over China scholarship in Taiwan since the 1980s, but, ironically, this disarray actually reveals a peculiar kind of China-centrism. Underneath this appropriation and reappropriation of Euro-centric theorization of China, there is an ulterior and yet ubiquitous China-centrism; after all, it is always the relationship with China that gives meaning to the adoption of the Euro-centric practice of classifying China as something that could be explained by the universalized laws of behavior. For proindependence scholars of China, membership of the Euro-centric circle is enough to prove Taiwan's separation from China.

For others, Euro-centrism is a shield that enables them to avoid scrutiny by proindependence reviewers. This most recent reappropriation of Euro-centric scientism in Taiwanese China studies is likely to be foreign to overseas Sinophone China experts. Moreover, their allegedly common commitment to the improvement of universal theory through China studies conceals their otherwise shared alienation from Euro-centrism, to the extent that everyone consciously feels that they are neither European nor Western.

The Possibility of China-centrism Realigned

Once they have tenure, some overseas Chinese experts are willing to think more independently and deviate from the mainstream, membership of which they once strived for. At this stage, the image of being scientific, which they tried to maintain in the early stages of their career, no longer seems as germane as it was before. A certain sense of difference that compensates for alienation from their subject of research, which used to be simply home, could lead some to look for realignment in China. Diasporic postcolonial Indian scholars used to experience similar reflections. However, overseas Chinese China experts seem to enjoy a warmer reception from their domestic colleagues. Scholarship embedded in post-1949 historiography has made possible a joint agenda for overseas and domestic Sinophone China scholars. Together, they have conducted research on reform socialism, an area in which Western social scientists have traditionally been weak. The meeting between successful reform and frustrated yet assertive overseas Chinese scholarship on reform likely goes along with a fear of China in some Anglophone circles, raising more alarms about a possible China threat. The typical Sinophone response is to convince observers that China is not a threat, in terms of both capacity and intention. Once an overseas Sinophone China expert takes up a defensive position on behalf of China to fight off accusations of the China threat, a potential alignment with domestic colleagues appears on the horizon, further aggravating the anxiety of some Anglophone China watchers.

The nascent attention to the Confucian notion of all under heaven suggests an alternative. This alternative has an even stronger potential for expanding the China-centric circle because "all under heaven" has its origins in pre-1949 historiography, hence a potential realignment with China scholars in Hong Kong and Taiwan. At a time when Euro-centrism in Taiwan is losing its intellectual productivity due to repeated appropriation that has reduced it to no more than a matter of political technicality, Confucianism could be attractive. Confucianism's cultural sensibility may further facilitate a non-Eurocentric realignment with other East Asian China experts in Japan and Korea who increasingly conceive of Confucianism as their forefathers' legacy. Most important, perhaps, when realignment of this sort attracts the attention of Western China watchers, who typically see Confucianism as a disguise for soft power (yet adherence to Confucianism does not lead to any deliberate response), a non-Euro-centrism that does not target Euro-centrism may eventually come into being.

In contrast, the advocacy of Asia as a method of China studies (see Chapter 7), especially popular in Japan and Korea, competes with the all-under-heaven perspective in exchange for a wider realignment among Japanese, Korean, and Taiwanese scholars. To see China as part of Asia would mean dividing national China based on regions, sectors, and ethnicities, thus implying transcendence beyond the sovereign statehood that reproduces confrontational identities in East Asia.[49] The motivation to shy away from *tianxia* is high since *tianxia* continues to value forms of hierarchy, order, and relationships—albeit in harmony.[50] In comparison, to conceive of China as part of Asia would celebrate the characteristics of ambiguity, fluidity, and reconstruction. Once they accept the narrative of Asia, scholars avoid embarrassing controversy over the historical understanding of war responsibility that has troubled Japanese China scholars ever since the end of World War II. Taiwanese scholars, divided between those who agonize over the loss of the Chinese Civil War and those who struggle with the proindependence and anti-China proposition, could similarly skip cross-Taiwan Strait relations when studying China. Implicit in the promotion of Asia as a method is, additionally, a hope for non-Euro-centrism, but so far this endeavor does not oppose Euro-centrism outright. In the coming decade, the promotion of Asia as a method will probably compete with the all-under-heaven perspective for disciples of East Asian China scholars, who would like to look for ways to escape Euro-centrism without really having to resist it.

PART III

China Subaltern and Different: Perspectives Below

CHAPTER 5

Urban Chinese: Self-Sinicization as a Method of Political Stability

This chapter reports on self-Sinicization, a common sensual mechanism that triggers the collectivist thinking of members of society, thereby favoring stability. This mechanism partially explains why the Chinese authorities are able to maintain stability amid dangerous political events,[1] including frequent township-scale demonstrations, widespread corruption, widespread liberalization of thought, and periodic ethnic uprisings. Self-Sinicization activates the schema that enables one to look at an incident from an imagined national perspective, usually advanced by the Chinese Communist Party (CCP). The mechanism depends on various cues. Through multisited observation, the chapter finds that popular and particularly powerful cues are characterized by a nationalist strand. Chinese citizens are cognitively prepared to refer to these cues when facing government calls for stability and support, and they therefore disregard otherwise perplexing appeals for political change.

The significant issue is whether China is on the rise or on the verge of collapse, whether there is political stability or chaos, social harmony or cleavage, economic growth or bubbles. In shedding light on this issue, researchers have used theories derived from elsewhere in the world and history-based predictions, as well as trends revealed by empirical surveys in China. These methods are endeavors to establish causal relationships between destabilizing variables and stability. Destabilizing variables are indications of the increasing possibility of drastic political change, but they cannot shed light on how the Chinese authorities are able or unable to avoid any drastic political change at a given moment or site. The current study contributes to the literature in two ways. First, it is a quest for a stabilizing instead of a destabilizing theory that explains why variables conducive to change have not resulted in any significant change. Second, it explores the actual mechanisms of political stability rather than the causal relationships between variables, and focuses on how individual-level decisions can make a difference.

The members of Chinese society are not simply agents of structures. With regard to political stability, the presumed macro-structure of the state versus society or the government versus the people is not valid because members of society internalize both structures and turn each into an individualized process of deciding which structure to apply on each specific occasion. To this extent, cadres do not always represent the state and the masses do not always represent society. Just as the masses can be active agents of the state so can cadres adopt the perspectives of society.[2] Because both sides of the political structure are built-in mechanisms, the cues that trigger specific actions are not always external. Shifts in perspective provoked by a change in choice can be internal. Similarly, actions that are triggered at one time can later be withdrawn because of internal revolving—a phenomenon that is not unique to contemporary Chinese society. For example, the actions of Japanese prewar activists and thinkers, as well as the Red Guards of the Cultural Revolution,[3] also indicate internal revolving.

A Note on Multisited Methodology

A study of variables involves studying structures that are made of variables, not of choices by members of society.[4] We operationalize variables as we observe them, so that operationalizing strategy may affect prediction. For example, a structure of action operationalized in accordance with the frequency and scale of social unrest contrasts with one of economic growth. All theories may provide useful observations of challenges to China's political stability. State–society theory highlights whether a growing middle class can accumulate sufficient resources to act autonomously and undermine one-party rule. Balance of power theory raises the issue of whether the pursuit of a hegemonic status by China will cause unavoidable confrontation with the United States. A theory of comparative revolution measures the threshold of collective action defined by dissatisfaction, organization, class strata, and ideological preparation, among others. Postmodern analysis emphasizes the shift between hegemonic cultural governance that penetrates daily life and social agency that creatively dissolves effective surveillance. Structures, in which how agents actually respond to situations, are unimportant and ultimately deductive. This perspective is true even for postmodernists.

By contrast, the onsite observation of agents allows the specification of actual mechanisms that enable agents to choose from a range of options provided by various structures, each assimilated by individual agents to different degrees. Maintaining political stability depends on members of society adopting the perspectives of the government in large enough numbers to avoid the repercussions caused by social unrest. A mechanism-based explanation assumes that agents have a choice; thus, mechanisms that prompt the application of one structure over another explain, to a certain degree, the government's capacity for political control. This approach is not a study of causal relationships between variables, but of the causal mechanisms of choice.

This chapter is the result of reading and rereading six researchers' diaries, which recount two to three months of travel in Beijing, Shanghai, Nanning, Xiamen, and Hangzhou between September 2010 and August 2011.[5] Multisited observation by multiple researchers presents two methodological advantages.[6] Unlike most types of social observation, in which the subject to be observed is fixed, multisited social observation does not necessitate subject specificity, thereby reducing intervention to a minimum. The drawback is that the mechanisms thus gathered do not enable researchers to empirically infer the boundary of society or claim objectivity when the mechanisms are reproduced by a different observer or on another subject of observation. However, if research is intended to gather as many mechanisms as possible, rather than exhaust all possibilities, then even one observed mechanism is worth the effort. The second advantage of multisited observation is that it allows comparison between the political stability mechanisms of different sites, thus enabling researchers to determine the existence of shared mechanisms. This method assumes that China cannot be defined geographically because agents are mobile and each of their individualized histories proceeds in its own way. Researchers cannot claim that their observations represent the cities that they chose to study. Nevertheless, China remains one shared identity if inferences on certain common mechanisms exist across time and space. Self-Sinicization is one such inference that makes China what it is.

Sampling is not important because the purpose is to gather, not represent. The scope of China is not definite because a lack of inference on common mechanisms would indicate that China could be an invalid identity.[7] The mechanisms of choice are not determined given that mechanisms are presumably two-way processes subject to agent reinterpretation. In addition, the mechanisms derived from observers' false imaginations are worth noting because these nonetheless represent forthcoming possibilities. Agents have no responsibility over their actions or the remarks written in their diaries. The consistency and accuracy of their beliefs are minor issues because the subjects being observed primarily inform us not about truth but about other evaluative possibilities of triggering or constraining political change.

The six researchers are graduate students conducting studies in academic institutions located in their cities of research. Five out of the six hosting institutions were fully aware of the researchers' side-projects in advance. One researcher was already in her city of research when she agreed to join. All of them have their own research grants and receive only meager honoraria for recording their observations in diaries. They were instructed to record as many observations as possible, particularly those that they believe reflected views on the state. The subjects for observation included public institutions, such as schools, hospitals, the CCP, the media, law enforcement, and so on. The researchers were also asked to observe public policy. Two diaries on Beijing reflect five months of observation. Two diaries on Shanghai cover three and a half months, and one on Nanning covers one and a half months. The diaries on Xiamen, Hangzhou, and Nanjing reflect one month, two weeks, and half a month of observations, respectively.

Two Styles of *Weiwen*

Weiwen, literally "maintain (political) stability," is the major responsibility of the CCP center because economic reform has generated frustration over the widening income gap, corruption, and consciousness of rights among the populace. The CCP leaders consider corruption the most dangerous issue because it paints the party as no more than another interest group.[8] The anxiety over loss of credibility, which is necessary for projecting the selfless proletarian image of the party, reminds the public of the post-Tiananmen rectification campaign.[9] As a result, people regard the CCP, which is presumably above all social contradictions, as in itself a cause and one splinter group of contradiction.[10] Increasingly frequent riots at the township and county levels, as well as in ethnic regions, should have alarmed the CCP, as *Renmin Ribao* (its sounding board) published a series of 25 commentaries on the deteriorating cadre–masses relationship in spring 2011. Reiterating the same message that has consistently appeared in self-examinations during all the previous political crises of the CCP, the warnings from the top-down this time continue to blame cadres for alienating the masses.[11]

Nevertheless, the CCP treats *weiwen* as a responsibility that points to style rather than structure. This perspective drives the CCP's continued focus on the attitudes and management skills of its cadres. This focus almost means that implementing *weiwen* is inevitably interpretive, inconsistent, and conjunctional work. It depends on how the cadres perceive a situation before they decide whether something or someone is creating chaos. Accordingly, *weiwen* is intended only as a prescription for immediate dangers rather than as the root of such dangers. When social unrest occurs on a large scale or very frequently, the manner by which *weiwen* is advanced will be more stringent and intense. This is exactly the perception of *Renmin Ribao* commentators.

According to one of the *Renmin Ribao* commentaries, "the wall of distrust" that allegedly stands between the people and the party demands a change in mindset and style. Specifically highlighted in these commentaries (which were previously unheard of) is the need for cadres to "tolerate heterogeneous ways of thinking" because such tolerance reflects empathy with various parties caught in the rising contradictions embedded in the social structure of multiple interests.[12] Otherwise, the CCP's unavoidable intervention will make it a friend of one but an enemy of all others. After all, the goal of *weiwen* is to resolve the causes of social unrest before they escalate into larger scale social conflicts. This prevention can be accomplished by detecting and then either preventing disorder or containing it at its inception,[13] depending on whether the issue challenges the CCP's role as ruling party.

Two different styles of *weiwen* can be inferred from multisited observations: reconciliatory intervention and preemptive intervention. The former targets events ex post in an attempt to resolve conflicts through persuasion and negotiation, so that everyone involved yields to some extent but no one loses out entirely. This style pertains to the management of potential triggers of social unrest, but not the deep-seated causes that require an outlet. When such causes exist, the CCP regards them as the consequence of poor management of previous issues. This perspective, however, may prevent the effective resolution of social problems. To illustrate, a field report describes a policeman bragging about his technique for beating suspects—this incident reflects the kind of attitude that the CCP should dread.[14] The CCP usually avoids interfering in institutional reform. Social unrest is largely spontaneous; thus, cadres are advised to exercise extreme caution and patience in managing an event in a public location or collective setting. Reconciliatory intervention can be implemented on issues such as traffic accidents, ticketing, firefighting, electrical power supply, pollution, and land use, among others.[15] Most of these issues are short term and individualized, but they can become components of long-term agendas. For example, the management of peasant migrants in cities is increasingly being treated as an item on the structural agenda, one that requires policy intervention.

By contrast, preemptive intervention applies to situations that potentially challenge the CCP's rule, and is therefore usually disproportionately stringent and scaled. Reconciliatory intervention aims to resolve issues and prevent escalation, whereas preemptive intervention targets people who can create problems ex ante. Preemptive actions do not target issues, which is why this style does not involve identifying deep-seated causes but identifying people who can stir up social unrest or oppose CCP leadership. The CCP does not yield when it comes to its preemptive actions as it would in its reconciliatory intervention. A case of minor preemptive intervention can be questioning anyone suspected of stirring up disorder at Tiananmen Square where many *weiwen* agents patrol.[16] A case of disproportionate preemptive action is the infamous government control of Internet access. This type of preemptive action can also target the innocent. A report notes the case of a research fellow who was imprisoned for inappropriately sending allegedly confidential documents to a foreign scholar by email in exchange for minor compensation.[17] His work unit learned of his act during a routine check of all the desktops in the office.

The strength and procedures of preemptive action are more a matter of judgment than one that considers the nature of an event or issue. In some situations, preemptive action may mean relaxing control to preempt overreaction, resulting in situations that others consider dangerous. For example, two diaries discuss the views of Han residents regarding the government's permitting Tibetans or Uygurs to constantly carry knives. The Han allegedly stated that they would rather avoid any close contact with Tibetans or Uygurs.[18] The discussion of control over religious activities is inconsistent between the diaries. The researchers provide different accounts of whether CCP members can engage in religious activities in their private lives. In most cases, ancestor worship through sacrifice usually necessitates no intervention. As a rule, however, preaching about religion in public is always banned. Religious gatherings easily draw surveillance, even Buddhist ones:

> [One] sincere believer in Buddhism always invites friends to chant sutras in my apartment. Many people come and go. The janitor of the apartment complex counts the number of people each time. Some years ago, the policemen began to pay attention to my home; so, we have moved a few times [since then]. The same old thing happens repeatedly. Janitors and policemen often remain in close contact. The janitor notes both the number of people visiting a home and how often. My family became a target of surveillance. Recently, the landlord politely asked us to move again. We are seriously considering buying a house in Shanghai.[19]

The authorities expect preachers to communicate with them regularly and attend policy sessions organized by the government. Visits by the authorities to a temple are called *shicha* (examining). One roommate of a researcher recounts a religious conference organized by the CCP, during which the party meets with Christians, both Catholic and Protestant. The researcher listens to his Catholic roommate calling it "soft kidnapping" because his acquaintance was compelled by the party to attend the sessions.[20] Another example is the abbot of the Shaolin temple near another researcher's residence who is also a member of a political consultative conference.[21] One clergyman emphasizes that his church is independent from the officially sanctioned Patriotic Three-Self Church[22] even though it is legally unlikely. In actuality, preaching and conversion are allowed as long as *weiwen* is not an issue. One report reads:

> My clan has over 300 people, who used to be Buddhists; they converted to Christianity. This [conversion] happened because of a family experience. An aunt of mine was once so ill that the doctor told my uncle to take her home. A Christian relative suggested having his [Christian] brothers come to chant sacred lyrics. My uncle was too stubborn to agree to the offer, believing this would mean disrespect for his own gods. However, there was no other way out and he finally consented. The relative threw away all the statues, which my uncle took again and hid. The chanting went on for days. My uncle began to pray alongside them after a period of alienation. He prayed for the chance to raise kids with my aunt. Unexpectedly, my aunt recovered . . . [23]

Sinicization and De-Sinicization

Reconciliatory and preemptive intervention aim to defuse emerging dissatisfaction. Neither directly generates active support for the government simply through intervention, which easily reinforces people's cynical attitude toward the authorities. Political alienation, if not aversion, is the consequence of *weiwen*. Given that *weiwen* depends on intervention, especially preemptive intervention, it can harm political support for the CCP in the long run. Theoretically, the CCP can appeal to economic growth for wider and more lasting support. In practical situations, however, political unrest is exactly the byproduct of the way that economic growth has caused corruption, poverty, and social cleavage. How then are ordinary Chinese people expected to support the CCP in its resolute implementation of *weiwen?*

The psychological process that is the opposite of political alienation is enthusiasm. *Weiwen* can gain support if the government is able to simultaneously invest in fostering a sense of pride in being Chinese through other programs, so that the masses find the representative of the nation (the CCP) commendable. Enthusiasm for the CCP arises from enthusiasm for the collective national identity. Using national pride to cultivate a sense of self-understanding among the masses, in which politics is viewed from collective interest rather than self-interest, can contribute indirectly, but possibly more powerfully, to the implementation of *weiwen*. A collective self-understanding presumably prompts spontaneous support for the CCP when it intervenes for whatever reason. However, if the CCP were to be the origin of cynicism in society because of its infamous intervention for the sake of *weiwen,* would not its attempt to nationalize self-understanding backfire? A young worker from the remote countryside thinks in a way that indicates the limited effect of CCP indoctrination:

> We are required to take political examinations beginning in childhood, reciting Marxism all the way through Hu Jintao ['s remarks]. Others will come to power in the future and future students will have to recite more remarks, take more examinations, and become more pitiful people. Everybody knows that all these are for brainwashing, but we have to study hard to get into better schools.[24]

One nascent theory suggests that the top-down force driving the involvement of lower-level government agencies in the central government's policy agenda is vertical Sinicization.[25] Conversely, horizontal Sinicization pertains to the assimilation of the idea that the world outside China can be made a more suitable place for the Chinese to live in. As the theory maintains, heterogeneity and fluidity are the characteristics of local China that rely on a shared policy and administrative platform to make them stay together in compressed development.

Vertical Sinicization Meets Vertical De-Sinicization

A local agent takes on multiple roles in various traditions, engaging simultaneously in Sinicization and de-Sinicization. An example of multiple roles is when the government rents out residences at below market rents. The local officials, who represent the state in administering this policy, rent the residence at the lower rate, but when these officials take on social roles, they rent out the residences to their friends, who sublet it at the market rate for a windfall profit.[26] In this textbook example of rent-seeking practice, vertical Sinicization is reflected by the typicality of rent seeking observed everywhere in China. This behavior results in de-Sinicization only as far as it revokes the national policy agenda. The balance of relationship between social and institutional roles and the balance of role playing between Sinicization and de-Sinicization unavoidably reinforce the wall of distrust between the CCP and the people.

In the same vein, granted that *weiwen* prompts officials to carry out national roles to Sinicize disruptive events for the sake of political stability, widespread corruption embodies de-Sinicization by assigning social roles to the state. The state's attempts to enforce vertical Sinicization so that people will enthusiastically respond to the CCP's *weiwen* backfire because these attempts reproduce vested interests and subsequently promote cynicism, alienation, and spontaneous apathy about, if not sympathy for, social unrest. Even if the symbiosis of *weiwen* and de-Sinicization is not logically inevitable, *weiwen* still clearly reduces enthusiasm for the CCP on some occasions:

> China is a place where power means everything. Even a little potato like me wishes to emigrate. The recent fiasco "My dad is Li Gang" is so disgusting. Many are mad at those children of officials. Take for example Li Gang's son who killed a pedestrian and fled in his car. He just left a line: "Try suing me if you can. My dad is Li Gang." He went away to find his girlfriend. A web search later revealed that Li Gang was no more than a mediocre vice bureau chief of a police division in municipal Baoding.[27]

Three types of responses to *weiwen* can be inferred from the discussion above. The first is resistance. None of the six diaries encountered resistance, but the focus of this chapter is support for *weiwen,* not resistance. The second response is alienation from or apathy about any national process, which is a widespread response in all the six diaries. This attitude is not conducive to reinforcing *weiwen.* Vertical Sinicization is irrelevant to those who feel alienated from the broader social meanings propagated by the CCP. Cynicism hinders people from believing in the CCP or its causes; to them, politics is merely a series of fake claims. A worse situation is when alienation is combined with self-centered calculation. Vertical Sinicization can even cause displeasure in people excluded from rent-seeking opportunities. The third response is complementing *weiwen* by adopting a national perspective that sympathizes with political stability. This response is as evident in the diaries in terms of frequency of inference. The rest of this section continues to draw on observations of the second response. By illustrating how de-Sinicization constrains *weiwen,* the second response sheds light on the importance of the third, without which *weiwen* can only be a process of destabilization in the long run.

We note a few illustrations. Alienation is easily shown in the discussion on housing. People living on meager salaries complain about high rents. Pressure at work also distracts people from paying attention to political campaigns. This pressure is enormous for professional drivers, for example. Four out of the six diaries mention incidents of drivers engaging in fist fights.[28] The income gap and poverty are also discussed in all the diaries.[29] One researcher witnessed beggars, both genuine and fake, asking for money or food on street corners. One report shows a photo of a potholed road in the suburb of a modern international city.[30] Another researcher witnessed a robbery, and yet another became a victim of that crime.[31] Fakes appear to be a social norm everywhere. For example, the bridge outside the east gate of the People's University in Beijing is notorious for peddlers selling fake college diplomas; some train or airline tickets purchased on the Internet are counterfeit; the well-known Buddhist Temple of Great Awakening (Da Jue) sells meat dishes in its vegetarian restaurant; the brand names on some products are possibly fake; nondisabled people rent wheelchairs outside the Shanghai Expo because people with disabilities are not required to wait in a queue; and inside the Expo, the beggars speak fluent English. On top of all this, the broadcasting of fabricated news is rampant.[32]

Cynicism toward the CCP is common. Two young men are quoted as saying that they joined the party not out of love but because they were "confused by enthusiasm" and "too young to understand things well."[33] After all, patriotism "has nothing to do with loving the CCP." Another young man specifically explained why he refused to join the party:

> For a while, I believed [in the party]. When I grew older, I began to feel that the information provided by the government is full of lies. In childhood, I still believed everything that the government had to say; sometime later, I began believing nothing the government says. I now learn to adjust and apply the Golden Rule. The TV news alone is full of lies and lacunas. Political news only features the perspectives of the CCP, but even social news is full of cover-ups. Just like the recent incident involving a college student majoring in music; he was hit by a car whose driver then murdered him. Other similar things must be abundant. The government only selectively reports. The kind of patriotic education which treats the CCP as the equivalent of China has been prevalent in our country for a long time. I strongly disagree with that.[34]

Another complaint about the CCP points to the privileges it enjoys:

> The road to my old village is very rough. The local CCP cadres only know how to collect money and put it in their own pockets. They sold trees recently to raise tens of thousands of RMB for road paving. Thank god that there is a good road to walk home on. I will tell you a joke. There were a few Chinese tourists who died in Taiwan in an accident. Many of us were pleased. Do you know why? It was because those people were tax collectors. In the eyes of ordinary people, tax collectors are merely woodworms of the state.[35]

People generally believe that what counts at the end of the day is money. This is applicable even to academics because "scholarship, which is funded by the government, is decided by the government." Schools try to dissuade parents from sending their children abroad on all types of pretexts as "parents may want to send children to an overseas school since the expense is now the same."[36] The government also seeks profit. One report cites an artist as saying, "art galleries only exhibit the works of those who pay a high price."[37] The government is willing to invest in short-term art gallery construction because high rents translate into huge profits and tax deductions, and rents for nearby apartments will also increase. These "phony galleries" "disappear in a few years." Money is more reliable than CCP leadership during a crisis, as evidenced by the salt pollution incident of spring 2011. One researcher heard the widespread rumor that certain salt products were exposed to radiation. A leader of a leading research institute reflected on how the government's denial of this did not ease panic buying at an outrageous black market price:

> Civil society lacks trust in the government. This is an important matter. Rumors spread much faster via web pages than does the official clarification and they gain more trust. This situation is worth serious attention. Along with the rapidly widening income gap, destabilizing elements potentially constitute a significant danger.[38]

Self-Sinicization

Three micromechanisms that directly affect the implementation of *weiwen* are the aforementioned alienation from vertical Sinicization, so that *weiwen* will not cause anxiety or alarm given passive acceptance; sufficient preparation for people to think from a national perspective so that *weiwen* can trigger enthusiastic support; and one's alternation between the first two mechanisms, so that acquiescence and support are alternate responses to *weiwen*. The first mechanism is one of familiarity, which enables carrying on with current tasks without distraction. Relatively speaking, older people who retire from public organizations and live on a state pension are familiar with CCP propaganda. They and their families have nothing to gain by getting involved in social unrest.[39] Young people focused on making a living can also apply the first mechanism. As a Chinese professor explained to his American guest,

> Most students are alienated from politics. They are burned up by the prospective challenge of survival that will come after they graduate. The majority have no energy to spare for (caring about) the degree of liberal democracy in China. The competition for survival among peers is far more pressing and real than the future of their country.[40]

The second mechanism is of self-Sinicization, while the third necessitates a decision in each *weiwen* situation. Hence, people are usually enthusiastic about agendas that they agree with and care about, and unenthusiastic about those that they disagree with. Decisions of this type create an ambiguous yet favorable condition for *weiwen*. In what follows, we illustrate three submechanisms of self-Sinicization derived from the six diaries. The first submechanism, which generates national consciousness through self-Sinicization, is thinking on behalf of China. The second submechanism is associating with opinion leaders who think on behalf of China, as well as engaging in activities that reflect one's connection with China and with officially prepared communication conducted on behalf of the country. The last submechanism is thinking on behalf of *part of* China, which presupposes one's identification or association with *national* China. Which submechanism is more familiar, comfortable, and available to people depends on their experiences and choices, making self-Sinicization a process of multiple possibilities and uncertainties.

With regard to the first submechanism, two countries that almost immediately went through self-Sinicization are Japan and Taiwan. This phenomenon would be immediately understandable if one were to visit the Museum of the Nanjing Massacre, listen to the CCP's revaluation of the Kuomintang's contribution during World War II, or read international reviews about China being a victim during its eight-year war with Japan.[41] However, international observers would not easily appreciate anti-Japan remarks in daily life or on blogs. Extremists even openly expressed joy over the catastrophic tsunami that hit the Pacific coast of Tohoku in spring 2011.[42] Widespread anti-Japan remarks similarly reflect a spontaneous and strong dislike. For example, Japanese food, which is actually popular in China, is often ridiculed. Another example is a boy who decided to break up with his girlfriend who was about to study in Japan.[43] A foot masseur confessed that he simply wants to beat any Japanese that he runs into.[44] A slogan that promotes China's indigenous merchandise says, "beat Japan's."[45] The territorial dispute between China and Japan over the Diaoyu Islands (called the Senkaku Islands by the Japanese) easily draws xenophobic attention.[46] An intern on a government training program, who comes from a remote village, commented on Japan's popularity in Taiwan:

> You Taiwanese like Japan because Japan left a positive impression on you during its occupation of Taiwan. You don't know what it was like during the Nanjing Massacre. I remember in my history class, the teacher's eyes looked like they were about to explode when [he] talked about this incident. Students on the downside of the platform were deeply touched.[47]

A researcher of cultural studies is uneasy about her fellow citizens' anti-Japan attitude and reflects upon her own feelings:

> In general, the Chinese rather dislike the Japanese, especially those from the Northeast, like me. The three Northeast provinces were the first to be taken over by Japan at the time. Before the Japanese troops left, they poisoned the

rivers with some biochemical stuff to kill all the villagers. My grandmother was the only one [in my family] who survived. I don't like the Japanese, either, but I am still rational in comparison. The Japanese are worth learning from in some aspects. I read about Japan. They are not all bad people. War was the mistake of the past generation and should not be a burden of this generation. It is not unlike the Chinese government cheating us; the Japanese government also surely cheated the Japanese.[48]

Taiwan is different from Japan. The typical Chinese attitude recorded in the diaries toward Japan is an example of simple aversion. Some people have mixed feelings toward Taiwan, but the Chinese immediately converge when discussions touch on the reunification issue. The reunification consciousness is, in all respects, conducive to self-Sinicization. An interesting case is a commentator who claims that he supports Taiwan independence, but this could be more a projection of his dissatisfaction with the CCP because he indirectly explained his attitude when he sarcastically asked who would want to be united with China.[49] All the other diaries present a unanimous position on unification. A speaker tries to think for Taiwan by sharing his concern that if Taiwan fails to seize the appropriate moment to come to an agreement regarding reunification, it may eventually experience armed unification.[50]

Most references to Taiwan compare the country with the Chinese mainland, providing a holistic identity for the CCP-ruled territorial mainland. People who are more satisfied with the current situation in mainland China are critical of Taiwan. An extremely successful female entrepreneur and a foot masseur, who are proud of Shanghai's internationalization, similarly believe that reunification will be advantageous to Taiwan because it significantly lags behind mainland China.[51] A policeman likewise holds the opinion that Taiwan has lost its competitive edge to China. A senior citizen eagerly tried to convince a Taiwanese stranger of the merits of unification, citing the CCP's leadership and success as beyond compare with anything anywhere else in the world.[52] A local foreign affairs official, who admires the CCP's step-by-step system of developing future leadership, is disillusioned with the democratization in Taiwan, which strikes him as only a waste of money and the destruction of government authority.[53]

On the other hand, those who are dissatisfied with their situation tend to have a romanticized image of Taiwan. The diaries record comments by a cleaning lady, a bus driver, and a jobless young man.[54] These comments refer to Taiwan as the land of decency, politeness, order, prosperity, and democracy. Some feel surprised to hear some Taiwanese speaking standard Mandarin. In addition to negative and positive images, comparisons that have little to do with evaluation also exist. Examples include comparisons of the pension systems or natural beauty. These evaluations and comparisons are spontaneous, alluding to a holistic identity of the CCP-led mainland that is represented by whoever compares Taiwan and the mainland.

The second submechanism is apathetic reliance on extant national perspectives, which are available during political incidents. The political indoctrination enforced by the CCP should favor *weiwen,* but the reality is that people may be bored by indoctrination campaigns. Nonetheless, whenever political indoctrination provokes nationalist emotion, it reproduces and sometimes reinforces a sense of togetherness among its audience, whether enthusiastic or not. In one research institute, all researchers have a copy of *The History of the Chinese Communist Party,* which, allegedly, no one would consult or even pick up on a normal day.[55] However, the book provides appropriate perspectives at times of need. This is especially true when people face criticism from a foreign country or a political dissident. They then have something to rely on, especially when they are emotionally disposed to defend the CCP. The same institute occasionally elects eminent party members, holds patriotic singing contests, and organizes tours in the name of patriotic education funded out of the monthly compulsory CCP membership fee.[56]

The second submechanism connects people to national symbols that enable them to refer to a national perspective when encountering a *weiwen* policy. Everything in daily life promotes national consciousness. For example, commercial soap operas have Civil War or anti-Japanese war themes. The China Central Television (CCTV) news covers events all over the world and invites comments on world politics and China's role in it, endowing people with a sense of pride in China as a major world power. The Beijing Olympics facilitated the appropriation of traditional cultural resources and recombined them with the CCP's patriotic education. The Olympic sites, as well as a variety of cultural activities on these sites after the Olympics, manifest the unification of different nationalities and historical periods, attesting to the quintessential mode of cultural governance.

The third submechanism is more sophisticated. It is about one consciously acting on behalf of part of China or discriminating against it. For example, big-city (e.g., Shanghai) residents often regard migrants from neighboring areas, such as Anhui,[57] Henan,[58] or Chongming Island, as lower class citizens.[59] Moreover, discrimination against ethnic minorities is common. Discrimination against a target population assumes a national perspective, even if it describes special incidents. Migrants from Anhui or Henan possibly respond by covering up their stereotyped provincial identity with a national identity. In recent decades, the urban–village divide has been substituted for provincial differences, thereby influencing the social conditions of discrimination. Unlike migration at the beginning of the reform (the early 1980s) when different provinces competed with one another, even to the extent of blocking one another, migration to coastal cities currently prompts less discrimination against provincial differences than against a village background.[60] Ethnic discrimination has become more significant in the twenty-first century because confrontation between Han and Tibetans, as well as with the Uygurs in Xinjiang, has intensified. The majority of Han suddenly adopted a common consciousness when the perception of foreign intervention or victimization of Han in Tibet and Xinjiang gained acceptance.

Choosing Sides on *Weiwen*

Weiwen is more than merely a policy for control. It requires all those allegedly benefiting from political stabilization to take sides, implicitly as well as explicitly. *Weiwen* policy, however resolute or scaled, does not unilaterally determine its results. It can cause displeasure, alienation, and sometimes resistance. The international media attends specifically to these psychological possibilities. A study of how *weiwen* can succeed necessitates examining the mechanisms through which people who are not directly involved in *weiwen* respond. These mechanisms prompt people to choose sides, assuming that structural factors, including economic growth, ideological justification, organization capacity, and income disparity, do not create immediate choices.

Multisited observation serves as a method for examining how ordinary people can embrace a national perspective that enables them to sympathize with the CCP's *weiwen* attempt. These national perspectives compete with other ideas that occupy people's minds in daily life. Taken together, these perspectives compel them to choose sides. Self-Sinicization is concerned with people's ability to view the world from the CCP's perspective at any given moment. The diaries cited in this chapter show that stereotypical Chinese nationalism is observed on topics regarding Japan, reunification with Taiwan, Tibet, and Xinjiang. When people from different sites can share a similar mechanism of self-Sinicization, their choice to side with the CCP is likely to continue as long as a trigger is present. This self-Sinicization also reproduces China as an observed and enacted identity, which remains valid against challenging odds, unless conditions dictate otherwise.

CHAPTER 6

Village Chinese: Anomaly as a Method of Chinese Transition

Transition Studies Top and Bottom

There is no dispute that China is in transition. But then, which country is not? The political science literature, which has limited its focus to two kinds of transition, namely democratization and liberalization, both embedded in individualism, excludes North America and Western Europe from transition studies. Furthermore, China's transition is from both socialism and underdevelopment at the same time. This involves a mixture of transition problems and has triggered a debate between the Washington consensus and the Beijing consensus and one over the pros and cons of the so-called China model.[1] Fortunately, from the point of view of the literature, the common end of transition for either a developing country or a former socialist state is the establishment of capitalist political and economic institutions. The liberalistic teleology reduces the complexity of transition studies of China even though the ruling Chinese Communist Party (CCP) leaders intend to stay in power permanently (see Chapter 5).

The teleology of transition to capitalism in general and China's turn to capitalism in particular prescribe for observers of China an academic agenda that is preoccupied with the conditions for establishing capitalism.[2] The larger questions may include "How different are China's practices from capitalism?" "Is China's route to capitalism unique?" and "How strong are the socialist and cultural legacies that can hinder capitalist development?" Specific topics of investigation include whether or not civil society has arisen in China; whether the CCP's centralized rule has given way to democratic participation, has disintegrated due to societal as well as local penetration, or has been challenged by ethnic consciousness in the border regions; whether

Chinese nationalism is a new threat to international security; and whether Chinese market practices conform to global norms of property rights.[3]

Outside of the English-language literature, there are indeed some completely different macro-approaches to China's transition. For example, some scholars treat China as an epistemological metaphor in order to appreciate the multiple transitional paths toward the human future,[4] some see globalization as a threat to China's political and economic security that calls for defense,[5] or regard Asianism as an alternative regrouping frame and transitional path that dissolves China's national statehood and/or resists the spirit of globalization.[6] Other approaches use Confucianism as an interpretive device for modernization that undermines the rationale of market incentives,[7] or see socialism as a nonprivate financing mechanism that continues to organize and motivate adaptation aimed at something other than accumulation or consumption.[8] Nevertheless, all of these approaches imply some teleology, albeit not toward capitalism, or at least allude to an essentially different path composed of certain historical stages.[9] These theories of historical stages have their roots in a particular school of thought or epistemic community.

In other words, identifying transition from the present stage to a future stage requires a perspective from somewhere in the future. The meaning of the present stage can be defined only after the future stage is first specified and then used as a comparison. Whatever this future stage prescribes for China, it is logically based upon an intellectual construction of experiences outside as well as ahead of China. Therefore, in spite of its analytical depth and complexity, it is a top-down prescription. Studies of transition in China have up to this point lacked bottom-up, past-oriented, and inside-out perspectives that would allow the formation of discourse for the village masses, presumably driven by the force of transition to respond from their indigenous positions. To discover what stories there could be if such subaltern perspectives that are not intellectually intelligible from the transition point of view are translated into transition narratives is the purpose of the following report.

The Metaphor of Transition Contextualized

Typically, agents of transition conceive of transition as movement from one historical stage that is passing into another, which is arriving. Conceptually, however, it is often the next stage that is identified first so that the direction of historical evolution has a reference point from which all previous stages and the present stage are accordingly identified. Those thinkers, policy makers, and/or activists who conceive of themselves as agents of the coming historical stages are always the first to name the current stage as passing into history.

Staging is an intrinsic component of European historiography.[10] Note that modernization theory, like Marxism, relies on some theme of staging to motivate, justify, and accomplish social transformation. Thus, toward the end of the Cultural Revolution, when reform began in China, it was called the "four modernizations." In the early 1980s, modernization theory had the upper hand in deciding that the next stage for China was market socialism. In fact, though embedded in an ostensibly socialist tone, socialist theorists at that time conceptualized the turn toward a market orientation in China as "making up the lessons of capitalism," lessons deemed to be indispensable for progression to socialism.[11]

Marxism and modernization theory nevertheless paralleled each other before the disintegration of the socialist Soviet Bloc. During the heyday of the Cold War, modernization theory would have been incapable of convincing the Chinese that their next stage would be narrowing the gap with the capitalist world. We should remember that before 1980, Communist totalitarianism and central planning were considered to be viable contenders against democratic capitalism.[12] Ideological, political, and military confrontation between the Blocs prevented transition from becoming an issue at all. Transition was a metaphor only for developing countries, not for those belonging to the Soviet Bloc. It was the breakdown of the Soviet Bloc that generated the notion of transition,[13] which in turn designated the socialist stage as a mistake.

To the extent that capitalism replaced socialism as the ethos of the time, modernization theory was able to expand its application into what was previously socialist territory. In the academic world, its contemporary expression is institutionalism. Despite various analytical notions in new scholarship, such as the rational actor, transaction cost, incentive mechanisms, and path dependency, the basic task for institutionalism experts is to observe step-by-step transition from socialism to capitalism. The transition to capitalism is not completely alien to Chinese society at large, both because socialism used to embody a similar process of historical staging and because the Chinese have for a long time taken for granted the superiority of Western civilization, the current manifestation of which is capitalism. In hindsight, the Communist takeover in 1949 was no more than the beginning of an interlude, as can be seen from the rapid return to worship of the West three decades later. Besides, a thousand years of Chinese cyclical historiography provided no teleology that could make sense of the notion of transition. Capitalism was the only readily available ideology when China transitioned away from socialism.

Once totalitarianism loses its analytical usefulness to academic observers considering potential alternatives to capitalism, the issue at hand is how to effectively foster a civil society that is strong enough to resist penetration by the state. For such a civil society to mature, it has to acquire and accumulate resources outside of the state arena. The institutional transition that would allow such accumulation to take place appears to be property rights reform. Property rights provide a reference point whereby the alleged mistaken stage of socialism could be designated as a passing historical stage that only hindered the institutionalization of private property rights. Consequently, underdevelopment in the Third World and the underdevelopment of property rights in what was the socialist world appear to belong to the same historical stage.

In other words, transition makes better sense after the free market, based upon the protection of private property rights, becomes destiny, allowing suspicion, indetermination, and inertia, reflected by forces resistant to transition, to exert no more than transient influence. Which social forces acting through what processes are necessary to move the transition forward is understandably contingent upon localized Chinese characteristics. However, these Chinese characteristics are primarily in terms of process, not in their ultimate destiny.

The fact that the issue of private property rights eventually becomes key to reform suggests that the institutional theory of modernization and its root in capitalism have provided reformers with a focus. This focus cannot be logically derived from the mistaken stage of premature socialism, nor can it be derived from China's underdevelopment, because neither has achieved the degree of capitalist accumulation needed to appreciate private property rights. Without such a focus, reformers had no clear direction aside from their vague determination to depart from the current institutional arrangement, that is, collective property rights.

Consequently, political struggles associated with factionalism and policy cycles unavoidably caused confusion regarding China's future for almost two decades.[14] Only after capitalism had won out could reform have a future or could meaningful transition begin. At the same time, only after capitalist private property rights started guiding the theory of historical staging could the reform faction establish stable leadership upon an ideologically justifiable cause. In short, the future stage must first be identified in order to label the present stage a passing stage of failure.

Therefore, transition is ultimately a metaphor, an intellectual maneuvering, and a political consequence. It is at the same time a comparative metaphor of how one society has to model itself on another society that is portrayed as having already experienced a stage similar to that of the former society, thereby indicating the former society's future direction. It is also a universalistic metaphor to the extent that the lead society is portrayed as the only possible model for the follower society. The comparative, universalistic nature of the metaphor of historical staging determines that the metaphor has to come from somewhere external to China. Transition that has a destiny is necessarily imported instead of being indigenous; hence it is a sort of Anglicization. Even though the left wing in post–World War II Japan painstakingly demonstrated that agency for change and modernization had existed in Chinese dynastic history and this was why China was able to progress to advanced socialism before Japan, it achieved at best limited influence among English-speaking academics. After the self-critical atmosphere among Japanese intellectuals reflecting on Japan's war behavior gradually dwindled, this left-wing historiography lost steam.

Nevertheless, the metaphor of transition runs into at least one problem. Note that China's current stage is not just underdevelopment, but underdevelopment under socialism. There is no historical experience of how socialism can be transformed into capitalism. In the sense of socialist transition, underdevelopment alone is not enough to guide China's transition. While transition from underdevelopment likewise requires the institutionalization of private property rights, there is less ideological opposition to private property now than there was under socialism. The institutionalization of private property rights is just one of many prerequisites for developing countries wanting to emancipate productive forces. However, in the Chinese transition from socialism, the issue of private property rights is the most critical one. Research on Chinese transition therefore tackles all aspects of the transition toward private property rights.[15]

The focus on private property rights in China studies suggests that the theory of transition has to be exclusively a capitalist theory, one that is preoccupied with the transformation of socialism as the opposite of capitalism. This focus omits the problem of underdevelopment as well as many other so-called barriers that hinder underdeveloped societies from taking capitalism seriously.[16] In the case of China, these barriers would likely include the religious factor that Max Weber saw as lethal to capitalism.[17] The metaphor of transition accordingly creates blind spots for reform theorists who are unable to appreciate the perspectives coming from the presumed agents of transition in China, who at the same time must additionally cope with both underdevelopment and China's Confucian legacy.

Agents of transition embedded in Chinese society cannot look at property rights from an established capitalist society's point of view. Their cognitive schemes come either from their experiences with socialism or from lingering cultural legacies such as Confucianism and Taoism, in addition to underdevelopment for which the theory of modernization prescribes a road map. Combination of these non-capitalist conditions creates uncertainty among students of transition as to what specific response they would get from those subaltern villagers whom they designate to be spontaneous agents of transition.

In spite of increasing marketization, concerns unrelated to property rights continue to direct market behavior. Village enterprises embedded in collective ownership, for example, remain the more trustworthy form of investment in places where the egalitarian legacy, be it socialism or Confucianism, is strong. In small cities, businessmen may still find that building social relationships is a necessary prelude to business relationships. Straight business could create embarrassment unless it is accommodated in a social setting. Any business beyond a certain scale would appreciate the installation of an internal Communist Party organization that can resolve conflicts more efficiently both within the business and outside of it. Even multinational companies typically agree to share certain social responsibilities when they begin to make a profit. In short, once business becomes an intrinsic element of social relationship, defining clear-cut property rights becomes an amicable process.

In studies of transition, agents of transition care about their "interests." They do not usually have their own "purpose," or if they do, their purposes are not really theirs because the larger forces of transition have determined that they can only succeed or fail in the pursuit of interests in the market-oriented political economy. Once the purposes that motivate agents of transition lose their relevance in making sense of reform, studies of transition easily orient themselves toward general theorization and methodological individualism whereby individuals differ in terms of measurement on the same scale of market value, not in terms of scaling that is foreign to market value.

From the point of view of transition studies, agents of transition can be peasants thrown back to a patron–client system of contract in spite of cognitive fixation within a moral, cultural environment; factory workers driven by a petty award system; rent-seeking cadres and officials looking for windfall profits; opportunistic businessmen taking advantage of loopholes during the transition from socialist collectivism; or citizens evading or taking advantage of the state apparatus for private gain. The thrust of research is to find out how different property arrangements lead to different behavioral patterns. Typically, which property arrangement is better or best is implied between the lines.

The metaphor of transition is thus both straightforward and strict concerning the ontological formation of a capitalist man who considers relatives, friends, and colleagues as social capital; the purpose of political and legal participation as resistance to state intervention in society; and the attraction of their nation-state for the rest of the world as soft power.[18] Accordingly, agents of transition are treated as ontological solipsists; their cultural and social indebtedness is external to their ontological beings. Once taught and familiar with the imposed destiny of market capitalism and liberal democracy, agents of transition lose those Confucian, collectivist, socialist, or nationalist discourses that reflect their emotional responses as well as the ulterior, alternative meanings of reform to themselves individually, making the theory of transition appear truer than it actually is.

Let us relax the ontological assumption that social relationships as well as market behavior are external to the formation of human beings. Entering the metaphor of transition or adapting to the forces of reform is now to be treated as ontological choices regarding how one wants to be a human being. Conscious or not, this choice compels one to prioritize one form of existence over another. Assuming the choice is in the hands of the peasant agents of transition, and even given how limited the extent of such a choice is under the enormous pressure of the craze for the lessons of capitalism, the meaning of their decisions would no longer be exclusively determined by the studies of transition. Evidence of such freedom of choice may be found by tracing those micro-transitions that still preserve a human ontology falling outside of the teleology of capitalist staging. If no such micro-transitions exist, then transition to capitalism becomes China's destiny.

Micro-responses to Transition

With their logically deducted teleology embedded in market capitalism and liberal democracy, studies of transition are able to determine the conditions for transition to succeed. Presumably, the absence of these conditions explains the failure of transition. Agents of transition are in no position to achieve transition otherwise since their destiny is not in their own hands, but is something they will eventually come to understand through the process of adopting capitalism. Responses incompatible with the assumed transition toward the given capitalist destiny are not included in the transition agenda. To make up for this omission, the following discussion reports on ten different responses from a few previous field research experiences by induction. These responses do not exhaust all the alternatives available to agents of transition. They are not predetermined or anticipated from any theoretical point of view, although some of them can be considered to be related to modernization theory. Rather, they are examples of transition that fall short of any given teleology (Figure 6.1).

Quasi-transition

This is a type of transition that begins with the hope of achieving full-fledged capitalism but stops before this hope is fulfilled. Homi Bhabha once described the embarrassment of inability to move forward or backward as being trapped

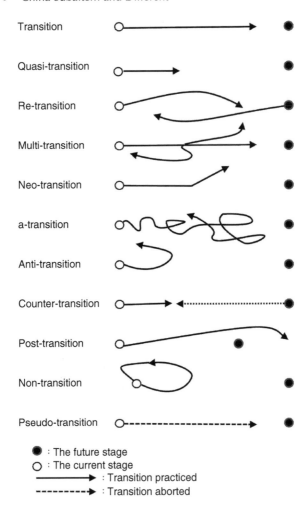

Figure 6.1 Micro-theories of Chinese transition.

in a condition of "in-betweenness."[19] As China is stuck in between liberal norms and socialist norms, West European and North American observers do not readily embrace China as one of their own. Conservatives in China are even more critical of the losing battle being fought by socialism. Even when the country appears to be moving toward the liberal end, practices always suggest that what appears to be conforming behavior actually means something else. Socialist and liberal values are more like layers that mingle with each other rather than one replacing the other. As a result, logically incompatible norms coexist and alternately exert influence depending on the time, the issue at hand, and the social relationship involved, as well as the personalities, judgment, and choices of the agents of transition.

Liberal norms came sharply into play against the backdrop of the Cultural Revolution, an example of extremism that backfired. Dialectical reform and transition started at a tremendous speed. This speed, together with the strangeness of transition from the perspective of socialist institutions, meant that agents of transition were unprepared for any transformation, so liberal values could not be substituted for collectivism. Besides, the craze for "traditional culture" that followed the Cultural Revolution provided another alternative to socialism that could compete with liberalism. As a result, in-betweenness is itself a social form as opposed to being post-transition in the capitalist discourse.

Taiwanese female financial controllers working for global firms constitute one example of these in-between actors. They do not usually try to resolve the constant state of confrontation between the manager of the firm and the local sales managers, as they are usually males. The female controllers are able to remain seemingly divided because neither side feels threatened by their exotic Oriental image when the demands of one side are not met due to opposition from the other. This capacity to tolerate inconsistency and negotiate on behalf of both sides testifies to a mode of existence that does not value a complete transition toward the global, liberal norm.[20]

Re-transition

Even when transition appears to have been effective for a period of time, there is still the chance that in the longer term a society will return to the original stage. Democratization is one such process. Democratic consolidation has become a popular agenda to resolve the embarrassment that occurs when countries that have been declared to be democratic return to authoritarian rule. It is equally possible that after transition takes place, re-transition will bring back the pre-transition behavioral pattern at a later date. This means that a transition may only be part of a larger cycle. This cycle could include a one-off re-transition as well as many instances of re-transition.

Re-transition suggests that even in Western Europe and North America, liberalism may be unstable if incidents such as 9/11 cause collective identity politics to prevail over individualist values. In reality, racism and religious politics have significantly affected electoral campaigns in the West since 9/11. Re-transition alludes to the reemergence of subconscious needs that are presently tamed by liberal processes. This is especially true for agents of transition who are under pressure or experiencing a crisis that destroys the promise of affluence or the protection they expect from capitalism.

For example, with respect to the reemergence of religious needs, the ethnic Hui people in rural areas of Litong City in the Ningxia Hui Autonomous Region lead a traditional way of life, whereas younger Hui who work in the construction sector do not practice Islam. It is only when they are much older that they begin to observe strict religious practices, such as going to the mosque on Fridays, praying daily, following a religious diet, or beginning to save money for pilgrimages. There seems to be a tacit agreement between them and the state that they will participate in the modern political economy approved and/or promoted by the state and, in return, the state will refrain from intervening in their religious life after retirement.[21]

Multi-transition

Transition creates new social conditions and, associated with them, multiple role conceptions that place agents of transition in situations of role conflict. With liberal democracy and market capitalism as their end state, studies of transition usually pay little attention to other motivations that are not directly detrimental to liberalization. However, agents of transition facing role conflicts have to cope with different social expectations arising from their increasing involvement in transition. Professional ethics, modern parenthood, nation-building, civic volunteerism, self-fulfillment, and gender equality all generate mutually incompatible self-expectations from time to time. Transition oriented toward liberalism in one aspect cannot predict the nature of transition oriented toward other values.

Liberalism assumes the existence of an integrated selfhood, which may not be the case when agents of transition do not enjoy the privilege of a long process of trial and error, like their counterparts in modern Europe for instance. The task of integrating modern values challenges one's intellectual capacity. As the old system of meaning ceases to be of relevance, the lack of integrated selfhood makes partial transition to liberalism no more than an incident without significant meaning. Multi-transition that undermines the foundation of transition is therefore deconstructive.

Professional women are the typical example here to the extent that they will need to fulfill multiple roles that only modern societies require. As a result, professional women also concern themselves with their children's education at home as well as parental participation in school. Their expected gender role is different from that of their coworkers or their spouses. Under socialism, women are, on the face of it, equal in the workplace despite being expected to perform other duties at home by the party-state. Traditionally, the role conflict between daughter, spouse, and mother resides in their dependency on males, which integrates their multiple roles. However, in the transition from housewife to professional woman, such integration is no longer achievable. Self-fulfillment in the liberal market and role obligations imposed by the state create incongruence.[22]

Neo-transition

Quasi-transition is not the only type of transition that is incomplete. And re-transition is not the only type that is cyclical. Liberalization may prevail in the early stages of transition; then there may be changes that are neither a return to the previous value system nor a whole-hearted embrace of liberal transition. Transition that responds to institutional rearrangement is not guaranteed to take only one direction. Although the adoption of private property rights explains the demise of socialism, it does not dictate what the new postsocialist behavioral pattern will be.

Neo-transition proceeds in a direction that is not clearly detectable to agents of transition. For example, traditional leaders or an authoritarian culture may consistently satisfy social needs better than liberal institutions. Calls for "socialism with Chinese characteristics," "scientific development," and a "harmonious society" reveal the desire for good governance as well as moral leadership that emerged in the aftermath of the Cultural Revolution in China. Good governance means small government under both traditional Confucianism and Western conservatism, but in China today, as well as elsewhere, it means big government. Good governance is always desired when the society encounters economic slowdowns, external threats, social crises, or natural disasters. Liberal democracy is not necessarily a desired end.

For example, democratic elections in Chinese villages often legitimate the leadership of the CCP, and the same party secretary could remain in control for decades; they are strengthened by the very same institutional devices that are supposed to keep them in check. Similarly, at the village level, market success expands the political influence of those entrepreneurs who adopt an organizational design in which the democratically elected village council is reduced to a branch at a level much lower than the business departments.[23] This happens quite frequently in the suburbs of big cities. Even a few officially designated "model villages" outside Beijing specifically list the village council as a low-level branch in their organizational charts.

A-transition

Once the extant historical stage is defined and then jettisoned, it is possible that the new stage is unavailable. Transition will never mean anything if there is no accepted teleology that provides hope to agents of transition. Transition presupposes a destiny, without which transition is no longer transition even though socialism has clearly run out of steam. In these circumstances, daily happenings do not assist learning because there is no credible system of references to provide them with meaning. Agents of transition who have no destiny are purely opportunists, dependent on any reference system that appears to be applicable in any particular situation. However, they will not show any consistency in their behavior. No macro-reference is available to help with comparison or recall memories fixed upon specific conditions.

A-transition reflects alienation from the past as well as lack of interest in the future. The theory of transition would consider these actors as failures unworthy of attention. Presumably, they should be taken care of by social welfare programs. However, the mere existence of a-transition indicates that market capitalism that rewards individual entrepreneurship is not a sufficiently strong incentive for people to answer the call for transition. Although Chinese socialism, which historically motivated hundreds of thousands of martyrs to sacrifice their lives and subvert their own values, has lost its ability to attract adherents, the Chinese people have yet to unanimously subscribe to capitalism.

For example, ethnic Bai women in the neighborhood of Dali often return to their villages after high school education because they are reluctant to migrate to coastal areas to the same extent that village women in Hunan or Sichuan have done. In fact, there is no urgent need for them to migrate, as Dali is not economically disadvantaged. The chance of marrying a college boy in the city is not a sufficiently attractive prospect to persuade them to leave. Eventually they return to their villages, marry less-educated peasants, and begin to feel sorry for themselves. In another example, in ethnically autonomous Xishuangbanna, young monks learning Buddhism run away from school and are then taken back from the temple by the village brigade and returned to school. Many of them have no interest in either school or Buddhism.[24]

Anti-transition

This type of transition treats transition as a strategy, a conspiracy, or a game of survival. Agents of anti-transition consciously conceptualize transition as self-strengthening with the purpose of defeating those who impose liberal values on China. The idea that China must learn from the outside world in order to defeat it even predates the Opium War of 1840. Under this kind of transition, the purpose of adopting Western technology, institutions, and values is precisely to defeat the source of the new technology, institutions, and values.

The goal of anti-transition is to acquire power for China in order to cleanse the sense of shame inflicted by Western imperialism. Even when liberal values are allowed to emancipate individuals from ideological restrictions, the rationale is nonetheless self-strengthening and anti-imperialism on behalf of the nation.

Anti-transition usually relies on patriotic education as well as ideological and moral indoctrination. While institutional rearrangements that protect property rights are strong incentives for agents of transition to keep an eye on market preferences in order to quickly adapt, indoctrination continues to influence the preferences of agents of transition. Indoctrination injects into their minds dedication to the welfare and dignity of all Chinese so that they will remember that the ultimate goal is not to achieve liberalism for all Chinese, but to achieve victory over imperialism. If it takes the protection of property rights to do this, then China will adopt the institution of private property.

For an alternative illustration of the "anti" mindset, take those peasant villages in northern China that have successfully turned themselves into affluent models of development. Under the village leadership, the peasants have effectively resisted the contract system that was popular during the agricultural reforms that were launched in 1979. However, they have been more prosperous than most other villages although collective property continues to dominate the village's political economy. These villages manage to make a profit without having divided the land. Actually, they have made use of their land in various clever ways under capable village leadership. Collectivism remains the spirit of village political economy. Equally importantly, liberalization is regarded as the ultimate enemy.[25]

Counter-transition

While similar to anti-transition in terms of its wariness of imperialist intrusion into China, counter-transition does not seek to defeat imperialism when engaging in reform and transition. Instead, although industrialization and modernization are highly desired, the agents of transition would use collectivism rather than liberalism to achieve modernization in China. While the studies of transition do not have to distinguish liberalism as a destiny from liberalism as an instrument, counter-transition clearly denies both.

For agents of counter-transition, resistance to liberalism, as opposed to resistance to liberal nations, is an important task. The confrontation between anti-transition and counter-transition could be politically deadly in that the former could expediently accept liberalism while the latter would oppose it vehemently. Could Chinese who adopt liberal values and liberalize their state, the latter would ask, still adhere to anti-imperialism? Counter-transition is therefore sensitive to the need to avoid the Western method. The debate over the "China model" vividly reflects this sentiment. The goal of agents of counter-transition is to counter the spirit of liberalism as a symbol of the West rather than defeating countries that physically represent the West.

For example, ethnic Miao villagers in Dehang, in an autonomous prefecture in western Hunan, put on performances that exploit Han tourists' expectations of exotic Miao culture. The purpose behind the performances is to make a profit, but the Miao still insist that the images they portray should be authentic. This particular phenomenon reveals a widespread mentality in China whereby agents of transition acknowledge their backwardness but insist on their difference while trying to catch up. Similar situations exist in diplomacy. Zhou Enlai, for example, was able to openly acknowledge China's cultural backwardness while asserting its uniqueness in catching up.[26] In short, the Chinese route to the common goal of modernization is allegedly uniquely Chinese, not liberal.

Post-transition

Among the various forms of conscious resistance to liberal-oriented transition, there is another sentiment associated with the rapid spread of postmodernism in China. Postmodernism, which is in many respects contradictory to Marxism, is in line with Marxism to the extent that they both reflect on and criticize liberal values from within Western civilization. Post-transition is a way of adopting postmodernism so as to deconstruct the modernity with which the Chinese seem to have preoccupied themselves. The task for agents of post-transition is to reverse the values that modernity promotes and that it despises. For example, while becoming rich is a modern value, post-transition would question it and even interpret it as being no different from the condition of poverty. In another example, self-fulfillment as a value is replaced by selflessness.

In practice, agents of post-transition do not have to be familiar with the postmodern literature. As long as they seek to bypass the historical stage that liberals consider to be the highest stage of history, their aim for transition is post-transitional. Deconstruction under post-transition is different from a-transition, which is indifferent, because agents of post-transition have reservations about liberalism. They may embrace positive feelings toward traditional values, be they socialism or Confucianism. For example, a notable development in those areas designated as "poor" is the invention of "ecological helping-the-poor" projects in which poverty that has resulted from an inability to utilize natural resources is lauded as achievement. Cultural backwardness becomes cultural progressiveness overnight. Public financing is available to those villagers willing to invest in preserving or even restoring degraded environments.[27]

Non-transition

This is a type of transitional frame that helps other microlevel transitions remain hopeful. Non-transition refers to behavior that resists any transition. There is no adjustment called for except actions to protect the current value system. It may be true that non-transition will eventually lose ground as successive generations adopt some form of transition. However, the mere existence of non-transition spreads the mood of resistance and is therefore conducive to anti-transition, counter-transition, post-transition, or other forms of transition that are alerted by perceived imperialist intrusion. Philosophically, non-transition may be in line with relativism, which straightforwardly opposes the universal claims of liberalism.

Although non-transition is usually denounced by reformers as overly conservative, the latter group overlooks the fact that non-transition is nonetheless only meaningful as a response to the pressure of transition, and hence is still a phenomenon of transition. Compared with counter-transition, anti-transition, and post-transition, in non-transition agents are indeed outwardly and strongly against liberalism. There is no pretense of accepting the liberal method, modernity, or postmodernity as a way of legitimatizing one's resistance to imperialism.

Perhaps, the best example of non-transition is the resistance of elderly, poor villagers who refuse relocation, which the helping-the-poor team considers to be the only way to alleviate their poverty. Some may consent to relocation to avoid embarrassment, but simply return to the mountains after the team leaves. Politically, there used to be some well-known "leftist kings" (*zuo wang*) who considered reform to be an outright national security threat to China. These leftist kings branded liberalization as a bourgeois strategy of peaceful evolution aimed at undermining socialism. They preferred to lose touch with society at large than go along with it. Their resolute acceptance of political bankruptcy as their destiny appears ironic to those celebrating the arrival of reform, manifesting a peculiar form of transition. Another example is that of ethnic Yi parents in autonomous Meigu County who, enlisting the official account that the Yi are only one step away from a slave society, seek to exempt their children from schooling. The children then raise sheep in the mountains as a hedge against hardship in the event of an unexpected family crisis.[28]

Pseudo-transition

In this type of transition, the purpose of transition has nothing to do with either transition as a process or liberalism as the next, highest stage of history. The motivation behind engaging in transition is the wish to be a member of the Western club, but winning recognition by the West is by no means relevant to liberalism. Transition has the goal of acquiring a Western identity. In other words, pseudo-transition involves the politics of identity and is a disguise that Chinese use in order to win respect from Western countries, although ultimately they remain inferior because of their subjection to recognition by the West. Pseudo-transition is about performance in the sense that technically all institutions that embody and reproduce liberalism in the West are like dramaturgical scripts. In actuality, the spirit of all these institutional arrangements finds no parallel in China.

Pseudo-transition is like a-transition to the extent that both are psycho-analytical processes. For observers of pseudo-transition, its symptom is not permanent alienation created by the conditions of transition, but anxiety about the loss of a relationship under the solipsist philosophy of liberalism. Such anxiety is resolved by being accepted by the West, although ironically through the pretension that China could also be solipsist. Intellectually speaking, performing liberalism for the West to see may contribute to real transition once liberal values are internalized through repeated practice, but since pseudo-transition is a personality and identity phenomenon, internalization is unlikely to take place.

For example, during World War II, Madame Chiang Kai-shek was able to paint China as a coming democracy and the coming democracy as the feminine dependent of a masculine America. Her sole purpose was to appeal to the sympathies of the United States; the adjustment was made for cosmetic purposes only.[29] Likewise, one important purpose of democratization in Taiwan is to win recognition by the United States so that Taiwan can be seen as part of the advanced world in order to legitimatize its claim to independence from China. This form of democratization stresses the holding of elections but ignores constitutional procedures. It substitutes moral leadership for limited government to the detriment of the protection of liberal values of any kind. Technical advancements in the electoral system are therefore to some extent cosmetic.[30]

China's Transition

The rationale for listing all the aforementioned anomalies is to suggest that neither transition in China nor Chinese conditions are teleological. It would be epistemologically obsolete to decide which of them represents a more probable model for China's future and why. Anomalies are no longer anomalies when methodologically one treats them as no more than cases or examples of certain universal laws to be discovered. The precise reason for using anomaly as a method is to move away from the teleological transition studies as prescribed by either modernization theory or Marxism. Nonetheless, a group of thinkers and practitioners can keep the metaphor of transition alive if they repeatedly preach transition to the believed end. They will not stop others from simultaneously embarking upon other routes, though. In other words, transition and its anomalies will always coexist in China.

Social scientists faced with anomalies typically look for a methodological solution in order to judge if an anomaly is an exception, a call for a law to be revised, or a harbinger of a different law. The move away from teleology is tantamount to the proposition that all of the ten anomalies together with the current transition studies and other additional anomalies that will be discovered or practiced compose an open range of responses that China is going to display in its future transition. Ironically, in the unlikely event that the liberal, institutional prescription for China's transition should completely monopolize the situation, this liberal institutionalism would be the ultimate anomaly.

Conclusion

If these examples of micro-transition continue for long enough to make the teleology of transition obsolete for village agents of transition, they would represent anomalous cases. Before waiting for a long enough time (100 years perhaps) to decide if they are genuine anomalies, there is an epistemological rationale for assuming that they actually are. First of all, there is no time duration that is long enough, since the possibility of re-transition indicates that there is always the possibility of renaissance, return, or cycling. Second, to assume that these anomalies are genuine anomalies is less risky than assuming they are not, as even if they are spurious, they may eventually become genuine. This assumption would be less risky because it would not prevent an ultimate move toward liberalism or modernity since acknowledging anomalies means leaving them alone. However, to mistake anomalies for deviant cases would call for some violent remedy, which would intervene in the selection of life models by agents of transition.

Epistemologically speaking, interpreting the case at hand as an anomaly could be a useful method for ameliorating the deterministic and teleological proclivities of the current literature on transition. In this way, agents of transition are more than agents. These villagers gain subjectivity through acquiring micro-perspectives on transition that are not allowed in the teleology toward liberalism. Agents of transition can participate in transition research by articulating, consciously as well as subconsciously, how they have strategically practiced transition, reducing researchers of macro-transition to equal partners in transition. Transition would no longer just consist of the technical issues of how well a group of peasants have done it, how far they are still from it, or how much better and how sooner they could achieve it. Instead, transition could become a philosophical issue of how they have faced it, responded to it, and reinterpreted the meaning of it.

PART IV

Worlding East Asia through China:
Multisited Perspectives

CHAPTER 7

Japanese Asian: The Absence of China 1997 in *Japan Times* Reporting

Granted that internal, subaltern responses to the rise of China are creative, uncertain, and divergent, their deconstructive effects are presumably not as clear as external responses. The rise of China is at the same time conducive to the deconstruction of China to the extent that the Chinas enacted at multiple sites outside territorial China do not coincide with one another and to the effect that no hegemonic discourse on China can monopolize debate or even gain respect any longer. This chapter presents the worlding and re-worlding of historical subjectivities in a Japanese site, hinting that China rising in the twenty-first century has no fixed destiny. For postsocialist, Asianist, religious (Christian, Islamic, Tibetan, or Indian) civilizational politics and international relations, this unusual Japanese practice is perplexing. By showing this particular possibility of remapping the past or the present China, the contending formulations of what China is in the mainstream English, Japanese, Russian, and Chinese literature can each find its own place in specific historical contexts, enabling China watchers to appreciate how their sites and China are mutually constituted.

Stylistic Reporting on China

The year 1997 may be seen as a threshold, beyond which conscious recognition of the rise of China began to emerge in the world's media. In that year, China witnessed events that had repercussions for years after. First of all, the death of Deng Xiaoping, who had single-handedly led China into the age of reform, prompted the international media to explore his career and speculate on the future of China. Next, there was the third "thought reform" in the Chinese Communist Party (CCP), which led to official acknowledgment of private property rights. The same party congress that launched the third thought reform also, for the first time in CCP history, included in the party's diplomatic mission the management of the "major power relationship." In doing this, the CCP was implying that China itself had major power status, and it set off a series of debates on major power diplomacy among China experts. The heroic return of Hong Kong to the motherland also occurred in this year, and that event was broadcast throughout the world by all the major news media. Last but not least, the onset of the Asian financial crisis challenged both the wisdom of Asian values and China's ability to hold onto Hong Kong, which was under the most severe attack. The crisis ended with the rise of the renminbi as the only currency that was strong enough to repel the speculators.

However, for readers of the *Japan Times* (*JT*)—the major English-language newspaper in Japan, which was founded in 1861 and acquired its current name in 1975[1]—these events may as well not have taken place. The newspaper carried no interviews or quotes from anyone in China, with the exception of sporadic remarks by overseas Chinese in Japan; there were no commentaries on the subject and few wires from international news agencies were cited. Readers of the *JT* were insulated from the major happenings taking place in China. The lack of curiosity or sensitivity of the *JT* toward events in China requires explanation.

What the newspaper failed to do—at least as much as what it actually did—provides valuable hints about Japan's views on China. This chapter examines this absence of China in Japan's leading English-language newspaper. In the following discussion, I will explore how modern Japanese thinkers may have laid the ground for the *JT*'s unique style of reporting, and will try to infer from the context of modern Japanese thought the meanings of the *JT*'s seeming lack of interest in China.

To begin with, there is certainly a significant difference between publishing an English-language newspaper and publishing a Japanese-language newspaper for local readers. In recent years, the *JT* has begun to promote its circulation among local students of the English language as a supplementary language-learning tool.[2] Despite this new marketing strategy, the *JT* continues to retain its primary function of serving Anglophone readers in Japan.[3] Given the sensitivity of Sino-Japanese relations and the ubiquitous and deep involvement of the West (primarily the English-speaking world) in constructing the historical path of these relations, Japan's English-language reporting on China is essentially a political device—the kind of China that is reported and Japan's approach to presenting that China to the West has a direct impact upon Japan's image in the West. There are four possible approaches to this politics of representation: (1) the *JT* should serve its non-Japanese readers by simulating how newspapers in their home country would provide them with news about China, (2) the *JT* should provide its readers with Asian/Japanese perspectives not available in the media of their home country, (3) the *JT* should do both, and (4) the *JT* should do neither. Consciously or not, the *JT* in 1997 obviously adopted the last approach, in contrast to the far more active and curious *New York Times* during the same period.[4] What does it mean when an English-language newspaper in Japan provides a narrative on China different from those that appear in English-language newspapers elsewhere or in the Japanese-language press in Japan?

A Thesis on Withdrawal

In this chapter, I argue that one dominant approach to modernity among Japan's modern thinkers was psychological withdrawal from Chinese conditions. Ever since Friedrich Hegel's concept of Oriental despotism reduced Asia to perpetual backwardness,[5] his Japanese readers have felt that they must overcome Japan's Oriental identity in order to achieve modernity. From the time of the Sino-Japanese War of 1894, these thinkers believed that the backward characteristics of the Orient were largely represented by China. Their challenge was to show the West that Japan was not China in order to win Western recognition that Japan was an equal participant in modernity.

Discursively condemning, and consequently separating themselves from, such Chinese backwardness met the call for modern consciousness embedded in Japan's quest for universal and eternal truth. From an object to be examined by the West for its strangeness, difference, and relativity, Japan became, through this paradigm shift, a subject that examined China's alterity.[6] Nevertheless, transformation of this sort was fundamentally a form of self-transformation, because the first step for Japan was to negotiate its way out of its own Oriental identity, while winning recognition from the "modern" powers. It is therefore Japan's duty to prove itself by showing that it is able to act just like any other modern/European country. As a latecomer, the only way for Japan to acquire membership of the West is by simulating the same "modern" characteristics already present in Western countries. To impress these Western forerunners, Japan must enact a role external to China. That explains why the whole range of approaches to modernity among Japanese thinkers reflected a common need to withdraw from Chinese conditions, be they historical, cultural, or political.

On the other hand, since self-transformation began with simulation, it was really the West, rather than China, that occupied the thoughts of Japanese thinkers. The similarity between Japan and the West has more importance than the difference between Japan and China, although distancing itself from China was instrumental in helping Japan catch up with the West. Ironically, Japan's attempt to withdraw from the traps of Chinese conditions entailed reentering China under some modern/Western guise, namely territorial expansion, capitalist exploitation, colonial civilizing, or simply international alliance building. The purpose of reentry was to simulate the modern behavioral pattern displayed in the West's imperialism in China. Reentry was a coordinated performance for the imagined audience in the West. It was therefore not what Japan needed, but what Japanese thinkers believed was necessary for it to become "modern." This is not unlike Chinese "harmonious realism" in which realism is, according to my argument in Chapter 1, more a mimicry than a preference. Only when Japanese political leaders perceived that Japan had no chance of winning membership of the Western nations did the whole purpose of entering China as well as the conceptualization of Japan's role in Asia take on a different meaning.

If Japan had to be Asian, it would have to transform both China and Asia to effect the process of self-transformation. Reentry into China was no longer from an imagined external position, but a reclaiming of what had always been Japan's scope of selfhood. The notion of East Asian coprosperity replaced the withdrawal theory, guiding Japan's self-transformation and leading to its subsequent invasion of China. The war and Japan's final defeat demonstrated that short-lived East Asian coprosperity was no more than imperialism. In the aftermath of the war, thinkers once again struggled with the idea of withdrawal. The following discussion shows how different approaches to Japan's self-understanding and concomitant views on China have led to different versions of withdrawal, which contextualize the *JT*'s unique absence of curiosity about China.

Withdrawal into Universality

Before discussing the specific narratives of withdrawal, a theoretical note regarding how the concept of withdrawal evolved is necessary. The discourse on withdrawal in modern Japan probably originates with the nineteenth-century writer and educator Fukuzawa Yukichi. Fukuzawa's well-known desire for Japan to withdraw from its association with its backward neighbors in Asia, primarily China and Korea, is cited even today.[7] He longed for a Japan that could embrace modernity like the European powers.[8] Since the criteria of modernity existed before he was conscious of them, the implication of his quest for modernity was that Japan had no alternatives other than complying and following suit. Neither did Japan have any say regarding what constituted modernity, or what the end of modernization ought to be. For

Fukuzawa, Europe represented the future "stage" for Japan, and Japanese leaders must learn from Europe in order for their nation to emerge from backward Asia.

Fukuzawa presented a possibility for Japan's future, even though many of his contemporaries disputed his vision. However, this vision eventually lost the battle, as the notion of East Asian coprosperity replaced Fukuzawa's proposition of withdrawal. However, a latent sense of withdrawal lingered on within narratives supporting the notion of coprosperity to the extent that there was inspiration for universality. According to the coprosperity narrative, to be universal meant being neither Oriental nor Western; therefore, the ability to withdraw from the partial Orient and the partial West was absolutely germane to achieving universality.

In a similar way, fear of a Fascist revival among postwar left-wing writers, who sought to compensate China, existed in the quest for universality. On the one hand, Japan could not be universal without being able to represent China, but on the other hand, Japan had to be somehow different from China in order to claim universality. Some peculiar measures taken to differentiate Japan from China have kept withdrawal implicitly on the agenda. One of these measures was the study of objective China from a position external to China. Objectivism called for Marxism, which was allegedly an objective science and, probably not by chance, also the official ideology in postwar China. How one could be objective or do objective research became more than an academic debate. It was concerned with the political construction of the modern consensus that Japan should be external to China. Not surprisingly, the discourse on withdrawal experienced a revival in the 1990s. The atavistic suspicion of Japan's Asian identity suggests that war has not cleansed the prevailing thoughts of the interwar period, hinting perhaps that the concept of withdrawal had a much older, premodern origin.

Withdrawal is to some extent a Buddhist trait. Methodologically speaking, thought on withdrawal from Chinese conditions was indebted to Buddhist learning while thoughts on entering Europe, to classic Sinology. During the Tokugawa period, Confucianism attacked Buddhism for the latter's passive attitude toward the mundane world in general, and specifically for its teachings on "nothingness" that deprived ordinary people of humanity.[9] However, the Buddhist approach prepared the modern proposition that Japan should withdraw from Chinese conditions and provided the tools for it. Indeed, Buddhist teachings carried an element of emancipation, in that nothingness symbolized unlimited space that had no boundary. Withdrawal from Chinese conditions promises Japan the unlimited freedom envisioned by Buddhism, thus enabling it to achieve universality. In fact, Zen Buddhism was able to rouse modern thinkers into exploring the concept of withdrawal as an alternative. Nevertheless, its passive attitude prevented it from motivating them to want something as badly as did the disciples of Western modernity.

Compared with Zen, which questions the appeal to any dicta or principles, Western modernity has substantive propositions and values. As a result, modernity was the substitute for tradition, individuality, and rationality, while interest was the substitute for collectivity, solidarity, and custom. In short, modernity enacts conversion by applying universal principles to specific situations and enforcing transformation. Conversion is in sharp contrast to withdrawal, whose goal is to achieve nothingness. Nothingness may connote a lack of soul that would be abhorred by Western Christianity, but for those torn between situations that incur incompatible role expectations, particularly self-role expectations, the imagined retreat to the state of nothingness sooths the anxiety of being caught between incompatible roles and images. Japan faced the dilemma created by the incompatible role expectations of Confucianism and modernity.

To withdraw, one has to fend off desires.[10] Self-discipline is essential to the process of withdrawal. Self-rectification campaigns are necessary from time to time. This is where Zen Buddhism and Confucianism coincide. Sinology could be helpful because the spirit of Sinology is that the individual encourages himself or herself to become an ideal, presumably a saintly figure. Therefore, having an ideal is the necessary first step in the self-disciplining process; it does not matter whether the ideal is a Confucian sage or European modernity. Before the arrival of modernity, Japanese Sinologists established these "sages" to guide the practice of withdrawal from each of their own specific situations of petty interests, making the reproduction of self redundant. In a similar way to Sinologists, who established a model of self-rectification, modern thinkers in Japan saw Europe as the "sage"—the Middle Kingdom that Japan should emulate. The methodology of Sinology enabled Japan to emulate Europe and effectuate withdrawal from China. This last extension was precisely why Takeuchi Yoshimi (1910–1977) denounced Japanese modernity as simply another Sinology, albeit without China.[11] The spirit of withdrawal remained evident—to the extent that modernity in Japan was not about individualist self-fulfillment but about collectivist self-rectification, hence simulation or counterfeit.

Ironically, the withdrawal from Chinese conditions—allowing Japan to open up to the West—led to Japanese colonialism in China. However, the colonialism implemented by Japan in China did not guarantee Japan's membership of the West. Japan's attempt to become a full-fledged Western nation drove it to challenge the West, in order to prove that Japan could be more universal than the West.[12] Consequently, Japanese thinkers believed that Japan had to group the West and China under a universal Japan. Following this line of thought, China would first have to be modernized in order for Japan to claim universality. And Japan, as the only modern country in Asia, must take responsibility for China's transformation. Transforming China was transforming Asia and, ultimately, alluded to Japan's self-transformation. In short, Japanese colonialism in China was essentially different from European colonialism there. Japanese colonialism was instrumental to Japan's image of being universal.

Western Orientalism, which treated the Orient as a homogenous backward, fixed, and dependent mass, was fundamentally different from Japan's version of Orientalism with regard to China. Japanese Orientalism is imbued with the spirit of Sinology, except that the role of the Middle Kingdom is played by Europe, which served as a model for Japan. Japan then forced itself to become the Middle Kingdom of Asia. Japan's Orientalism was a "simulated" Orientalism; it modeled itself on Western modernity but also replicated the West's ambitions in China. There was no proposition of a universal norm or law in Japan's Orientalism, with the exception of establishing Japan in the image of being universal. It was thus about self-disciplining. If simulated Orientalism was a kind of Orientalism, it was nonetheless selfless, as contemporary right-wing writers in Japan continue to assert.

Japan's Orientalism, so to speak, was not the Western Orientalism that presupposed differences between the European "self" and the Chinese "other." In contrast, when Japan was denied entry to the West, Japanese Orientalism quickly evolved into a force for assimilation, rather than differentiation. The Japanese military wanted to assimilate both China and the West to expose the false nature of European universalism. They appealed to the method of withdrawal by claiming the highest level of universality—which, in reality, was a mix of Confucian Sinology and Western modernity. Japan embarked on the mission of modernizing Asia and taught the West the spirit of nothingness, as well as the method of withdrawing from the particular, relative West.

Asianism as Synthetic Universalism

Japan was the only country in Asia that had achieved modernity, hence the only place in the world that could achieve universalism. Stefan Tanaka records how Shiratori Kurakichi (1865–1942), the founder of the Tokyo school, struggled to demonstrate Japan's access to universality.[13] Shiratori resorted to a scientific discourse, identifying Japan as a synthetic civilization able to learn from both Confucianism and progressive modernity. Additionally, Okakura Tenshin (1863–1913), also known as Okakura Kakuzo, was able to reconcile Confucianism, Buddhism, and Hinduism in an English text aimed at introducing to the West the true spirit of the Orient.[14] While Shiratori used modern science to translate the seeming difference of the Orient into something on the same universal template as the West, Okakura used the English language to achieve universal representation. These early thinkers painstakingly devised Japan's synthetic roles by reading universal implications into the intellectual legacies in Japan that were allegedly informed by imported Confucianism, Buddhism, and Hinduism. They tried to bring Japan closer to the West, to the point of placing the West in the role of the Middle Kingdom.

Although the West's refusal of Japan was shocking, the reaction of Japanese thinkers was to suspect the universality of the West rather than question the quest for universality. The general reaction was to enhance Japan's universality—to the extent of challenging the West to see who was more universal.[15] The notions of "the princely way," "the earth under one roof," as well as the "Greater East Asian Coprosperity Sphere," were examples of how Japan could be at the center by appropriating the meaning of the West. They were not so very different from Shiratori's mission, which was to show how Japan and China were connected and yet how Japan had not been trapped in this connection. Post-Shiratori thinkers developed different strings of thought over a span of at least three generations. These included, among others, Nishida Kitaro (1870–1945), founder of the Kyoto school; the literary critic Takeuchi Yoshimi; and the multiculturalist Mizoguchi Yuzo (1932–2010). Thinkers of different schools and generations together promoted the method of freely entering into and withdrawing from specific situations. In any case, a claim of universalist Asianism would have to both include and exclude China in order for it to denounce Western universalism as insufficient.

The simultaneous representation of modernity and an Asia that included a backward China created a dilemma. Thinkers of the time had to worry about how to maintain internal consistency. Nishida renovated the teachings on Zen into a place of nothingness, hoping to avoid substantive situations that would inevitably be inconsistent with each other. Having retreated into nothingness, situational conditions dissolved into nonexistence, as did the inconsistency associated with these situations. The West was unable to withdraw from situational conditions, since selfhood in the West came from Western universalism achieved through the entering and conversion of specific situations. For each of these situations, no matter whether the West represented individuality, rationality, or interest, what Japan was—in nothingness—remains unexplained. Nishida did not bother to answer this question; it was as if Japan's existence needed no demonstration or representation. It appeared to him that Japanese physical bodies were more relevant than any ideology in terms of providing the meaning of existence in nothingness.[16] The Goddess Amaterasu granted the physical bodies; therefore, they needed no ideological explanation or justification. This ease with nothingness and the ulterior conviction concerning Japan's inexpressible existence have been present in the thought of most thinkers, whether conservative, socialist, postmodern, or relativist. Inexpressible but stable, Japan has exclusively resided in nothingness; as for all the Western "others" that Japan regularly met, they existed only in specific situations.

Takeuchi employed the same logic in interpreting Asia in a way that excluded the characteristics of a territorial entity. Instead, Takeuchi's "Asia" comprised a temporal process of continuing synthesis as well as self-denial.[17] Mizoguchi similarly advocates treating China as a method, rather than as a territorial entity. He points out that Japanese China experts should observe China only from a position unrelated to Japan, thereby ensuring Japan's externality to China. He believes that China, as a method of disconnecting Japan from Chinese conditions, will eventually exempt the world from pursuing one dominant view and lead to a world that has no destiny.[18] For Mizoguchi, the permanent lack of destiny is destiny itself.

By withdrawing from Chinese conditions, Japan enters a place of nothingness where it can easily accept the synthesized Western modernity. Even though Japan appears to be learning Confucianism or modernity in specific situations, in the realm of nothingness, Japan engulfs and assimilates all factors into its inexpressible, intangible, and subconscious selfhood. Nishida's "place of nothingness" performed the same function as Takeuchi's process of Asia or Mizoguchi's externality to China. Nevertheless, the latter two were a response to the embarrassing reification of Nishida's nothingness into the all-encompassing coprosperity sphere, withdrawal into expansion, and the princely way into imperialism during the war.[19]

Takeuchi's solution was to dissolve Asia into a process of self-denial, where one struggled against becoming the representative of something concrete. As long as Japanese self-knowledge was kept from preoccupation with a particular geographical or ideological scheme, presumably Asia would be safe from future Japanese imperialism. Becoming Asian, accordingly, would not be about becoming bigger, stronger, or more modern, but about refusing fixation on selfhood. His Asia would be a peculiar conceptual device for resisting Europe. There was no concrete Asian entity refusing imperialist Europe; rather, it was a universalist Asia, where everything could be possible, that refused a particular Europe under the guise of universalism. In this sense, to be Asian would be functional to withdrawal from a particular European universalism. Asia would be the place of nothingness under a different name, because Asia was where Japan would be after its withdrawal from China and Europe. Asia could also be everything, since self-denial would guarantee that Japan would not deny any particular condition in the name of another condition. Whatever one would want Japan to be, becoming Asia would help one stop Japan from being just that.[20] Ironically, the constant process of self-denial should prove that there is an undeniable Japan, in the position of nothingness, directing those momentary, situational Japans to withdraw from specific conditions. No one could possibly touch or deny such a pervasive and yet disembodied Japan.[21]

Mizoguchi still detects a China string hidden in Takeuchi's narratives on Asia. According to Mizoguchi, Takeuchi's motives for gearing up his methodological Asia came from his sense of guilt toward China. Indeed Takeuchi's preoccupation with self-denial came from reading the Chinese literary critic Lu Xun, whom Takeuchi praised for having executed the most effective resistance to becoming oneself. Mizoguchi sees Takeuchi's purpose as compensating the China that was once deprived of selfhood by imperial Japan.[22] For Takeuchi, not only did China possess a selfhood, it actually successfully resisted the West by refusing to emulate it. This was something Japan failed to achieve. Mizoguchi dislikes a Sinology conducted for the sake of compensating China. This approach would permanently trap Japan. Japan can only be Japan when Japanese Sinologists stop studying China for their own purposes.

Mizoguchi acknowledges that he is indebted to Tsuda Soukichi (1873–1961), a student of Shiratori, for his strategy of taking Japan out of Sinology. Tsuda was the first ardent opponent of the notion of "the Orient." He contended that not only did Japan not belong to the Orient, but also there was no such thing as the Orient. What he wanted to say was that Japan and China were completely different, and ancient history and the texts of the Chinese sages were all fabrications. Any seeming similarity between China and Japan was actually a result of the universal law of development, not the diffusion of Chinese culture to Japan.[23] Mizoguchi does not subscribe to Tsuda's loathing for all things Chinese; nonetheless, he finds it enlightening due to Tsuda's adamant conviction that it is possible to understand "Japan-ness" outside anything Chinese.[24] This partially explains Mizoguchi's reluctance to participate in the construction of Asianism, even though it is a place of nothingness. He believes that if one could view China from the perspectives of how China has been China, Japan would no longer be trapped in Chinese historiography. As long as Japan's knowledge of China does not come from Japan's own conditions, Japan will see China from a universal, objective position. This method of China would lead Japan to the goal of universality.

These are thinkers who have adopted different identity strategies: Fukuzawa's entry into modernity by simulating colonialism in China, Okakura's translation of the Oriental spirit that appropriated Confucianism, Shiratori's synthetic science to enhance Japan's universality, Nishida's retreat to nothingness by allowing anything Chinese to be transformed, Tsuda's breaking up of the Orient in order to welcome relativity, Takeuchi's disembodied Asia that empowered China but sneered at compliant Japan, and Mizoguchi's quest for a Japan outside of China studies to universalize Japan. However, in one way or another, they have all narrated Japan into somewhere outside of China. That said, some of these approaches to China have had fatal political consequences.

The Contemporary Shinto Method

The contending approaches to China during the Taisho period (1915–1926) witnessed (and fueled) political suppression of these theories in the subsequent Showa period (1926–1989). Knowledge of China has never stayed within the circle of intellectuals since then. Fascism suppressed left-wing narratives on China, which rebounded after the war to the point of achieving a monopoly among academics. The left-wing writers were also vehement opponents of American imperialism. However, they failed to influence Japan's generally conservative politics, or even to reform right-wing historiography. Right-wing writers waited in the ivory tower and bided their time, which came when the Cultural Revolution put the leftists into disarray.

Postwar Japan was bounded by the security treaty with the United States, the nation that had backed the prewar conservative politicians against Communism. The US containment policy incorporated Japan. Prevailing narratives fell back on the territorial meaning of Asia. During this period of left-wing narration, Asia was neither politically a base for resistance to the West nor Takeuchi's process of self-denial. In contrast to Japan's submission to American occupation, China was ruled by socialism, and it was the adversary of the United States. This gave left-wing writers reasons to feel anxious about Japan's negative role in building Asianism. Again, Asia appears to be a concrete and tangible target of political occupation, resulting in a kind of Asian consciousness parallel to the prewar coprosperity sphere, and both embody the essence of resisting the West. In the beginning, postwar Asianism was China-centered and left-wing-oriented, but throughout the twentieth century, the puzzle over China's identity was never really solved between the left and the right, though it affected other nascent schools of thought as time went on. In the 1980s, after the Cultural Revolution had discredited left-wing writers and as studies of Chinese Republican history began to substitute some continuity for the change stressed by works on revolutionary history,[25] the conservative forces launched historicist campaigns to reinterpret the history of the war. In this conservative atmosphere and amidst Fascist revisionism, Fukuzawa's shadow/enlightenment returned.[26]

Despite Fukuzawa's liberal tone, what remained influential in his writings was actually his advocacy of withdrawal. Obviously, there have been strategic disagreements among conservative writers, especially on the attitude toward the United States.[27] Connected with these disagreements is how Japan should reenter world history. None of the contemporary narratives appear to be truly fresh, though.

The inability to solve the China puzzle brings one to Maruyama Mazao's (1914–1996) criticism of Japan's modernity, that it was no more than "corporal modernity," lacking a true liberal spirit.[28] Maruyama was an admirer of Fukuzawa.[29] It is not surprising that the contemporary postmodern critic Koyasu Nobukumi remains unimpressed by Maruyama's criticism, worrying instead that Maruyama's dedication to Western modernity only repeated the familiar story of prewar imperialism. Koyasu especially dislikes Maruyama's famous view that Ogyu Sorai (1666–1728) was the premodern root of modernity for Japan. Instead, Koyasu indirectly echoes the quest for a Japanese perspective outside of modernity.[30] Along the same lines, Koyasu also derides Japanese thinkers for living under the shadow of China. He proposes to confront the notorious notion of East Asia by disembodying East Asia into a fluid process of reinterpretation. Nevertheless, the common agenda of withdrawal still prevails between the oppositional Maruyama and Koyasu, although neither was a Sinologist.

The various attempts at withdrawal that lack a clear narrative connection between them are worth noting. First of all, there is no realization that there has been a common epistemological tendency toward withdrawal. Second, there has been no anxiety about what will happen to Japan after withdrawal, to the extent that Japanese thinkers all feel comfortable with it. Clues of what may happen after withdrawal may be found in views at very different extremes. Liberal Maruyama, for example, saw an ancient layer that supports Japan's quest for modernity,[31] while Nishida resorted to Shinto discourse. Maruyama denied that his ancient layer that could have prepared Japan for modernity had anything to do with Shinto. Nevertheless, the notion of an ancient layer played a similar role to Nishida's recourse to Shinto—namely, reproducing a sense of Japanese-ness that needs no representation, and alluding to a Japan that is inexpressible, intangible, and mysterious, but undeniable. This conviction concerning Japan's irretrievable and yet undeniable origin supports both Tsuda's and his follower Mizoguchi's treatments of China, in which something exclusively Japanese must have existed beyond doubt. The same under-narrated Japan that engaged in scientific synthesis for Shiratori, as well as the Japan that should have practiced self-denial as hoped for by Takeuchi, must likewise be amorphous but unquestionable. Although few contemporary writers still use Shinto narratives, the irretrievable and yet unquestionable origin of the Japanese people in which all these thoughts are similarly embedded is implicitly a Shino method.

The Year of no Significance for the *Japan Times*

The approach of the *JT* to China is characterized neither by its perspectives on the nation nor by its treatments of the people or events in China. Rather, the style of reporting on China may be summarized as "quite removed" and lacking in obvious references. This inattentive style was particularly apparent in 1997, a year of many challenges for the Chinese people who had to cope with such dramatic incidents as the death of Deng Xiaoping, the third "thought reform," the return of Hong Kong to China, and the Asian financial crisis. Each of these events was in itself worthy of in-depth research by historians. However, they do not seem to have aroused as much curiosity for the *JT* as they did for other major newspapers around the world.

For example, there were only two mentions of the death of Deng Xiaoping in the *JT*;[32] in contrast, the story surfaced 12 times—including one front-page story—in the *New York Times* during the same period. The reports were typically much shorter in the *JT*, too. In another example, on July 1, 1997, the day of Hong Kong's return to China, there was no reference to the event at all in the *JT*. Analyses of Hong Kong's return appeared on other dates, but these articles focused on other countries' concerns rather than the return itself.[33] The Asian financial crisis—a major issue that even the *New York Times* followed closely—merited a grand total of one report in the *JT*.[34]

There were only a limited number of articles covering topics such as China's possible entry into the World Trade Organization, social issues in China, and specifically China's relations with Japan. In July and August, special care seems to have been given to reports involving conflicts of interest with China—perhaps triggered by Japan's Memorial Day marking the end of the war on August 15.[35] On the other hand, two articles were printed that day reflecting the mood in Japan.[36] These articles listed the points of conflict between the two nations. Sizable portions of the articles were devoted to the sufferings of the Japanese people during World War II. Other articles touched on China's role in maintaining peace in the Asia Pacific, including triangular interaction among Japan, China, and the United States. The positions of the United States were included to explain issues regarding Japan's relations with China or its role in East Asia. However, China, in contrast, was usually depicted as a minor player, while the leading roles were taken by the United States and Japan.

Even if Chinese narrators were featured in the reports, they rarely mentioned China, even though the *JT* had reporters stationed in Beijing. Chinese government spokespersons were not cited in the news on China, nor were staff members of the Chinese embassy in Tokyo interviewed. Chinese scholars were not consulted, and the Chinese cited in the *JT* were primarily overseas Chinese living in Japan. Typically, it was Japanese scholars who presented Chinese positions in the *JT*. Likewise, readers learned about China's positions by reading quotes from governments of third countries.

As a result, readers had no access to China's official narratives on Mongolia, Taiwan, or human rights issues. Yet there was an abundance of reports on what other countries would like China to do on specific issues. China appeared in the narrative, but it was never the narrator. Chinese positions were always presented by a Japanese analyst. It should come as no surprise that recognition of China's human rights achievements in social welfare or gender equality came from Japan. As for controversial historical issues, no contemporary narrators were ever quoted—neither Chinese nor Japanese. The only narrators were older Japanese who had experienced the war.

Conclusion: Explaining the *Japan Times*

Two themes that are theoretically viable but empirically inapplicable are the Shiratori theme and the Mizoguchi theme. The Shiratori theme would expect a style of reporting engaging in synthetic universalism; the Mizoguchi theme would expect a style engaging in local Chinese contexts unrelated to Japan. However, it is obvious that the *JT* adopted neither of the two themes in 1997. The two broad themes available for interpreting the *JT*'s lukewarm approach to events in China are the Maruyama theme and the Takeuchi theme. According to the Maruyama theme, the *JT*'s style of reporting is no more than the practice of corporal modernity, in that it is neither Western, nor modern, nor Anglophone in the spirit of those others who use it elsewhere. According to the Takeuchi theme, the *JT* refrains from adopting any perspective so as to avoid fixation on what events in China may mean. The Takeuchi theme would expect a style of reporting on China that satisfies neither the Chinese nor the Anglophone mainstream views.

Both themes involve withdrawal; the Maruyama theme concentrates on withdrawal from China without a simultaneous adoption of the spirit of English-language reporting; the Takeuchi theme avoids both the Chinese and the Anglophone discourse. The interviewees from the *JT* may provide some clues. These were Keisuke Okada, the newspaper's director and managing editor, and Sayuri Daimon, the director of its news division. According to them, the *JT* would like to become both a source of news for Japanese society at large and an English-language learning tool. They stress one important feature of the *JT*—its reports are actually written by *JT* staff. In contrast to *NHK* or *Asahi Shimbun*, which typically depend on international news agency wires, the *JT*'s bilingual staff can obtain and write first-hand accounts. In addition, they know Japan much better than foreign correspondents working for the international media. In this sense, the interviewees claim that the *JT* owns its news as well as its commentaries, and therefore has a better professional quality.

The interviewees acknowledge that they have never thought about the *JT*'s Asian or Japanese features in their editing and reporting. They consider that the *JT* is closer to the *Washington Post,* albeit on a much smaller scale, than the *Taipei Times.* However, the *JT*'s reports on Japan are better than those of the *Washington Post,* although they resemble each other in other respects. The *JT,* they claim, takes a different approach from the mainstream newspapers in the West on critical issues such as the war on terror, Jews, ethnic politics, and so on. This is because the *JT* is independent from sponsors or a board of directors that might require it to take a specific perspective. They agree that perhaps the most appropriate description of the *JT* is that of a "window on Japan."

In short, the staff mentioned two key points in their interviews. First, the newspaper's articles are provided by Japanese reporters writing in English. This is different from many other English-language newspapers in Asia, which rely on the international news agencies. In other words, its special feature is not its perspective, but the national identity of its reporters. This is almost a direct reflection of the aforementioned Shinto method, in which the Japanese body alone is enough to guarantee the Japanese identity in the place of nothingness or in Japan's adoption of modernity. Second, the *JT*'s editors do not serve the kind of political purpose that other editors of other newspapers do, since the *JT* is not under the influence of politics in the West, or of the newspaper's owners in Japan. The *JT* is financially independent. This freedom from intervention is also freedom from Western perspectives, so that the *JT* can be a window on Japan. And being a window on Japan is in no significant way related to events in China. This is almost the other side of the Mizoguchi theme—one that promotes a deep understanding of China that is not related to Japan. It is also significant to note that the lack of curiosity about perspectives from within China is a powerful practice of withdrawal.

In this chapter, I do not argue that *JT* journalists actually have these philosophical themes in mind when they are composing or editing a narrative. Rather, I am attempting to match a philosophical perspective to their subconscious style of inattention to Chinese narrators. The purpose is to determine the range of meanings available to the average Japanese reporter writing in English when he or she is dealing with China. In this sense, the readers of the *JT* can decide for themselves if the *JT* is nothing more than an English newspaper or whether it is an attempt at universal Asianism. In 1997, what the *JT* was doing was tantamount to practicing the re-worlding of Japan through its representation (or absence of representation) of what the Chinese considered to be significant events in the rise of China.

CHAPTER 8

Korean Asian: The Sinic Tribute System of China and Its Equals

In this chapter, I look at Asian responses to Mizoguchi Yuzo's (1932–2010) notion of Sinic *kitai* (i.e., the basic substance, body history, underlying concepts, and essential being of China) through a multisited approach. Mizoguchi's notion refers to a China that has a life of its own and does not follow modernist historiography. Politically, recognition of the Chinese *kitai* neutralizes Japan's own modernization as that of an outsider and demolishes the legitimacy of its intervention in Chinese affairs on the pretext of Asian modernization. The *kitai* method involves a critical reflection on the East Asian international relations (IR) scholarship that is embedded in modern Asianism. While early Asianism coped with the collapse of the Sinic world order by proposing the conquest of China, contemporary Asianism copes with China rising by deconstructing it. This chapter gathers those narratives that, taken together, allow one to move beyond the typical epistemological collusion between social science and history that treats China as a distinctive, substantive subject of inquiry, tangible or intangible, modernist or *kitai* oriented.

The following discussion juxtaposes Mizoguchi's strategy for reconstructing a historical path that can reconnect Japan to the Sinic world order as an outsider and those strategies adopted by the colonized communities in the rest of East Asia for releasing their own subjectivities from within the same order as insiders. Specifically, I present the multiple sites of China studies that de/reconstruct the Sinic world order through the worlding of historical subjectivities from Korea, Vietnam, Mongolia, and the Chinese communities in Southeast Asia, demonstrating that China rising in the twenty-first century contains no fixed destiny for East Asian IR. By showing multiple possibilities for remapping the past or the present Sinic world order, the contending formulations of what China is in the mainstream English, Chinese, and Japanese literature find their own places, each in its own specific historical context, enabling students of China studies to appreciate how China studies and China scholars—as well as the Sinic world order and China scholarship—are mutually constituted.

According to Edwin Reischauer (1910–1990), the higher cultures of all four East Asian countries, namely, China, Japan, Korea, and Vietnam, are derived from the civilization of ancient North China, as shaped over the millennia by Confucian ethical concepts and the tradition of a centralized empire.[1] Several contemporary social scientists have focused their attention on the Sinic world order, each of them thus forming a stance on Chinese and East Asian foreign affairs that contrasts with realist scholarship in its own peculiar way.[2] As the reimagined Sinic world order has inspired students of contemporary IR theory to look for an alternative that restores the historical subjectivity of a silenced order on behalf of China, similar attempts have been made to reestablish the historical subjectivities of modern Asian nations, supposedly once belonging to the Sinic world order, from within their own Sinic world orders.[3] The first such effective attempt dates back to the Meiji Restoration in Japan (1868). One common strand from Meiji Japan through the beginning of the twenty-first century, which has enabled self-discovery by a wide-ranging school of thought, is the rediscovery of a kind of Chineseness, as opposed to Japaneseness, especially with regard to the uniqueness of China's lineage, that has indirectly proved Japan's own distinctiveness.[4] Given this distinctiveness on both sides, the idea of forming one East Asian identity that once justified Japan's civilizing intervention in East Asia becomes devoid of meaning.

The obsession with a historical lineage that exclusively belongs to China has dangerous political and cultural implications for epistemological communities that do not feel responsible either for Japan's expansion and conquest during World War II or for its thinkers' quest for intellectual rebirth in the aftermath. For example, Mizoguchi Yuzo's effort to formulate an exclusively Chinese historiography that is not contingent upon Japan's political needs rings no bells for those who were once physically, rather than just intellectually as in Japan, colonized or marginalized in world history. No such worries about returning to an imperialist or war-prone expansionist identity exist in contemporary Korea, Vietnam, or Mongolia, or in the Chinese communities of Southeast Asia, as they do in Japan. Instead, the historiographical sensibilities of these countries/communities are oriented toward an all-encompassing Sinic world in the Chinese historiography, in which their own paths resemble those of derived, alienated, rebellious, or lost children. Reappropriating

Chinese history in these other communities to meet the contemporary need for a reconstructed national or communal history is as politically meaningful for them as puzzling over how they can avoid the appropriation of Chinese history for Japan's own purposes is for Japanese thinkers.

The following discussion begins with contemporary Japan's quest for a Sino-centric China studies, which is independent from outsider Japan's own national conditions, enabling the discovery of the Chinese way of evolution. A few examples then show how the mainstream literatures in English and Chinese collude with each other epistemologically by unanimously assuming such an ontologically distinctive and substantive China. In contrast to the imaginations of China-by-itself, this chapter shows how some Korean, Vietnamese, and Mongolian China scholars argue or concur by presenting their own re-readings of the Sinic world order as insiders from within Chinese historiography, as well as how the literature on Chinese overseas presents multiple Chinas in exile. Together, with each worlding their own objective China, they suggest that there is a need for an epistemological platform or metaphor that will enable multiple Chinas to understand one another.

From a Place to a *Kitai*

An increasing number of contemporary Japanese thinkers subscribe to a temporal epistemology of places. Places used to be the focus of the Kyoto School of philosophers, who were determined to transcend Japan's liminality between the Orient and the Occident, especially and specifically the Hegelian designation of a despotic Orient from which other modern Japanese thinkers similarly endeavored to exclude Japan. For example, Nishida Kitaro (1870–1945), a founder of the school, proposed that nothingness is the place where the true spirit of universality lies. From nothingness, one can enter either the Oriental or the Occidental conditions without having to resolve the obvious differences between them, as a Hegelian thinker would be inclined to believe.[5] One can achieve universality by practicing withdrawal from specific conditions rather than by converting different others.[6] This withdrawal allows one to claim a world history standpoint in which a seemingly liminal Japan takes the lead in achieving universal nothingness.[7] Although nothingness is meant to be inclusive rather than transformative, the pre–World War II regime hastily adopted this worlding discourse as a philosophy of both counterintervention and intervention. Accordingly, the world history standpoint had to defeat the partial history of the Occident represented by the White race and transform the partial history of the Orient represented by the Sinic order.[8] Thus, the postwar reflections on place focus on how to dispense with the drive for intervention as well as counterintervention prepared by the self-neutralizing idea of universal place/nothingness, which allegedly justifies all existing possibilities as they are.

To remedy the distorted Kyoto quest for transcendence, contemporary thinkers have painstakingly conceptualized Japan and its others as temporal beings that are distinctive and substantive, yet intangible. A place can become a target of occupation only because it is tangible. Thus, Japan can take China or Korea only if they are delineable territories. In contrast, a temporal being cannot be taken. The Kyoto approach, which lays out civilizations geographically, means that a universal Japan can only plausibly exist in nothingness if neither the Occident nor the Orient accepts Japan as a member. Universal Japan is the dream so ably synopsized in Fukuzawa Yukichi's (1834–1901) galvanizing slogan "departure from Asia for Europe," which equates Europe with the universe.[9] Fukuzawa's approach was rejected when it was realized that Europe refused to accept Japan as a member. From then on, this self-suppression of Asian identity became a world history standpoint, according to which Japan could idealistically be anywhere. In comparison, the reflexive temporal approach preserves for every existent being its own becoming from the past to the future, hence implying the impossibility and meaninglessness of any plan for civilizational expansion or territorial conquest. By becoming, no civilized being can remain unaffected by others, and no one can take over anyone else, since everyone else has their own process of becoming that is rooted in the past.

Accordingly, Takeuchi Yoshimi (1910–1977) suggested the concept of "Asia" as a process of becoming, through which one can only be oneself by constantly denying one's past self.[10] In his formulation, Asia, the conceptual foundation of the pre–World War II Greater East Asian Coprosperity Sphere that inspired Japan's military expansion, should be contested by the multiple beings, including Europe, which make up contemporary Asia and its constant becoming. Asia, as constituted by multiple beings and their constant becoming, loses occupiability. Together with other Asian beings, Japan's distinctive being and becoming are automatically justified; they can do without intellectual engagements. Both Maruyama Masao (1914–1996) and his contemporary Koyasu Nobukuni rely on premodern thought to demonstrate the lineage of a Japan uninterrupted by the adoption of modernity.[11] Koyasu is particularly keen on linking premodern Edo (old Tokyo) to modern Tokyo in his reconstruction and recollection of the Edo perspectives. Koyasu's line of logic aligns him with Maruyama's discovery of the "ancient layer" as an intangible ingredient of Japanese modernity, despite his suspicion of Maruyama's liberal stance.[12]

In the same reflexive atmosphere, Mizoguchi Yuzo, whose work is well received in the Chinese worlds,[13] came up with the idea of the Chinese *kitai*.

Interestingly, his method is also a reading of the classic literature, which seeks to appreciate an original Chinese source of modernity in terms of historical progression upward from feudalism. For Mizoguchi, this original source exempts China from the staging of European historiography; he urges everyone to study China from the point of view of the Chinese *kitai* so that China's entry into the capitalist stage can have a life of its own not premised upon European experiences. By approaching the Chinese *kitai*, students of Chinese history are also transcending their own limited conditions embedded in their national history, eventually meeting in a truly universal world condition. This is why Mizoguchi saw in his China a worlding method by which Japan could merge with all the differing beings in the world. This world is an epistemological one where Japan's own *kitai*, or that of anyone else, is dispensable. Yet Japan also achieves an ontologically undeniable *kitai* by becoming an object of study unrelated to anything else. Neither conquest nor Westernization is necessary for Japan to become modern because Japan, like China and its *kitai*, by definition has its distinct path toward modernity.

Mizoguchi's Chinese *kitai* is a result of both his in-depth reading of the Chinese classics and his epistemological stand. In his reading of the classics, Mizoguchi first differentiated China from Japan through an analysis of the notion of "the public."[14] He found that for the Japanese, the public is contrasted with the private, and that an undeniable private space exists in Japanese civilization. Thus, the public refers to the space between individuals, each of whom possesses an impenetrable private space. This finding is in accordance with Nishida's use of *kitai*, which ultimately indicates the place of nothingness in between everything. Institutionally, the public can be represented by the governing body. However, Mizoguchi continued, the scope of the Chinese public is flexible and can be extended endlessly; thus, the Chinese private can ultimately be revoked completely. This finding is related to Mizoguchi's study of Chinese modernization, which he further differentiated from European modernization. According to Mizoguchi, Chinese history did not progress through Hegelian synthesis. For example, the local landed gentry was not an outdated class. Rather, it became the agency for capital accumulation. The relationship between the masses and the court was not feudalist, but was instead an ideological site of constant negotiation, to the extent that decentralizing institutions at the county level, sanctioned through the gentry, served to preserve Chinese culture and ultimately the long-lived belief in a Chinese all-under-heaven regime. The gentry were the leading force of historical progression into the next stage rather than the resisting and eventually purged class. They could be both public (i.e., the court/the county/the state) and private (i.e., individual households). They embodied the discursive foundation of Chinese modernity in contrast to their progressive European bourgeois counterparts.

Epistemologically, Mizoguchi was heavily influenced by Tsuda Soukichi (1873–1961) and Takeuchi Yoshimi.[15] The former abhorred China, whereas the latter adored it. Tsuda adamantly denied the validity of the identity called "the Orient," which he argued never really existed.[16] He deconstructed the seeming parallels between Chinese Taoist literature and Japanese Shinto classics, and gained himself the reputation of being a "China despiser." Mizoguchi learned from Tsuda his determination to differentiate Japan from China and Europe. In fact, his notion of *kitai* was based on his criticism of the China scholars of his time, whom he believed either loved or hated China too much to present China in China's terms. A successful mutual distinction should exempt scholars from self-involvement in China studies. Mizoguchi's interpretation of the Japanese public space echoes Takeuchi's interpretation of Chinese subjectivity, which, Takeuchi believed, had reproduced itself by exercising constant self-denial.[17] Takeuchi's ideal of Asianism is also a constant process of self-denial. Mizoguchi considered Takeuchi to have romanticized China. Nevertheless, Takeuchi's Asia cannot be taken over by the entire nationality, as Mizoguchi's public in Japan was never taken over by the private. This finding contradicts Mizoguchi's treatment of the Chinese public, whose space could justify whoever acted in its name virtually to intrude on the private of all others.

For Mizoguchi, China's evolving substantive entity, the *kitai,* is even capable of wanting to detach Japan from Chinese historiography. Mizoguchi's peculiar approach to the controversial issue of the Nanjing Massacre is worth noting here. For a long while, right-wing writers in Japan vehemently disputed the death toll in the massacre given in Chinese sources. According to Mizoguchi, the issue was not the death toll or its validity.[18] He considered the number of dead given in Chinese sources to be representative of the harm felt by the victims. Thus, he advocated an understanding based on the Chinese consciousness instead of Japan's internal needs.

Mizoguchi's quest for access to the world, as his destiny, is bizarre from a social science point of view, in which China, studied independently of Japan's needs, is a given. Despite sporadic reflections on the political context of China studies in North America, the scientific pretension that scholarship should be independent of the individual scholars' identities continues to prevail in the literature. The charge that China is a demonized, feminized, and Orientalized object in the mainstream literature meets the counter-charge that China is a relativized, romanticized, and revolutionized subject in critical literature.[19] This issue is not a question of whether China is a distinctive and substantive subject of inquiry but predominantly one of whether the substantive entity is so different that a China-centric methodology is necessary to understand it. Mizoguchi could either join the China-centric side or not care about the debate at all, as his worlding concern was not about the comparability of China with other national communities. On the contrary, he would have dreaded such a comparison, lest it should rest upon a cross-national standard that necessarily places either China or the other compared *kitai* in an ostensibly universal but certainly wrong gauge.

Epistemological Collusion

Mizoguchi's work has been properly received by a highly divided Chinese audience in a sense not necessarily appreciated by Mizoguchi himself. His discourse on *kitai* has impressed Chinese academics, whose search for ways of self-understanding has not been helped by European experiences. Granted that his instrumentalizing epistemology reduces China to Japan's route to universality, his worlding method, which defends China from modernist historiography, can provide inspiration for Chinese colleagues who suffer from the over-application of Anglo-Americanized jargon to China. In fact, the political narratives on socialism with Chinese characteristics in the Chinese Communist Party's quest for pragmatic solutions in the early 1980s appeared roughly at the same time as Mizoguchi's new worlding method for Japan. Note that the call for "Chinese characteristics" embodied a political conviction that prompted a determined search for such characteristics before there was any evidence that they even existed. The nascent quest for a Chinese model in all disciplines in the twenty-first century proceeds from the same spirit.[20] The nationalist or relativist temperament compares China with Europe or North America. However, this obsession with Chinese characteristics in China's low moments, as well as the China model in China's high moments, is not merely a contemporary strategy. With or without Mizoguchi, the image of a different China satisfies the Chinese people.

Confucius (551–479 BC), for example, claimed that he could only record the thoughts of the sages who had gone before him and shied away from claiming to be an original thinker. This important disclaimer, which effectively constrained innovation among future generations, is premised upon an intangible and yet authentic spirit of *dao* (or tao). The Tang Dynasty scholar Han Yu (768–824) reproduced this authenticated spirit in his essay "The Original Dao," which was still read over a thousand years later. The Song Dynasty official Wen Tianxiang (1236–1283), who was imprisoned by the triumphant Mongol invaders, wrote "The Song of Justice," in which he instilled an imagined spirit of *dao* into anything considered Chinese, including heaven and earth. Mizoguchi's analysis of the Chinese public space is particularly pertinent here, as this space can expand to take over every corner of existence, leaving no room for private space at all. Even the totalitarian rule of the Chinese Communist Party rests upon the assumption that the proletarian party has, by definition, no private interests, as if all cadres are imbued with the all-pervasive spirit of *dao* disguised as collectivism. In a nutshell, the Chinese political *kitai* is reproduced in the continuous claim of power holders that they are selflessly serving all under heaven.

Moreover, the imagined spirit of *dao* is always coupled with an imagined kinship, leading Confucius to declare that "all men are brothers." According to this imagined kinship, all Chinese are descendants of the emperors Yan and Huang, a racist narrative that appeals to Chinese overseas. Sun Yat-sen (1866–1925), the father of Republican China, was attracted to this kinship narrative, while at the same time his dedication to Confucius allowed him to claim a hold on the chain of *dao* stretching back to the emperors Yao and Shun whose ideas were recorded in the Confucian classics. Post-1911, Sun skillfully substituted a mixed kinship theory for the anti-Manchu ideas that inspired his revolution.[21] However, Sun's new kinship theory of "five nationalities in one republic" (*wu zu gonghe*) is abrasive because there were more than five nationalities in the newly established Republic of China. Fei Xiaotong (1910–2005), the highly regarded official/scholar of the People's Republic, became popular because of the same belief.[22] Fei extended Sun's kinship theory to include 56 nationalities in one Chinese body, making a modern orthodoxy of the "pluralistic integration" (*duo yuan yi ti*), which is still in force. The blood of each of these nationalities is to some extent mixed with that of some of the other 55, so being Chinese remains a matter of both kinship and spirit.

John Fitzgerald finds that the Republican narratives of various schools share the assumption that there is an a priori Chinese nation that can be awakened.[23] This imagined Chinese substance embedded in Confucian *dao* and kinship, far from being welcomed, is a cause for anxiety in the English-language literature. This a priori civilizational identity led Lucian Pye (1921–2008) to denounce the Chinese state as fake[24] and Samuel Huntington (1927–2008) to foretell a clash between China and Christianity.[25] Thus, the racially and ideologically self-involving Chinese regime is caught between apologizing for its history of perceived victimhood and triumphing in its perceived superior civilization, resulting in what William Callahan calls the "pessoptimist nation."[26] While each has his or her own theoretical foothold and political agenda, China scholars generally accept the challenge of representing China in a language that is friendly to an English-language audience. Although preoccupied with an entirely different concern, the literature on the China threat (civilizational, economic, and military) actually colludes with the aforementioned Chinese sources that celebrate the emergence of the China model to the extent that all seek to represent China as an antagonistic regime.

Although Tibet is non-Han Chinese and Taiwan has favored independence, a clearer and more substantive image of China is visible whenever these two areas are able to provide an external standpoint. The civilization of Tibet is certainly not Confucian. Students of Tibetan studies cannot escape an imagined authentic China. In his detailed comparison of Tibetan studies in Australia and India, Wu Tsong-han contends that in Australia, Tibetan studies is an intrinsic component of China studies.[27] Activists usually assume that the solution of the Tibetan issue lies in China, incidentally echoing the theme of pluralistic integration. Wu also finds that Indian students of Tibetan studies sometimes acquire a perspective on Chinese civilization from their study of Tibet—"othering" China through Tibet. Either by considering Tibet as part of China or rediscovering China through Tibet, China becomes substantively authentic. Considered a vicarious site of China studies, Taiwan was the place where students of China went before China opened up in the 1980s. The proindependence politics of the past two decades has generated a political need to demonstrate that Taiwan is not part of China and therefore cannot understand China in Chinese terms. Accordingly, Taiwan's knowledge of China should not differ from that of its American ally. This line of thought encouraged a kind of scientific scholarship that presumes it is possible to present China objectively, creating an epistemologically universal position of Taiwan, the observer.[28] Either way, China was an objective being, which Taiwan struggled to represent before the 1980s, but since then has pretended to know little more about than any American social scientist.

The Challenges of Multisited Studies

Unlike the generations of Japanese thinkers who tried to explain Japan's passage to modernity ahead of the rest of the Sinic world by formulating a distinctive Chinese *kitai* in a spirit of awe, disdain, or detachment, other communities in their literatures considered the possibility of self-rediscovery from within the Sinic order. A similar process can be found in the Japanese literature: Naito Konan (also known as Naito Torajiro; 1866–1934) is well known for his depiction of Japan as the new Sinic blood revitalizing the aging Chinese culture, which also places Japan inside the Sinic world.[29] Naito's "new-blood" stance is no longer popular or even legitimate today because of his politically incorrect favoring of a Sinic world order, if not a Chinese one, in the postmodern age of multiculturalism. Taking the Sinic world order as a given constituent of their history, Korean and Mongolian scholars have led the rediscovery of a completely different historical trajectory that crossed, rather than belonged to, the Sinic world during the latter's heyday. And although consciously belonging to the Sinic world, some Vietnamese scholarship nonetheless contains the possibility of regarding such belonging as a positive component of self-empowerment. Finally, the literature on and from overseas Chinese in Southeast Asia demonstrates the possibility of being an essentially different Chinese in the same Sinic world order. All these worlding strategies together comprise the multisitedness of the Sinic order.

At least two seemingly opposite ways of regaining historical subjectivity are observed in the Korean literature. One involves claiming a Korean origin for things that are widely considered Chinese. These range from the Chinese script, sages such as Confucius, and cultural festivals such as the dragon boat festival to other traditions shared by people from a much wider area than just China proper. For example, Jin Taeha is known for his linguistic research that traces some of the most significant traits of the Sinic world from Korean sources.[30] According to Jin, the ancestors of modern Koreans are the Eastern Yi (Eastern aliens), the inventors of divination using oracle bones. If his interpretation is accurate, the overlapping of Chinese and Korean history would pose no threat to the independent and equal status of the Korean historical trajectory vis-à-vis China. This view parallels the view of Sinic history in classic Vietnamese scholarship. This separate discourse focuses on an origin of its own earlier than the Sinic order. However, the second and majority view in the Korean literature subscribes to a separate trajectory instead of an original (or singular) one.

The Korean literature is particularly keen on the meaning of the tribute system in the Chinese and English-language literature, especially as it was recast by John King Fairbank (1907–1991). It was Fairbank who established the orthodox interpretation of the tribute system as a form of uneven trade between the superior, generous Sinic court and submissive, peripheral reward-seekers.[31] The Chinese literature is not interested in Fairbank's preoccupation with trade but generally concurs with his view that Korea acted like a vassal under Sinic suzerainty. The Korean rediscovery of Korea's equal, rather than subordinate, status is primarily a response to this last point. Compared to Japan, with its different Shinto religion and relative independence in premodern history, the Korean peninsula's adoption of Confucianism and the tributary status of its kingdoms make its relationship to China much clearer. As a result, restoring Korean historical subjectivity requires a different strategy from simply granting China its own *kitai* from an imagined external site, epistemologically, territorially, and institutionally. The goal is nonetheless the same as that of the Japanese thinkers: that is, the equalizing of the relationship between Korea and China. However, this is not really feasible in the current historiography in Chinese or in English.

Instead of refuting the validity of the tribute system or simply giving another side of the Sinic world story that is more to the liking of contemporary Koreans, the Korean literature constructs as a rediscovery the intention behind the peninsula's participation in various kinds of tribute systems. Considering the factor of intention, the constitution of the tribute system involves inter-subjectivities. Therefore, this site-shifting rediscovery that rejects inter-subjectivities offers a history of another tribute system rather than another aspect of the same history. Accordingly, the meanings of the tribute system in Korean history belong exclusively to Korean history. These meanings are not responses developed within the Chinese tribute system, with Korea as either its original member or incorporated by someone into the system unintentionally. The tribute system that Korea joined is Korea's own tribute system from a historical path separate from that generated by the Sinic tribute system. Although there was only one tribute system between the Sinic court and the peninsula, the two historical paths converged to make the tribute system a platform where the Chinese and the Korean met. Interpreting and performing the role played by each of them had unavoidably complicated psycho-cultural implications beyond the control of any single scriptwriter or director because of the existence of at least two streams. Despite the seemingly hierarchical roles, the scriptwriters that produced the two simultaneous dramas behind the scenes had to be equals.

Chun Hae-jong led the rediscovery in an article featured in Fairbank's well-circulated volume *The Chinese World Order*.[32] In his subsequent writings, Chun consistently denied that Korea's subscription to the Sinic world order implied a submissive stance of any kind.[33] At most, Korea slowly became a vassal state toward the end of the Ming Dynasty (1368–1644), and vassal status was institutionally consolidated during the Qing Dynasty (1644–1911). However, Chun traced Korea's practice of the tribute system back to the period of the Three Kingdoms (57 BC-AD 668), the Goguryeo, Baekje, and Silla, at which time all the parties to the Sinic tribute system were largely equal. He contended that the rise of the Manchu tribal forces during the Song Dynasty (960–1279) disrupted the tribute relationship in the Sinic world, facilitating the tribute relationship between Goguryeo and the synchronous non–Han Liao (907–1125) and non–Han Jin (1115–1234) courts. Both were much more demanding than the Song court, but no one ever claimed that Goguryeo was under their suzerainty. According to Chun, it was during the Mongol Yuan Dynasty that a much strengthened, strictly enforced tribute system was imposed. Goguryeo's tributes during the Yuan Dynasty, including women and eagles, were more expensive than those they sent to the

Qing court. The kingdom also served as the Yuan's military base and weapons producer for its war with Japan. The fluctuations that took place throughout these dynasties, with Korea being treated sometimes as an ally, sometimes as a tribute nation, and on other occasions as an equal, virtually destroys the vision of a Sinic *kitai.*

The Yuan's overwhelming influence reinforces Chun's argument. The tribute system, which was the core of the Sinic world order, was most powerful during the non-Han dynasties, including the Yuan and the Qing. Together with Goguryeo's experience during the Song Dynasty, what happened during the Mongol and Manchu periods made Chun question the idea of a Sinic world order. He noted that the peninsula was a faithful subordinate in the tribute system only under non-Han dynasties, which came and went, so it hardly counted as a Sinic regime. The Korean elite had, to say the least, strong reservations about considering the Manchus or the Mongols as Sinic. However, Chun found that when the system centered on a Sinic court, the peninsula regimes relied on the tribute system to deter invasion by non-Han forces. To this extent, the tribute system was neither cultural nor economic, as the Chinese and English-language literature would have its readers believe. For the peninsular kingdoms, their participation in the tribute system had a predominantly political motivation. In fact, in one of his detailed accounts, Chun demonstrates how neither the Sinic court nor the Korean kingdoms benefited materially from their tribute exchanges at all.

Veteran Sinologist Lee Choon Sik of Korea University further questioned the Chineseness of the tribute system. In other words, he refused to accept that Korea was part of any Chinese system.[34] Rather, it was part of a human system. He argued that the system was no more than an exchange between a state of higher cultural status and its surrounding states, of a kind that historically existed elsewhere in the world—for example, in the Middle East. Cultural superiority requires acknowledgment; thus, the system is reciprocal, not unilateral. According to Lee, only someone of an "arrogant, selfish, and exclusive" mindset can deny the equality between the Han and non-Han nations,[35] as seen in the treatment of non-Han nations as vassals in Chinese literature. Lee then cited examples dating back to the Zhou Dynasty (1046–256 BC), a period that literature on the tribute system largely ignores. During the Zhou Dynasty, the relationship between the court and the surrounding tribes was one of equality, and the tribes usually wanted to acquire goods from the Sinic world. Occasionally, non-Han nomads raided Han communities. A more peaceful way of acquiring goods and culture from the Han was through the tribute system, so participation in the tribute system was one of a number of available options. The decision to join was always based on calculation. In other words, invading nomads and peaceful Koreans adopted different methods to achieve the same ends, with neither treating the Sinic court as a suzerain.

Chung Yong-Hwa, a professor of Korean studies at Yonsei University, disputes China's suzerain status in the peninsula even during the Ming Dynasty.[36] The early Ming rulers rapidly sought to establish a tributary relationship with their Korean contemporaries, the Goryeo Dynasty (918–1392) with the purpose of strengthening the legitimacy of both sides and deterring the Mongols from striking back. The Chinese calculation included the fact that the Goryeo had once attempted to take over Liaoyang, an area to the north of Ming territory that had not yielded to Ming control. In other words, the tribute system was a form of alliance in this instance. At the beginning of the Korean Choson Dynasty (1392–1910), Chung maintains, national security continued to be the prime motive behind the Korean rulers' pro-Ming policy. Korean literature records the statecraft of the time as being concerned with positioning between the Ming and the synchronous late–Jin Dynasty (1616–1636). The decision was to take a *sadae* (serving the great) approach toward the Ming and a restrained approach with regard to the Jin. This is the interpretation given in Korean history, not Chinese history, which portrays the *sadae* approach very differently.

Other Intellectual Paths Compared

Korea's rediscovery of its own historical path, which has enabled its contemporary thinkers to claim ownership of the tribute system, parallels the long-existing displeasure among Mongolian scholars toward the Chinese monopoly over the history of the Yuan Dynasty. Mongolian scholars have an easier task in that they do not need to resort to intention to prove that the nomads did not belong to an agricultural civilization. To this extent, Mongolian scholarship holds a binary view premised upon a *kitai*-like historiography. However, for the Chinese, the Mongolian Yuan Dynasty was part of the Sinic world order. It is not disputed that the Yuan was a Sinic dynasty, but the question is whether Mongolian history is also part of the Sinic world order.[37] During the Cultural Revolution, Chinese maps included Mongolia within China's borders, presumably in accordance with feudalistic historiography, and this enraged Mongolian scholars. Thus, the Mongol conquest of the world was distorted into the glorious record of the Sinicization of the Yuan Dynasty.

Contemporary Mongolian scholars regard the Yuan Dynasty in the same way that contemporary Korean thinkers view the tribute system—both of them provide a platform on which different historical paths meet. These scholars point to both Mongolia's history of independence in the early twentieth century and the emergence of a Mongolian worldview that gave the Mongol nation a comprehensive history of its own.[38] One dimension of these reflections by Mongolian scholars involves a series of studies on the ethnic minorities living in China's border areas, especially in neighboring Chinese Inner Mongolia.[39] Mongols living in Inner Mongolia are the main focus of this research campaign. In a sense, this nascent historiography of Mongolian nationality gathers many Chinese components. In short, with these different discursive trajectories, there is no single Yuan history to be studied. The Yuan Dynasty belongs to at least two distinct historical paths.

According to Jamsran Khereid Bayasakh, the Mongols were nomads belonging to a prairie civilization.[40] The Chinese dynasty was simply an institutional instrument that the Mongol conquerors of China used to rule the Han Chinese and the Sinic world order, including neighboring kingdoms such as that of Korea. The Korean ruling families secured their place through intermarriage with Mongols. According to Bayasakh, the Mongol rulers consciously avoided mixing their blood with that of the Han. They established their seat of government in Beijing specifically to prevent the Han from migrating to the great steppes and even allowed themselves to be called *hu* (savages) in Chinese in order to protect their Mongol identity. Some Sinic measures, such as the tithing system, were expediently employed, and this was misperceived by Han Chinese dynastic historiographers as a sign of the Sinicization of the Mongols. For example, these historiographers speculated that the tomb of Chinggis Khan (1162–1227) was beside a river, while according to Mongol tradition it was in the mountains. Although acknowledging that Chinese civilization was superior to that of the Mongols, and that the Mongols could learn from it, Bayasakh holds that it would have been impossible for an agricultural civilization like that of China to assimilate the Mongols.

Restoring subjectivities by constructing their own paths is not the only strategy adopted by communities that share part of their history with China. Strangely enough, celebrating the convergence, rather than the divergence, of histories can also be useful in worlding subjectivities. Many Vietnamese scholars are suspicious of Beijing's intentions toward its Southeast Asian neighbors, but the Sino-Vietnamese war and the historical dominance of China do not monopolize their contemporary narrative on China. Nguyen Huy Quy and Phan Van Cac, both veteran social scientists, have a great appreciation for the common history of Vietnam and China. Their scholarship is embedded in both family traditions and their training in the humanities. Instead of feeling threatened by a politically, economically, and culturally overwhelming neighbor, they both regard the 1,000 years of shared history as an asset that contemporary Vietnam can deal with skillfully. Knowing China better than anyone else is even a source of pride. This is a dramatically different attitude from that of the aforementioned Korean or Mongolian scholars who always find proximity a threat to self-identity. Nguyen and Phan do not feel that Vietnam would lose its own identity by acknowledging that it shares a historical path with China.

These two scholars do not derive a sense of security from the possibility of a different historical path for Vietnam. Rather, their sense of security is increased by their confidence in their knowledge of China. For them, if there were a Sinic *kitai,* it would have already split into China and Vietnam. This self-confidence encourages them to deal with the evaluative comparison between Korea and Japan, thus insinuating Vietnam's externality to China as an observer. Nguyen is comfortable having both Chinese and Vietnamese identities in his own scholarship, as he indicates in the following:

> Because Vietnam belonged to Chinese proper and was under Chinese administrative jurisdiction for a thousand years, the Chinese and the Vietnamese cultures have for long converged into one despite the fact that Vietnam is politically independent. The relationship is still intimate although there have been a few confrontations. The exchange relations between China and Vietnam were so early that Vietnamese today are able to write Tang-[618–907]style poems in Han characters. The Koreans and the Japanese have adopted a different tonality, resulting in their inability to write Tang-style poems. For example, one kind of Tang-style poem is the eight-line poem, which Vietnamese can write. Vietnamese write beautiful Han characters. Vietnam could proudly announce that Vietnam's China scholarship ranks number one in the world.[41]

The Chinese identity provides the basis for Nguyen's Vietnamese identity. This view is in sharp contrast to that of the allegedly calculating and opportunistic Korean kingdoms, which sought to separate Korea from the Sinic world order. The reason for these differing attitudes toward the Sinic world could have something to do with the more than two decades of conflict between China and Vietnam that confirmed their separate identities. In the same vein, the Korean literature takes pains to record examples of Korea politically outwitting China to subdue or deny social and cultural meanings, which in reality have obscured the difference between China and Korea that the Koreans desire. Contemporary Vietnamese IR literature draws a veil over China–Vietnam relations during the three decades between the demise of Ho Chi Minh (1890–1969) in the mid-1960s to rapprochement in the mid-1990s.[42] This gap, which is sanctioned by the regime, works to the advantage of the two abovementioned scholars of the humanities. The humanities are a worlding vehicle. Presented in a universal spirit, they provide a way both for the Vietnamese nation to cope with an overwhelming China and for Nguyen and Phan to transcend the socialist politics of the past and reconnect with their family and cultural legacy. According to Phan,

> Chinese poems should not be restricted to my personal liking. They are for the whole world. The Chinese should feel good about Chinese poems. Tang-style poems are a human treasure. I was born into a Confucian family. My father taught me to write Han characters when I was five or six. I heard him chant poems. Tang-style poems imperceptibly, powerfully influenced and attracted me. Once grown, I went to China to perfect my Chinese. My only goal at the time was to teach Chinese one day at home. As I went along, I immersed myself in Chinese literature. When I had no classes, I spent all my leisure time in the library reading Chinese novels.[43]

Besides reconstructing their ancestors' calculating intentions, incurring the civilization of the steppes, or recalling a shared humanity, studies on Southeast Asian Chinese communities present additional possibilities of sited knowledge that undermines Mizoguchi's *kitai* perspective. A number of these authors work in Singapore. Suryadinata Leo, a Chinese Indonesian, is head of the Chinese Heritage Institute at Nanyang Technological and Science University, where he records the evolution of the Chinese in Southeast Asia. He is particularly interested in studying the identities of ethnic Chinese of Indonesian nationality.[44] Although they vary in background and origin, they are by no means "overseas" Chinese. They worship Admiral Zheng He, a Muslim eunuch who led treasure fleets to Southeast Asia. Assimilation and localization are Zheng He's legacy to the extent that 600 years later, Wang Gungwu, after a lifetime of research demonstrating the impossibility of categorizing Chinese in Southeast Asia today, urged the abandonment of all the terms used by native Chinese to refer to people of Chinese origin overseas, such as diaspora, overseas Chinese, *huaqiao* (Chinese nationals living abroad), and the like.[45] De-Sinicization is intrinsic to the worlding of Chinese in Southeast Asia.

As Chineseness continues to be an issue and an alienable part of identity in Southeast Asian communities, students of China studies should not be indifferent to the epistemological implications of the term *Chinese*. The force of identification among ethnic Chinese makes them respond enthusiastically to the rise of China in the twenty-first century. Admitting to some Chinese roots is popular among public figures. According to the recent literature, a multidirectional Sinicization is taking place. The Beijing Olympics, increased business opportunities in China for Chinese in Southeast Asia, and higher education exchanges are just a few of the numerous reasons for the mounting awareness of one's own Chineseness.[46] Thriving Chinese-language programs also encourage identity politics. Chinese newspapers in Southeast

Asia have begun to adopt the editorial perspectives of the Chinese domestic media, some to the extreme extent of becoming a sounding board. However, Caroline Hau denies that these signs of the revival of Chineseness indicate the return of a "Chinese empire."[47] Instead, the enhanced interest in being Chinese in various sites should alert territorial Chinese nationals to the fact that they are really not the Chinese they think they know. Thus, Hau observes, "no single institution or agent, not even the putative superpower People's Republic of China, has been able to definitively claim authority as the final arbiter of what constitutes Chinese and Chineseness, or even, for that matter, China."[48] This would be a *kitai* tracker's nightmare if she is correct.

When one tries to extend the deconstructive analysis from Chinese Southeast Asia to the Chinese domestic domain, similar, if not clearer, challenges arise. It has been claimed that China is a temporal concept in which Chinese exist only in "China moments"; that is, the name of China is incurred by someone acting in the capacity of authority.[49] There are many who act in that capacity but each has a different understanding of China and a different purpose. In the same vein, the Australian journal *Provincial China* encounters the conceptual problem in which the provincial level, proven to represent neither the center nor the local, cannot sustain fluid, multisited actors. The territoriality of Chineseness becomes less relevant where the Taiwan issue is concerned; here, sovereignty is passionately contested, regardless of the Beijing authorities' apparent success in containing proindependence Taipei. This situation leads one to suspect that China cannot be academically defined. Tracking the Chinese *kitai* is futile except in the sense of Douglas North's notion of path dependency. Even this notion accepts that multiple paths are inevitable. A prior disclaimer is required for whose path is adopted.

The Sinic *Kitai* as a Multisited Possibility

In order to rescue an imagined substantive China from Japan's own political and psychological needs, manipulation, or identity process, many Japanese thinkers look for discursive mechanisms that can detach Japan from their observed others. For social scientists unfamiliar with Japan's recent past, this rescue attempt seems bizarre. However, for Japan, pretending that there is an externally substantive China is a departure from its imperialist history, the associated civilizing burden, and its unwarranted sense of superiority. Thus, Japan does not have to be obsessed with the backward identity of Asia or responsible for remedying it. The seemingly natural objectivism of European and North American social science is neither natural nor neutral once Japan's quest for a China-centric methodology is put in perspective. An encounter with the scientific world supported by gun boats eventually led Japan down its own imperialist path, which proved to be a mistake. The civilizational embedding of scientism inspired the Japanese elite to take a "departure from Asia to Europe" approach, rendering Japan's Confucian cultural heritage an intrinsic liability and China an object of projected self-hatred. This explains why a Sinic *kitai* becomes an epistemological prescription for Japan's obsessive drive toward modernity, incidentally exposing the political nature of Western social science.

China's many colonized neighbors cannot appreciate the *kitai* discourse. Their otherwise insignificant choices, meaningless to the mainstream literature, nevertheless constitute a variety of creative worlding possibilities. In their quest for subjectivities from within the Sinic world order, the things that used to define the Sinic world order—for example, the institution of the tribute system, the philosophy of the *dao,* mixed ethnic kinship, political territorial sovereignty, and so on—no longer hold true or are no longer practical. However, this finding does not mean that they coordinate these deconstructive exercises or that deconstruction is incompatible with nascent Sinicization. For the majority of Korean thinkers, a Korean historical trajectory that eventually mingled with the Sinic world has an origin of its own, which carried the tribute system through its vicissitudinous past. For the majority of Mongolian thinkers, there exists a Mongolian historical trajectory in which the Yuan established a great empire, foreshadowing the eventual reunification of a great Mongolian nation. A small group of veteran Vietnamese Sinologists cling onto a Sinic identity to support a distinctive national position. The work of deterritorialized Chinese scholars in Southeast Asia deeply undermines any attempt at a centered arbitration of Chineseness. In hindsight, Mizoguchi's *kitai* is no more than another example of nuanced scholarship that ironically reveals his site to be in Japan, something *kitai* historiography tries to shun.

Multisited reinterpretation of the Sinic order challenges the singular text of "China rising" as well as "the China threat" and points to a different East Asian IR and, ultimately, a different global IR. China rising has already generated multisited understandings both inside and outside the territorial borders of China. Chongqing, the leading municipality in central China, has consciously developed a China model that contrasts with the Western model. In some sense it parallels Canton, which has deliberately combined liberalization with one-party rule. Before a political coup toppled the Chongqing leadership in 2012, both models had been under capable leaders possessed of confidence and vision, who kept an eye on each other, not to mention their competitors in Shanghai and Beijing or any other smaller, allegedly unique site that seemed to be developing its own kind of socialist reform. Further challenges come from Tibet, Xinjiang, Hong Kong, Taiwan, and other places where the borders of China become increasingly blurred territorially and socially, as well as politically. Transition from one territorial Chinese site to another usually means a new and distinct understanding of what China is. How China is continuously becoming another China is therefore contingent upon how each site—at the lowest level an individual household, and at the highest a national regime—creates its own historical trajectory. Neighboring nations certainly join in this continuous process of becoming part of China rising and of China becoming part of their own becoming. The way that borders and sites multiply in this complicated manner almost certainly undermines high politics in the imagery of the IR literature.

Sites are where identity strategies emerge. The multiple Sinic orders arising from various sites, which appear to belong to one singular Sinic order, reflect different identity strategies that meet in their interaction. These strategies, derived from different historical trajectories, construct their own China out of the mechanism of encountering and choice. Through encountering, each site is constrained by the physical and discursive contexts from which its strategies emerge; through choice, it combines and recombines cultural resources to give meanings. This is how no site monopolizes the meaning of the Sinic order. All sites are able to come up with new meanings or to recycle old meanings. The Sinic order ironically survives in name or imagination, if not in substance, as all strategies interact and adapt continuously. In short, what is important in Mizoguchi's quest is not just his advocacy of the Chinese *kitai* for Japan in order for it to avoid recreating the Sinic order of the prewar era, but also the mechanism of choice and the appropriation of cultural resources that enables the quest for or rejection of such a *kitai*. The same is happening in East Asian IR that is witnessing both the recalling or preempting of the Sinic order and the mimicry or misappropriation of liberal IR.

CHAPTER 9

Global Asian: China as Position between Host and Home

Following the multisited knowledge production that constructs the intellectual images of China across various communities, the current chapter substitutes the traveling agents for communities to study how one's knowledge of China evolves along with individual choice over identity strategy. Sinicization describes processes of civilizational evolution that adapt both internal needs and external contacts with various agents who substantially, though not fully, share worldviews, values, self-understanding, and life practices. Appropriating knowledgeable practices across civilizational boundaries encourage adaptation. Sinicization thus rests on the readiness of its agents to conceptualize and practice new ways of self-understanding.

As already stated in Chapter 3, encounter and choice are the mechanisms that define agency. Encounters embody civilization in process. Sinicization is premised upon the encounter between Chinese and other civilizations. Encounters push agents to adapt as they must choose between resistance, teaching, learning, or a combination of all three. Consciously or not, each agent thus is constantly involved in choosing different strategies of adaptation. If encounters thus can generate fresh possibilities for innovation and recombination, Sinicization is multisited. In processes of cross-civilizational encounters, no two agents will adapt their practices in exactly the same way. And although such encounters are occurring all over the world, on account of the size of China's population and China's peaceful rise, Sinicization is of increasing significance.

Chapter 2 discusses Anglicization of China's Africa policy. Anglicization has enhanced the vitality and resonance of Sinicization. It has facilitated the spreading of American practices of market capitalism to China's economy, nationalism, and rights rhetoric to Chinese politics, balance of power to China's foreign policy, and multi-culturalism to China's global diasporic communities. Conceptual and institutional adaptations to Anglicization and the different forms of resistance, re-appropriation, and feedback they engender have made Sinicization more important. All responses push agents to be cognizant of the positions they occupy between different civilizations, and all require knowledge of both Euro-American and Chinese civilizations. And invariably, agents of Sinicization cannot do without the use of English, which has unavoidable ideological, practical, and institutional consequences.

Anglicization as well as Sinicization often implicates not simply China as a nation-state, but also the Chinese in Indo-China and Taiwan who are mediating between Chinese and their various forms of identity. They act as both producers and consumers of civilization who maneuver between collective, familial, and individual centers of allegiance. Self-knowledge is the foundation of Sinicization of international relations. Sinicization and Anglicization are multisited processes that deconstruct stereotypical notions of China's rise in the twenty-first century. Chapter 9 introduces four scholars have actively participated in Sinicization under a social science disguise (John Wong), anxiously wished the best out of it to make geo-civilizational Chindia (Tan Chung), managed it from an imagined place of inbetweenness to achieve peace (Akira Iriye), and shifted attention from incorporating China to incorporating his own home country (Samuel Kim). Their strategic choices are shaped by their specific historical contexts, and their adaptations thus vary widely. Positioned at different sites, agents do not respond in a similar manner to China's rise.

Home and Host

Sinicization proceeds in the mind rather than through territorial expansion. Sinicization is thus composed of processes of increasing mutual self-knowledge as well as increasing knowledge about China. Processes of Sinicization that accompany the rise of China have triggered a recombination of, rather than a rupture with, established patterns and practices.[1] Although Sinicization is not just a territorial expansion of influence, recombination is more visible in areas located close to China's territorial state. Since one needs to make sense of China's rise and what this implies for one's relationship with China, the understanding of China is intimately tied to one's self-understanding. Mutual constitution is normally invoked as an abstract category and is rarely itself interrogated, as based on a discursive analysis of the work of these four scholars.

Mutual constitution is central for Asian diasporic scholars who usually take on identities addressing their relationships with China, the country of origin or residence. Their home and host countries are important geo-cultural contexts of Sinicization at the micro-level. However, the designation of home country is often a complicated matter since in many cases a person could have lived in many different places; home identity is a complex and situational choice complicated further when it involves territorial China: self-identity can then become a matter of the periphery or the center. The responses of Asian diasporas outside Asia can offer valuable insights into processes of Sinicization.

A comparison of each of the four possibilities thus generated permits their readers to make some conjectures about processes of Sinicization. Cultural Sinicization thus concerns discourses and how these discourses emerge from a specific social and cultural context. Since individuals make strategic choices, their decision to move in one direction or another is never simple or neat. The coincidence of individual strategy and a larger conjuncture are unavoidable. More specifically, the diasporic dimension of Sinicization invites us to answer two questions: how does one view China and how does one think that others view China. The two answers focus, respectively, on identity and image.

The chapter will rely on a comparison of their writings as well as interviews to accomplish two tasks—to gather evidence that their intellectual position can be traced to a larger context *and* that their position always entails making meaningful choices. The meaning of Sinicization, accordingly, cannot be determined in advance. In brief, Sinicization is thus made possible through mutual constitution. Moreover, by no means is the background of these four scholars sufficient for characterizing their thematic choices. The following discussion shows instead how their choices are well grounded without precluding that other choices might have been possible.

In short, background gives meaning to texts. Not unlike most intellectuals growing up in a postcolonial society, Asian diasporas have generally experienced an identity dilemma involving home and host country.[2] On issues involving their home country, members of the Asian diaspora should think and act like fellow citizens in the host country. At the same time, they also need a home country that enjoys respect in their host country so as to reduce the anxiety that their status as a diaspora might become a liability. The worst case occurs when the host and the home country are in conflict. Were it to involve a serious conflict, the rise of China thus could put Asian diasporic scholars to the test.[3] Their views of China would then reveal their choice between home and host country. Colleagues and readers would watch carefully especially in times of conflict.

When diasporic scholars construct the image of China through their scholarly writings, they are at the same time presenting their self-images.[4] First, they need to decide if China should be evaluated by the often universal standards accepted in the host country. These standards typically concern democracy, human rights, capitalism, and peace. Second, if these norms are not applicable, then they need to make sure the other norms are intelligible to the host country. In brief, diasporic scholars incur social costs for any analysis that gives the impression that China does not have to conform to widely accepted norms. By no means, though, do diasporic scholars have to agree with the mainstream view of the host country. Invoking a cause larger than China, however, is essential to demonstrate independent scholarship to the audience in the host country.

It appears from the limited number of cases in this chapter that one's portrayal of China indirectly answers to the question about one's own personal identity and social image. Identity concerns itself with the type of the home, image with the type of host country. If the home country used to be peripheral in the Sino-centric world, the need to differentiate from China should be comparatively weak on questions of identity; if equivalent in status, that need should be strong. Diasporic Korean scholars, for example, should be less interested than diasporic Japanese in differentiating China from their respective home countries. Analogously, if the host country is a Western state, the expectation that China should conform to specific and allegedly universal norms should be relatively strong; if not in the West, it should be weaker. Thus, the Chinese diaspora living in North America or Western Europe would probably be more attuned to China's failure to abide by the norms of liberal democracy.

To understand the rise of China thus asks for the actor's judgments on questions of both identity and image. To understand how individual judgments are embedded in a scholar's background, the following discussion relies on interviews with four Asian China experts, all teaching outside of their countries of birth: Samuel Kim (an "idealistic" Korean living in the United States), Akira Iriye (a "defeated" Japanese also living in the United States), Tan Chung (a "betraying" Chinese living in India, who is used to placing the family in front of the given name), and John Wong (an "objective" Hong Kong China watcher living in Singapore). Mutual constitution of self-knowledge and knowledge about China thus involves identity and image, with self-knowledge telling the actor how to view China and with the knowledge of others about China telling the actor how China is viewed.

Sinicization processes expand the China discourse in ways partly determined by biography and partly by individual choice. Their different conceptions of China reflect both their diasporic social positions and hybrid cultural bearings as well as their specific choices about their identities (Table 9.1).

To begin, Akira Iriye sees China as different and ready to conform. He is originally from Japan, which is relatively equal to China in status, but lives in the United States. Iriye's position is in line with as well as different from

Table 9.1 Self as position between China and the West

Image \ Identity	China is identical to self	China is different from self
China is identical to the West	Synthesis/Sino-centrism Kim	Centrism/solidarism Iriye
China is different from the West	Statism/nationalism Wong	Civilization/commonwealth Tan

that of Hedemi Suganami's. Samuel Kim views China as similar and ready to conform. Kim's views are in line with and also different from David Kang's Sino-centric analysis. He is originally from Soviet-occupied Korea, which is peripheral to China, but lives in the United States. John Wong is originally from peripheral Hong Kong but lives in Singapore. He sees China as quite similar to other states and does not insist that China should conform to the universal standards defined by others. Wong's view is in line with as well as different from Zheng Yongnian's nationalism metaphor. Finally, Tan Chung sees China as different from other states and sees no need for China to conform to the norms propounded by others. His views both agree with and differ from Wang Gangwu's commonwealth metaphor. Tan Chung is originally from China. He used to live in India before his retirement.

Career Trajectories and Perspectives

The Centrist[5]

Akira Iriye's scholarship always points to possible avenues that seek to accommodate seemingly irreconcilable positions. He calls himself a centrist. He places himself between the United States, Japan, and China and is committed to individual diplomacy. He argues that culture offers such possibilities since the love for culture is universal. He thus uses music as the quintessential example of a universal culture. Iriye does not attempt to mediate through consensus building. Rather, he seeks to breed confidence in a universal humanity that transcends mundane conflicts of interests. His scholarship expresses the view that conflict among states takes place over superficial issues that are based on ignorance. A deeper sharing of common values is made possible by redirecting attention away from political and economic issues toward cultural ones. Other than reducing enmity, Iriye is not interested in changing anyone's position. Iriye thus hopes to unstiffen existing and at times bitter policy disputes. He resorts to simple facts and simple logics that may have limited theoretical appeal. He insists instead on the realization of the simplicity of a universal human spirit.

Iriye's scholarship avoids controversial issues. And he calls his approach centrist. He is therefore more ready than many of his Japanese colleagues to sympathize with China's nationalist mood, rooted in deeply felt grievances caused by the violence Japan inflicted on China during World War II. This does not mean, however, that he is ready to blame Japan. Iriye's scholarship on Japan shows no sign of placing blame on Japan for its past policies.[6] Building an integrated and unified Asian Community is the best way to achieve genuine peace.[7] It requires China's and Japan's reconciliation. For him, misunderstanding is the root of all problems, and cultural exchange is the only method to resolve misunderstanding. China is an important place to begin retrieving universal humanity. If Japan and the United States are to achieve genuine peace, he argues, then East and West must come together.

Understanding and respecting China in the context of the historical evolution of its policy choices is the first step to bridge the gap that separates China from its opponents. China's rise is a phenomenon of globalization, not a threat to or disruption of it. To achieve that end, Iriye's scholarship does not advocate a change in or transformation of China. History shows how misunderstandings have emerged. And history shows why China is a nation that possesses a character different from Japan and quite legitimately adheres to policies informed by its own interests. In short, Iriye's centrist position makes him see China as ontologically different. But he does believe that China could achieve a deeper self-confidence if it were to retrieve some universally shared values. Both Japan and the United States should and could accomplish this as well.

The UK-based English School Solidarist Hidemi Suganami adopts different approaches while stressing China's distinct status and insisting on conformity with specific principles. In comparison to Iriye's centrist approach, which resolves conflict by recognizing a shared humanity, Suganami sympathizes with a Japanese School of International Relations. Although he rarely touches in his writings on China, Suganami notes the different international principles that pervade ancient Chinese history.[8] His curiosity toward a national school of international relations and his appreciation of different national histories make it easy for him to readily accept China as a distinct nation. His solidarism, however, predisposes him toward China conforming with globally shared human rights standards.[9] A comparison of Iriye with Suganami shows similarity in their designation of China in accordance with their home (equal with China) and host (in the West) country identities. Nevertheless, their expectations differ. Iriye stresses peace more than the kind of human rights that Suganami cherishes. Furthermore, for Suganami, war is not unthinkable. Iriye prefers micro-level communication while Suganami focuses on macro-level management. Sinicization would compel Suganami to think seriously about intervention in China's human rights policy. It poses a practical challenge to solidarism and the principle that defines him as a Solidarist.

The Synthesizer[10]

Samuel Kim's involvement in world order studies fostered the argument that China has to fulfill its duty when it conducts its international affairs. Kim thus began to write about how China has acquired its sense of membership in international organization and sought to fulfill its international obligations. He began his career by writing about Christian missionary Anson Burlingame, who later served as China's ambassador to Europe.[11] If China could be represented in Europe by an American missionary, it simply could not be all that different from the West. Contrary to conventional opinion prevailing in the 1970s, he argued that China was not a troublemaker in the United Nations. To the contrary, China painstakingly chose political gestures that signaled its disagreement with specific policies without disrupting UN procedures.[12] Even in areas whereas legacy of deep conflict remained, China acquiesced and gradually came to adopt UN procedures it had vehemently opposed before. At the same time, China tried hard to adhere to the stance of most Third World countries. Kim also notes how attentive China has been to improving its own image. From the perspective of world order studies, there exists no great difference between China and other states.

Kim likes to combine all different analytical perspectives on China into one composite model. Kim calls his scholarship synthetic. Kim edits a book on conflict that incorporates virtually all related theories. Similarly, most theories about China are included in Kim's edited books and he discusses a broad spectrum of bilateral and multilateral arrangements.[13] Specifically, Kim sees different theories account for different aspects of Chinese foreign policy. It almost appears that both world order and China are arenas to display his collection of theories. In the era of globalization, his scholarship is instead to understand how China adapts to new challenges such as the rules of the World Trade Organization. The attention Kim pays to the negotiation process suggests that he views China as just another state. To the extent that Kim does not support or oppose specific theories, his work resembles Iriye's. But synthesis differs from centrism. In his synthesis, Kim develops his own theoretical perspective. It is typically well rounded and rarely provokes others. In this he resembles Iriye's writings. However, in contrast to Iriye, Kim does not hesitate to articulate his own position. Kim's quest in scholarship is combining and reconciling different intellectual positions and thus to transcend the limitations that specific theoretical perspectives inevitably entail. In scholarship Kim does not view China as a country that is seeking to demonstrate its uniqueness.

For Kim, Sinicization offers opportunities to incorporate previously excluded regimes such as Pyongyang into the world order. For David Kang, Sinicization consolidates an alternative to realism that promises a world order actually desired by today's major powers. US-based Kang is an ardent defender of a Chinese worldview unfamiliar to Western theories informed by the Westphalian state system, as opposed to Kim's synthetic approach. Furthermore, he considers China's neighbors to agree with, indeed embrace, a hierarchical world view.[14] This agreement generates collectively shared expectations about relationships that even China, located at the top, must comply with. Both the US scholars Kim and Kang are critics of all versions of realism. Instead, Kang argues that the East Asian order has been maintained not by balancing but by bandwagoning. Located at the center, China has always been a familiar phenomenon to its East Asian neighbors who started fighting one another only during periods of China's weakness. Although far from a synthesis, Kang's criticism of realism is a plea for peace, stability, and prosperity,[15] everything that Washington would cherish. For Kim, the establishment of a world order requires practical work. For Kang, realism is the main danger that threatens to cause conflict and war.

The Scientific Watcher[16]

John Wong's stress on scientific methodology and detached and yet informed analysis of China's situation gives a clue to his alert at any perceived linkage between Singapore and China. His China is usually placed in a macro-structural context often reflected in the titles of his many publications. He takes a problem-solving approach and puts himself as much as possible in the shoes of Chinese leaders. In his writings Wong addresses Chinese economic, social, and political problems. His scientific sensibility often shows on statistics as well as models that seek to describe the situation faced by the Chinese leaders in objective terms. Occasionally he is willing to propose policy solutions. Although his analysis is always problem centered, Wong rarely, if ever, shows any interest in the notion of China's collapse. Instead, he is interested in why and how Chinese leaders are coping with difficult challenges. And he does not romanticize their ability to resolve any of them. He is particularly sensitive to China's relationship with its Southeast Asian neighbors[17] John Wong publishes more on China's economic development than any other issue.

In their Chineseness, Singapore and China share common sensibilities. Wong's analysis rests on the recognition that China's rise offers Singapore a unique opportunity.[18] Singapore's relationship with its Southeast Asian neighbors is vulnerable because of domestic ethnic quarrels that center on the existence of important Chinese minorities. Wong understands and presents China's policy toward its Southeast Asian neighbors as one of caution. In Wong's depiction of East Asian international relations, there exists no Sino-centric world. For Wong, China is just another country. His analysis is based on national statistics. However, to the extent that China could not simply apply experiences gained elsewhere to resolve the problems it faces, China's experience and capacity are specific and distinctive, illustrated by issues such as leadership succession, socialist reform, and crisis management such as SARS.[19] China's distinctiveness becomes a professional rather than cultural identity for Singapore, in English, with easy access to Chinese informants, to make contributions to social science scholarship on China. In short, the reason that he wants to understand the contemporary challenges Chinese leaders face is that this kind of knowledge is put in the service of the Singapore government.

For Wong, Sinicization is illustrated by Singapore's greater sensitivity toward and compliance with Chinese practices. For Zheng Yongnian in comparison, Sinicization is illustrated by China's pragmatic nationalism. China-born, US-trained, and currently Singapore-based Zheng Yongnian takes Chinese scholars very seriously as a vital source of knowledge. Zheng argues that Chinese nationalism has both pragmatic and emotional aspects.[20] Both Wong and Zheng agree that China can be studied objectively. China is not different from other countries that similarly abide by realist logic (for Wong) or subscribe to nationalism (for Zheng). However, Wong and Zheng differ from each other on the subject of empathy with Chinese feelings as an essential ingredient to the understanding of China. Sympathy with China could mean deep trouble for Wong's Singaporean host. Zheng is less sensitive to the ethnic issues that surround the position of Chinese in Southeast Asia. Both agree, however, that China has its own way of doing things. This explains why both rely on Chinese sources. Neither lives in the West now, and both have lived in Chinese settings—Wong's Hong Kong and Zheng's Zhejiang.

The Anti-imperialist[21]

Tan Chung began his professional career by criticizing John Fairbank's study of the tribute system, and ends by criticizing Samuel Huntington's thesis of the clash of civilizations.[22] After his retirement, Tan Chung has been promoting the image of an Indian elephant dancing together with a Chinese dragon.[23] Tan Chung's father, Yun-shan (1898–1983), helped Rabindranath

Tagore establish the first China studies institute in India. He has adopted Tagore's conviction that China and India are two civilizations that could not possibly threaten each other. Tagore treated individuals as meeting places of civilizations. Tan expanded on that theme. Tan believes that both Fairbank and Huntington have misread China profoundly. Tan has consistently tried to argue how harmonious and peaceful Chinese political thought and practice has been. He debates some of his Indian colleagues about their concerns over the threat China may pose to India. For Tan, the historical relationship between the two countries centers around two civilizations, each capable of giving to and learning from the other. To him it is inconceivable that either China or India could pursue imperialist or hegemonic policies and become enemies. At the same time he debates Chinese and Taiwanese colleagues by insisting that, besides exporting Buddhism, Indian civilization is an important source of Chinese civilization, illustrated by its export to China of the image of the dragon and the idea of equality.

Tan criticizes geo-politics for its obsession with power competition, and agrees with geo-economics about the importance of interconnections between China and India. Civilizations highlight rather than threaten one another. Neither India nor America needs to worry that a powerful China would compel them to follow a specific model of life. Tan looks to the Himalaya as the origin of four great river systems, two of which laid the foundation for Indian and two for Chinese civilization. To substitute, he developed the concept of "geo-civilization."[24] He develops the concept of "Chindia" to convey the existence of "great harmony between China and India." In the rise of China, Tan discerns a different model of international behavior that will show the world how it is possible not to challenge anyone. India is a good example since in its long history and despite its superior strength, China has never tried to conquer it. In short, China does not have to treat India or any other state as a rival. Instead China is a civilization that has its own inner logic and spirit.

Sinicization bears witness to China's enhanced capacity for more learning for Tan. For Wang Gungwu it could yield a thickening of Chinese identity and a reversal of hybrid identities. In comparison with Tan's strident anti-imperialism, Wang Gungwu—born in Indonesia, raised in Malaysia, trained in England, and having taught in Australia, Hong Kong, and Singapore—shows no stridency in his scholarship. Yet he sees China inhabiting a different world that contrasts with the West. Wang views the Chinese in Southeast Asia fractured into different kinds.[25] For the sake of convenience, one could categorize his approach to China with a "commonwealth" metaphor. Wang's analysis recognizes differences in each locality without denying that together they share a thin layer of Chinese identity. For Wang it is a mistake to judge all Chinese by one standard. As a concept, "Chinese" is much broader than the notion of a territorial state and thus not suitable for judgment based on a single standard. Through his scholarship, Wang personifies a perspective that is very tolerant of hybridity, fluidity, and uncertainty. Tan strongly defends China's uniqueness. Wang instead would like to see hybridity as a result of local conditions evolve into difference. Tan argues that the intermixing of civilizations stems from all kinds of interconnections.

The Personal and National Contexts

Akira Iriye

Without him being necessarily fully aware of it, the philosophy of nothing-ness and the world history standpoint are epistemologically embedded in Iriye's centrism, his idea of the importance of inter-cultural relations, and his commitment to an Asian Community. Some members of that school sup-ported the war fought in the name of the Greater East Asian Coprosperity Sphere.[26] Although a pacifist, Iriye takes an epistemological stance quite sim-ilar to that of the Kyoto School of Philosophy. According to their philosophy of nothingness, Hegelian contradiction needs no synthesis. To be univer-sal is the ability to be both Oriental and Occidental. This means that one must exist in a place of nothingness. Retreat to nothingness philosophically brings one back to the origin of civilizations and enables reentry into a differ-ing cultural context so that one would appreciate all without changing any. In its time the Kyoto School inspired important scholars such as Takeuchi Yoshimi, once Japan's most influential literate critic. He suggested that Asia should be conceived of as a method of self-denial that would shield us from being preoccupied by any specific values or being committed to any specific standpoint.[27] Today Koyasu Nobukuni, in particular, carries on the legacy of the Kyoto School legacy. He argues that East Asia is a method that reveals itself through an unending process of becoming.[28] Since it is a process, East Asia can never be a piece of territory that is to be occupied. Hence, there exists no conceptual room for a revival of imperialism. Late Mozoguchi Yuzo similarly advocated treating China rather than East Asia as a method, thus enabling the Japanese to learn how to view others without taking into account Japan's own condition. Thus, Japan can aim to become truly universal.[29] This preoccupation with attaining the universal without resolving obvious contradictions echoes the Kyoto School's view of both Orient and Occident as partial. To follow the logic of nothingness, the rise of China is a devel-opment that does not affect Japan as it occurs in an altogether different context.

Iriye's favored civilizational relationship preserves all cultures and would not have a chance to become a reality if China's rise were political. Conceived of as a bridge, Japan facilitates inter-civilizational understandings. It thus might lower the chances of a future confrontation that would force Japan, and Iriye, to choose sides. This particular scholarship owes a great deal to his mentor John K. Fairbank, who helped him throughout his career. World War II posed the question of whether Japan, his home country, or the United States, where he made his life, was to blame for the war. He resolved that difficult question by insisting that the war resulted mostly from colossal misunderstandings on both sides. Thus, he was able to sidestep the issue of who was right and who was wrong. Even at a time when war between China, Japan, and the United States is highly unlikely, Iriye continues to be an advocate for peace as if the threat of war was real. It is, of course, real for anyone who bears the burden of war in their choice of identity. Without China's participation, Japan can never become the representative of the East, seeking genuine peace with the United States and the West. The rise of China could pose an intellectual threat if China feels no need of Asia joining the world. If this were to happen, there would be no East to engage in cultural exchange with the West. The idea of an Asian Community that includes China, the United States, and Japan would be impossible. That should be a sufficient reason why Iriye tries to persuade his audience that China is a rising civilization that poses no threat whatsoever. Rather, it offers a historic opportunity.

Iriye appreciates the merits of both sides of this civilizational divide. His peace is not as bitter as that of the war-accepting Kyoto School. For Iriye war would betray consciousness, which is to validate and secure all sides to all possible conflicts. The cognitive capacity of the prewar Kyoto School to tolerate that incongruence between an older China-oriented Japan and a modern Western-oriented Japan coexists does not yield the same bridging result. Since Iriye does not accept the dictates of various situations, he clearly differs from the Kyoto philosophers to the extent that he does not just abide by various situations as given. To favor Orient at one time and Occident at another is not simply a spontaneous act. Consciousness has to be taught and cultivated. Furthermore, war would pose a threat to his relationship with his mentor. Iriye is thus quite aggressive in preaching peace. He teaches us how to appreciate other civilizations. Iriye thus tackles directly the mutual animosities in Chinese and Japanese society. He urges both sides to adopt an inter-civilizational rather than a national perspective. The rise of China confirms his idea that China is a civilization rather than a state. This makes him appreciate Japan and China as civilizations that can and need to build their inter-civilizational relationships, thus protecting his own centrist position. He transcends his Japanese identity by making it politically irrelevant or universal. Iriye respects all perspectives he deals with, potentially including both the Kyoto School and the contrarian position of Iriye's, which advocates personal diplomacy.

Samuel Kim

Kim learned English on his own so that he could teach Koreans and translate for Americans. Thus, he was able to scrape together enough funds to buy an airline ticket to America. Kim supported himself from the beginning as he entered the field of China studies. Before settling in the United States, Kim was constantly on the move. Born in what later became North Korea, he learned Japanese as his first and Russian as his second foreign languages. But he was determined that he would live in the United States. Since it would make it difficult to find a job, he made the shrewd decision to avoid Korea as his main focus at the outset of his career. China appeared to be a better choice. Thus he began to learn Chinese as his fifth language—after having studied English and French in college. In his scholarship he shied away from a power politics perspective and instead favored a normative approach. The normative high ground allowed him to avoid making judgments about political developments that had previously pushed his personal life into directions not under his control. Later he became the first American Fulbright Professor teaching in China. Throughout his career, he has had no enemies. When he was upset about the Tiananmen uprising, as a scholar he did not act.

It is hardly surprising that Kim insists that China is simply too complicated a subject to be encapsulated in a nutshell. A description of China must be nuanced and qualified. This approach mirrors his own career. Kim always looked for the confluence of diverse factors that would help him explain complicated events. Concerns over human rights in China simply could not yield one general assessment. Similarly, the rise of China does not push Kim to embrace one simple theory as is true of many other intellectuals. In any case during the past decade, his attention has shifted away from Chinese to Korean politics. If Communist China failed in shaping China's destiny in the past, China's rise surely would not have a teleological destiny either. The Cold War, the division of Korea, and the containment policy were the context in which Samuel Kim made his career choices. They were shaped by a mixture of cultural and social forces that offered numerous opportunities that Kim seized with alacrity. Kim is very much aware of the deep puzzle posed by his own identity. And he is also cognizant of and sensitive to his seemingly inferior social position.

Kim is comfortable with the notion of Sinicization, which for him is an open-ended process. And he readily acknowledges that Korea and Japan were both deeply influenced by China. His attention to and sympathy for North Korea is embedded in his never-alarmist views on China.[30] In North Korea he recognizes something he would have actually characterized himself with when he says that North Korea is no longer a shrimp because the shrimp has learned multiple languages. Kim is a self-professed pacifist. He wants China to become a democracy but without external pressure. He pays great attention to China's increasing conformity to the norms of international organizations.[31] Unlike realists, and especially offensive realists, he is not alarmed by China's rise. In his writings he shuns extreme positions such as "China threat" or "China collapse." Instead of adhering to a neutral and centrist position, as does Iriye, Kim draws useful lessons from all sides. Since his scholarship on China is always synthetic, Kim's understanding of China does not point to one clear path. Interestingly, his self-conscious avoidance of any and all teleologies is rooted in combining many different teleological arguments.

John Wong

Because of China's potential intervention in local ethnic politics,[32] Singapore's government has traditionally tended to discourage the study of China. Its anti-Communism and ethnic sensibility both help explain this aversion. However, facing the rise of China, this city state, which so heavily relies on international management and financial flow, simply cannot afford to lag behind in the analysis of developments in China. The first analysis of China was disguised as Confucian studies. Since 75 percent of Singapore's multi-ethnic population are Chinese, Singapore's relations with China are very delicate. Some scholars of Chinese origin writing in Singapore on Southeast Asian Chinese affairs dispute the very notion of a Chinese diaspora. They insist instead that Southeast Asia's Chinese are native. Subsequently, it was carried on under the name of East Asian studies. As a matter of fact, nevertheless, East Asian studies is primarily about China and secondarily about Taiwan. To desensitize further the study of China, the Institute of East Asian Studies now virtually monopolizes all of Singapore's resources in the field of China policy studies. To this end, Singapore's government has decided to rely exclusively on overseas Chinese, temporary appointments, English writing, and social science approaches. In relying on these four institutional traits, it hopes to prevent the knowledge on China produced in Singapore to become a political linkage to China. Born in China, raised in anti-Communist Hong Kong, trained in English, and accustomed to annual reunion with his emigrant family in Canada, John Wong offers an ideal fit to assuming a leading position in the field.

Anti-China sentiment never factored into Wong's research, which also includes the study of Southeast Asian Chinese. His interest in and concern for Chinese and China is very evident in his policy analysis. To him the rise of China is largely a Chinese matter and should not be a matter of concern to any other state. China's rise has caused Chinese problems and Chinese ways to resolve them. Both Wong's Hong Kong background in which individuals had no say about their political future and his experience as an immigrant cultivated a self-awareness of having escaped from a Communist takeover. This helped create a feeling of distance from the object of his studies. Recruited from a foreign country, with little intellectual connection to the local community, and without the protection of tenure, Wong could rely on no one but his direct superior, then Premier Goh Keng Swee, and indirectly, on then President Lee Kwang Yew. Wong recruits researchers who stay for no longer than five years. An increasing number of these scholars have come from China in recent years, and he coaches them to write policy papers. His superiors expect a pragmatic approach in the East Asian Institute's (EAI's) publications so that the institute's research is of benefit to the government.

However, the more the EAI's research succeeds in preparing Singapore's participation in China's rise, the less Wong is keeping Singapore away from China. In short, the rise of China is enticing Chinese identity consciousness and eliciting responses from neighboring states. Wong has shown little nationalist emotion in his writing. He began to recruit Chinese scholars only because Prime Minister Goh insisted that it was important to develop perspectives on China from within China. Goh also believed that anti-Communism would not work. This also has affected Wong's approach. He has faithfully observed Lee's pragmatism and Goh's strategic thinking. Consequently, EAI's research on China has no connection to Singapore's society. Wong thinks that Southeast Asian Chinese are increasingly becoming less Chinese, while his work makes him increasingly be in touch with China. Wong sees it as his main task to present China to Western audiences.[33] Like Lee, his position on China is friendly and neutral. Lee wants the EAI to copy neither Western nor PRC perspectives. Wong is able to achieve this objective because he can justifiably claim that the EAI knows more about China through its Chinese researchers and that their objectivity results from reliance on social science models and English language.

Tan Chung

The historiography of Tan's anti-imperialist epistemology preserved the civilizational sensibility in Tagore's and his father, Yun-shan's, worldview. His politically incorrect ethnic identity was neutralized by his politically correct anti-imperialist standpoint. Note that Tan began his career in Tagore's tradition. The outbreak of the Sino-Indian war in 1962 cost him his job as an interpreter affiliated with an organization funded by National Defense Ministry. His Chinese origin raised suspicion because it was thought to be incompatible with the loyalty required by his position. Tan Chung has devoted his career to criticizing imperialism and American scholarship on China. He succeeded in convincing his Indian colleagues that it was possible to use Chinese history to establish a perspective outside of the mainstream literature. This orientation is appreciated in the Indian academic world since Indian intellectuals are especially sensitive to their indebtedness to British perspectives, which many struggle to resist. Specifically, he demonstrates how premodern tribute paid to the Chinese court was sheer etiquette rather than a system of trade.[34] Tan shows how the imperialist desire for trade had led Fairbank to misunderstand the meaning of tribute for the Chinese. Through his historical scholarship on China, after the 1962 war, Tan reoriented Indian perspectives on China in general toward an anti-imperialist approach to China studies.[35]

Tan's life-long struggle for better Indo-Chinese relations rests on his insistence that ancient China borrowed from Indian civilization to become today's China. Furthermore, India has much to learn from China in order to make a genuine break with its painful experience with Western imperialism and colonialism. This is a remarkable parallel with Tagore and Yun-shan, who cherished the fact that in the past Buddhism was exported from India to China and who promoted the return of Buddhism to India from China in the future. Tan has not only tried to improve China's image in India. He also tried to encourage his Chinese colleagues to take India seriously. In their times Tagore and Yun-shan tried to do the same with little success. Tan follows Tagore's approach by tracing India's contribution to Chinese civilization. This begets serious criticism from Chinese and Taiwanese colleagues but fascinated his audience nonetheless. Tan wants to prove that Chinese civilization is capable of learning and adapting without sacrificing its authenticity. The first argument reconnects China with India; the second assures China's independent position outside the West. Tan wants his Chinese colleagues to be mindful of the rewards that China has reaped by learning from India in the past.

While others see China's rise as posing a challenge to India, Tan sees a new opportunity for reminding his audiences of the importance of civilizational interconnections. Four decades after the 1962 border war had created enormous pressure on anyone who wanted to stop the two states from further confrontations, the rise of China provides Tan with a new opportunity to reconnect the two civilizations. His writings on geo-civilization have, since his retirement, been hastily published in a number of books that reiterate his long-held views.[36] The Shanghai Academy of Social Science's bi-annual World China Forum, initiated in 2004, has featured Tan as a keynote speaker addressing over 1,000 participants. Here Tan enjoys the opportunity to be part of China's rise among Chinese colleagues enjoying their improved self-image and self-confidence. His writings have gained attention as he introduced his civilizational analysis through book and newspaper publications and, most efficiently, through Chinese web pages.[37]

Embedded and Multiplying in Individual Careers

When they contribute in their writings to the scholarship on China, the four scholars take an active part in processes of Sinicization. Note, though, that Asian diasporic scholarship typically is written in English. English is a prerequisite that shapes the audience it primarily serves. While this common feature is shared by almost all diasporic scholars, those involved in Sinicization differ from other diasporic scholars in at least two ways. First, sensitivity, if not sympathy, toward Chinese history registered among Asian diasporic scholars in the domain of scholarship gives substance to the process of Sinicization. Second, this sensitivity has repercussions inside and outside of territorial China. Chinese audiences thus appropriate and re-appropriate the interpretations and insights diasporic scholarship provides with the effect that China and so-called Chinese concepts encounter all kinds of interventions.

Their scholarship in English makes Sinicization a total experience. Each of the four scholars discussed in this chapter has his own intellectual agenda. Wong's preoccupation with greater China's economic development, Iriye's advice on the propriety of a Japanese apology to China for wartime crimes, Tan's celebration of Chinese anti-imperialism, and Kim's support of China's entry into international organizations, all share to different degrees a profound sensitivity and at times sympathy for China. In addition, each spends a good deal of his professional career as well as leisure time in either his home or host country. That said, the Anglo-Chinese scholarship of Tan and Wong differs from the Anglo-Asian scholarship of Iriye and Kim. Anglo-Chinese scholarship deals with the English world, the hosting society, and China, while Anglo-Asian scholarship with the English world, the home society, and China. Sinicization processes that make the world adapt to Chinese values are only one part of the lives of these four scholars. There are also attempts at influencing those acting on behalf of China by supplying them with certain larger analytical causes the four scholars choose to represent their academic independence.

Nonetheless, the national contexts intertwine with career trajectories to generate different challenges that motivate the evolution of research agenda for these four scholars. Wong stresses scientism so that he can justify his core proposition that China's distinctive national conditions call for indigenous treatment; Iriye emphasizes peace and humanist values to justify his criticism of the insensitivity of the Americans and the Japanese conservatives of different national and cultural perspectives; Kim articulates an idealist world order to justify his refusal to support either China after the suppression of the pro-democracy movement or Western sanctions imposed on China in the aftermath; and Tan supports a geo-civilizational connectivity to justify his optimistic articulation of the hope for a long-term human evolution away from egoistic nationalism. These larger causes more than their substantive interest in and preoccupation with China also help define their scholarship. This is not to deny that Wong's preoccupation with the greater China is shared by many who do not trust Western scientism; that anti-imperialism has been used to justify China's confrontation with India, putting into doubt Tan's central claim; that China's participation in international organization has failed to bring about the world order Kim is advocating; and that widespread Japan-phobia in China might not be assuaged by the kind of apology that Iriye is advocating.

All four scholars demonstrate a kind of concerned scholarship toward both home and host countries, in addition to China. Wong must pay heed to Singapore's strategic, objective participation in the Chinese market; Tan has endeavored to establish respect for India in China; Kim wishes to rectify the distorted image of Pyongyang; and Iriye wants to persuade the Japanese people not to change its Peace Constitution. All four feel a profound obligation to help their Asian home or host country. For the two Anglo-Chinese scholars, Wong and Tan, their self-image is deeply implicated by their relationships with China and their respective Asian host country. For Wong, professional work and emotional loyalty have led him to discover a China that the West does not fully understand. And for Tan the West that embodies an imperialism should be eliminated in Asia. For the two Anglo-Asian scholars, Kim and Iriye, their connections to China are linked intimately to their personal identities. For Kim, China and North Korea are basically in the same camp in world politics. For Iriye, China is a somewhat foreign land to be coped with by means of an idealist and personal diplomacy.

Historicized China in Four Life Histories

Encounter and choice are constantly present in diasporic scholarship. Traveling that often resulted from previous encounter and choice and resulting in further encounter and choice connects them to home. Our four diasporic scholars typically have avoided direct involvement in the politics of their host societies. Dealing with China remained for all of them a strictly academic subject. This was less true, however, when they were connected back to their home countries, either while visiting or while greeting visitors from back home. But since all four spent most of their careers abroad, politics tended to be the exception. Nonetheless, their frequent travels and their stature as internationally renowned scholars confronted them with all kinds of practical inquiry, often political in nature. This happened, for example, when Iriye began to return to Japan regularly as a guest lecturer in universities, in the course of his globe-spanning travels, and when he accepted invitations to China for giving interviews. The same has been true for Kim, who is often in South Korea; Tan, who now lives in Chicago while also organizing and attending events in China and India including receiving prestigious Lotus Award in New Delhi; and Wong, with his frequent professional meetings in China, his constant engagements with Chinese scholars in Singapore, and his annual family reunion in Canada.

The possibility of confrontation or rapprochement between the home and the host as well as between either of them and China appears to incur different affective reactions among diasporic scholars. There appears to be some anxiety in Iriye and Tan, passion in Kim and Wong and also Tan. Anxiety centers on a possible confrontation between the host and the home country: the United States and China for Iriye, and India and China for Tan. Both Iriye and Kim had their host society, the United States, in mind in the early stages of their careers as they self-consciously refused to take a specific theoretical and political position. Now they do not question China's rise and demand the United States and Japan to adapt. Tan and Wong are facing China without a top-down perspective when they travel from India or Singapore. English plays a smaller role in their China travels than for Iriye and Kim. Iriye operates in English when in China and in Japanese when in Japan, while Kim lectures in English wherever he goes. Passion reflects the presence of growing opportunities. For Tan it is the opportunity of China fulfilling its civilizational ideal and also of him continuing his father's legacy in China. For Kim it is the opportunity to give North Korea a fair treatment. And for Wong it is the opportunity to celebrate his identification with China.

Interestingly, in speaking to a Chinese audience, Iriye argued that a still powerful United States would no longer be a superpower. His Chinese hosts are invariably interested in his criticism of Japanese nationalism. However, when in China, Iriye encourages his audience to attend to China's civilizational rather than political influence and in that spirit he describes this as "China's twenty-first century."[38] In his early scholarship, Iriye had written about what had gone so terribly wrong to cause war in Asia. Later, while traveling especially in China he encountered the very same forces still at work. Continuing to view China as a victim today is no longer an adequate response to the forces transforming world politics. Rather the most urgent task is to persuade China not to choose the path of political competition by showing how other states, especially the United States and Japan, are not fearful of China's rise. Promoting the civilizational correlates of a rising China thus acts as a substitute for the earlier empathy with China's victimization in the past two centuries. Iriye's recurring guest teaching career in Japan began in 1997. He has consistently expressed strong disagreements with Japanese nationalism, military build-up, and constitutional revision when in Japan. He once criticized former Premier Abe Shinzo as a second George W. Bush, Jr. and expressed his preference for the peace advocate Yasuo Fukuda over nationalist Aso Taro, both once a Premier. He also has taken exception to the notion that the United States was in decline on account of the vibrancy of American civil society.[39] He specifically welcomed the more recent Premier Yukio Hatoyama's call for an East Asian Community, which, Iriye argued, should include the United States. In fact, he hopes the East Asian Community might eventually evolve into an Asia-Pacific Community.

In contrast with Kim's ambivalence about the United States, Tan's anti-imperialist engagement shows some ambivalence about China's rise. Tan welcomes the rise of China because he believes it embodies a non-imperialist way of being a great country, yet he also worries about the negative attitudes toward India that it may engender. When he had settled down in Chicago, Tan had primarily written articles for Chinese web pages, criticizing the United States and promoting India. Among our four scholars, Wong is the only one who has found complete satisfaction in his increasing contact with China, where he is able to make policy suggestions openly without worrying about anxious Southeast Asian neighbors, receive respect, and meet key policy makers. More recently, he has organized delegations to China, spanning over weeks each time he travels. Kim's increasing contacts with Korea are also reflected in his increasing interest in and concerns over policy issues on the Korean Peninsula. In contrast to Iriye, however, this shift in attention has led him to step away from China since few Koreans regard China as an actual or potential threat. Kim's analysis of the Korean situation is subtly critical of U.S. policy.[40] On the one hand, this is made easier because China's rise restrains Washington's dominance in the region. On the other hand, the US dominance is taken for granted.

Whether or not China has its agency for action, change, and resistance above all is an epistemological decision any writer on China must make, consciously or not. The four scholars treat China differently over time.

To different degrees in the early stages of their careers, they have viewed China as an object—of imperialism, misperception, Cold War, or ignorance of how to get things done internationally. But with China's rise their perceptions have shifted and they all now recognize that China has become the subject of its own future. Both Kim and Wong thus view China as having unquestioned and rightful agency over its own future. Tan leaves no doubt that China has taken full ownership over its India policy. Despite his advocacy of a harmonious order of "Chindia," he is keenly aware of a possible future filled with conflict and recrimination. Kim and Wong take China's rise very much for granted. For Kim what matters is not his support of China but the support the world assumes China gives to Pyongyang; this makes his writings about Korea so useful for American audiences. Wong is the only one of the four who feels that he enjoys clear support in China. Iriye, likewise, is very sensitive to the openness of China becoming the master of its own future. For Iriye, it swings between the poles of civilization and power politics. Although Japan has a clear responsibility to avoid China choosing the path of power politics, Iriye is telling his Chinese audiences that the choice is theirs alone.

Given the constraining civilizational positions in which they found themselves and the empowering cultural resources at their disposal, all four scholars have to decide, discursively, professionally, as well as personally, how to formulate their own identity strategy and style. In form as well as content, Sinicization thus has changed over time for all four. Discursive analysis shows that these four academics consciously manage their liminal positions through scholarship: Kim's synthetic analysis, Iriye's centrist mediation, Tan's geo-civilizational critique, and Wong's scientific Chineseness. In their work on China, there appear at least two common puzzles that call for answers. How do they place themselves in the Sinic world: does China belong to an identical or a different ontological order? And how do they want China to be evaluated: should China conform to a Western standard expressed in values that are claimed to be universal? Kim's and Iriye's professional affiliations in the United States seem to push for a universalist prescription for China's place in the world; the peripheral relationship between Kim's and Wong's home, on the one hand, and China, on the other, pushes instead for a shared ontological identity. By contrast, freed from both American affiliation and a sense of belonging to the periphery leaves Tan with a different and more innocent sense of China.

Conclusion: Serious Hypocrisy

A Westphalian system is presumed to be one that upholds equal sovereignty. In practice, however, its stress on power and national interest occasionally makes this nominal recognition of equality obsolete. In fact, it is always the more powerful nations that dominate international relations, and historically, these have been the countries of North America and Western Europe. In addition, these major powers share a common ideology as international relations proceed into the postmodern age of globalization. Based upon this shared ideology, they hold that in order to be granted equal sovereignty, countries must adopt value systems and collective identities that conform to liberalism and belief in the nation-state. The rise of China challenges both of these: it insists that other national values should be able to coexist on an equal basis with liberalism,[1] and it revises the notion of the nation-state by proposing the unfamiliar ideology of a harmonious world. The combination of nominal sovereign equality and practical power hierarchy is the irony of current state of international relations that originates from the Westphalian system. In the twenty-first century, the rise of China directly attacks this epistemological hypocrisy.

The theory and practice of the Chinese harmonious world likewise present a paradox. Although according to this ideology, different values and identities are permitted to coexist, there is always an imagined center or apex of a hierarchical world order. The center is a moral concept defined by selfless leadership. Making concessions and sharing benefits are the norms to be observed by selfless leadership. Harmony is maintained by demonstrating that conflicts of interest with the center are unlikely. Furthermore, the center should have no interest in actually controlling the rest of the world.

The center is satisfied by a ritualized acknowledgment of the hierarchy. In the past, this meant submitting tributes, to which the court's response was to give more in return. Nowadays, welcoming the establishment of a Confucius Institute in one's country may be seen as a creative substitute for the tribute system. The irony is that it is not legitimate to refuse all-encompassing harmony, especially after China has conceded on its national interests. Ironically, harmony is punitive for those who refuse idealistically beneficial arrangements. The harmonious world is philosophically more tolerant of differences than are liberal-statist international relations. The tradeoff is that equality is not valued in the harmonious world, which rests upon ritualized worship of a selfless leader.

Marginal, postcolonial, and other subaltern communities in East Asia face double pressure from both the lingering and even reemerging harmonious worldview and the liberalizing sovereign order. Many of them have not subscribed to liberalism or possessed great power; instead, they struggle to gain respect in international relations. At the level of their choice—be it individual, familial, communal, ethnic, national, gender, religious, linguistic, or civilizational—the equality they seek has two aspects: exemption from both cultural submission to China and submission to Western power. On the one hand, the Westphalian system is unsympathetic toward the subaltern groups and communities that lack national power, while the notion of a harmonious world protects nonliberal values from harassment and intervention, thus indicating that China could be their ally. On the other hand, the Chinese harmonious world jeopardizes their equal status by requiring them to accept a peripheral position in relation to the Chinese center. In these circumstances, the sovereign order gives them the courage to face China on an equal footing, so the West could be an ally. Can they ensure respect for their own, not necessarily liberal, values in the harmonious world and at the same time avoid succumbing to the Chinese center? Alternatively, can they—as participants in the Westphalian system—assert their equal sovereignty without facing intervention aimed at exposing and converting their long-held values that are deemed incompatible with liberalism?

Reflections from below could take a variety of positions at various levels. This book has glanced over individualized intellectual trajectories of diasporic Asian scholars, community-based Chinese academic immigrants in the States, the first Kuomintang generation in Taiwan embedded in Chinese Civil War historiography, postcolonial Taiwanese intellectuals strategically adapting to constantly recombined identities, open-ended profit seekers in mountain villages driven by a top-down development imperative, urban residents ready to engage either in self-Sinicization or in alienation, veterans of Chinese studies in Vietnam recollecting their common Chinese roots, national groups enacted by concerned Korean and Japanese writers, and so on. There are many other potential sites that could emerge in response to the rise of China that are absent from this book. The re-worlding of these possibilities has reconstructed the seemingly powerful and self-sustaining circles that began with the Westphalian system and the Chinese dynastic world, characterized by the harmony of "all under heaven," and have reached subaltern communities. Thanks to the widespread recognition of the rise of China, which shakes the liberalizing statism of the postmodern sovereign world, the reexamination of Sinicization and its practices at multiple sites is not just possible but inevitable.

As the lives and scholarship of the individuals examined in this book illustrate clearly, the meanings of international relations and its Sinicization are complex, multidimensional, and contested. International relations refers to deeply entangled conceptions of the self and the other, as well as to practices—discursive and otherwise—that signify either the broadening or the narrowing of social and cultural distances. Many of the developments shaping the contemporary world, such as globalization, capitalism, nationalism, and multiculturalism, are providing the context in which China encounters and engages both East and West. The Sinicization of international relations in East Asia in its various guises, involving the self and the other, is about influence and interaction among people as much as among states, about Chinese and their self-understanding as much as about China and its sphere of influence, and about China and its diaspora beyond the category of territorial China.

Moreover, Sinicization focuses one's attention on those elements and agents that mediate between China and the world. Consumers of China-made products, Taiwanese advocate of independence, Chinese villagers struggling with transition, and indigenous Chinese loyal to Southeast Asian states can all act as cultural brokers involved in processes of encounter, engagement, and clash between different civilizational complexes. The Sinicization of international relations is a concept that summarizes an important process that, in turn, leads to self-discovery and self-interpretation. Without it, the economic, security, and political dimensions of Sinicization are devoid of meaning. This book focuses attention on academics whose lives and work demonstrate the importance of the processes of Sinicization and of international relations in East Asia.

Specifically, the book tracks the identities and associated practices of diasporic intellectuals who, for the most part, communicate their scholarship on China's economy, politics, history, and culture in English and in their native language. Their careers and intellectual evolution, along with the simplifications and complexities in their work, offer us a window into their understanding of identities and practices in the Sinic world. Their careers are not representative in any way. However, they do indicate the possibilities that structures provide for self-reflexive agents to make meaningful choices, thereby shaping their environments to a certain extent without ever fully determining them. Writing outside of China and for an English-speaking audience, these intellectuals clearly present the liminal positions they occupy between China and Asia, and between East and West. Their lives and work thus show China's international relations to be multidirectional, multisited, discursive processes that include variants of de-, re-, and self-Sinicization. In short, Sinicization presupposes agency as well as the appropriation and reappropriation of Chinese phenomena by Chinese and non-Chinese agents for their self- and group-interested use within an Anglicized world.

The lives of these intellectuals exemplify a variety of geographical, linguistic, and temporal possibilities. They were born into different Asian communities—Taiwan, Korea, Mongolia, United States, China, Hong Kong, Vietnam, and Japan. They have lived and worked in various countries, including China, the United States, Korea, Singapore, Vietnam, and India. Although they have read and written mostly in English, their occasional reliance on other languages shows that Sinicization does not have to proceed in either Chinese or English.[2] Rather, third languages can be useful in making a statement about who one is, where one comes from, and where one is headed.[3] In brief, Sinicized international relations reveal, in one person, the existence of multiple cultural-geographical selves. Later in their careers, many of these intellectuals experienced a growing concern for their home countries, often reflected in their frequent visits and the shift—undertaken consciously and rationally—of their academic and political agendas. This fact provides a healthy antidote to the common preconception that structures are all-determining. As these individual and communal lives show, nothing could be further from the truth.

Even far-reaching views that seek to associate China with very specific images, such as its "rise," "all under heaven," or "Chinese characteristics," represent choices, not inevitabilities. The lives and works of these intellectuals contradict any such notion of inevitability. If one sticks to the idea of the nation-state as the only viable civilizational actor in world politics, Huntingtonian clashes of civilizations may have some plausibility. However, intellectuals who have had transnational lives and careers are free to choose practices that are unrelated—even resistant—to the constraints and opportunities that nation-states provide.[4] Promotion or denial of Chinese distinctiveness always involves choices. Therefore, no views on China can be politically neutral. As such, Sinicization is unavoidably shaped and influenced by conceptions of identity and political practice.

This does not mean, however, that actors have full control either over their scholarship on China or over the self-identifications that implicitly or explicitly inform their perspectives. None of these intellectuals could control the larger forces that have prompted their civilizational encounters or the liminal positions they have held.[5] Their choice of language, for example, would never go unnoticed by one community or the other. Home and host countries impose structural constraints simply because they differ from one another, and any narrative strategy about China could not help but activate those differences. Yet meaningful choices have persisted, including choosing sides and avoiding taking sides altogether. Structural determinacy, therefore, fails to take away the capacity for strategic indeterminacy.

Notes

Introduction: Transcending National Identities

1. One notable comparison is that presented in David Shambaugh, Robert F. Ash, and Seiichirō Takagi, eds. *China Watching: Perspectives from Europe, Japan and the United States* (New York: Routledge, 2007).
2. For example, see Yu-wen Chen, "Xinjiang 13 Revisited," *Asian Ethnicity* 13, 1 (2012): 111–113; Chih-yu Shih and Yu-wen Chen, eds., *Tibetan Studies in Comparative Perspective* (London: Routledge, 2012).
3. See Peter Katzenstein, *Sinicization and the Rise of China: Civilizational Processes beyond East and West* (London: Routledge, 2012).
4. Zhijun Ling and Licheng Ma, *Jiao feng: Dangdai Zhongguo san ci sixiang jiefang shilu* (Cross Fire: The Three Thought Liberations of Contemporary China on the Record) (Beijing: China Today, 1998).
5. Xuetong Yan, *Ancient Chinese Thought and Modern Chinese Power,* ed. Daniel Bell and Zhe Sun, trans. Edmund Ryden (Princeton: Princeton University Press, 2011); Jeremy Paltiel, "Constructing Global Order with Chinese Characteristics: Yan Xuetong and the Pre-Qin Response to International Anarchy," *Chinese Journal of International Politics* 4, 4 (2011): 375–403; Tingyang Zhao, "A Political World Philosophy in Terms of All-Under-Heaven (Tian-xia)," *Diogenes* 56, 1 (February 2009): 5–18; Tingyang Zhao, "Rethinking Empire from a Chinese Concept 'All-under-Heaven' (Tian-xia)," *Social Identities* 12, 1 (January 2006): 29–41.

Chapter 1

1. Note the literature on Sinicization in recent years, for example, Peter Katzenstein (ed.), *Sinicization and the Rise of China: Civilizational Processes beyond East and West* (London: Routledge, 2012).
2. Hence, the notion of the China model. See, for example, Stefan Halper, *The Beijing Consensus: How China's Authoritarian Model Will Dominate the Twenty-First Century* (New York: Basic Books, 2010); Martin Jacques, *When China Rules the World: The End of the Western World and the Birth of a New Global Order* (New York: The Penguin Press, 2009).

3. Weiwei Zhang, *The China Wave: Rise of a Civilizational State* (Singapore: World Scientific, 2012); Xuetong Yan, *Ancient Chinese Thought, Modern Chinese Power* (Princeton: Princeton University Press, 2011); Ross Terrill, *The New Chinese Empire: And What It Means for the United States* (New York: Basic Books, 2004).

4. For official perspectives on the harmonious world, see "Build Towards a Harmonious World of Lasting Peace and Common Prosperity," Statement by Hu Jintao, president of the People's Republic of China, at the United Nations Summit, New York (September 15, 2005).

5. For a critical assessment of these themes, see Daniel Vukovich, *China and Orientalism: Western Knowledge Production and the PRC* (London: Routledge, 2011).

6. For more optimistic perspectives, see Gordon White, *Riding the Tiger: The Politics of Economic in Post-Mao China* (Stanford: Stanford University Press, 1993); Merle Goldman, *From Comrade to Citizen: The Struggle for Political Rights in China* (Cambridge, MA: Harvard University Press, 2007). For pessimistic views, see Richard Bernstein and Ross H. Munro, *The Coming Conflict with China* (New York: Vintage, 1998); John Mearsheimer, "The Gathering Storm: China's Challenge to US Power in Asia," *The Chinese Journal of International Politics* 3 (2010): 381–96.

7. See Information Office of the State Council, *China's Peaceful Development* (Information Office of the State Council, September 6, 2011).

8. Liu Yawei and Justin R. Zheng, "The Rise of China and Its Consequences," *The 9th Annual APSA Pre-conference on Political Communication* (August 31, 2011).

9. Lucien Pye, "China: Erratic State, Frustrated Society," *Foreign Affairs* 69, 4 (Fall, 1990): 56–74.

10. For a discussion on how Chinese civilization improves the world, see Zhao Tingyang, "A Political World Philosophy in Terms of All-Under-Heaven (Tianxia)," *Diogenes* 56, 1 (2009): 5–18.

11. Stephen Hoare-Vance, *The Confucius Institutes and China's Evolving Foreign Policy* (Saarbrücken: LAP Academic Publishing, 2010).

12. Chih-yu Shih, "Assigning Role Characteristics to China: The Role State Versus the Ego State," *Foreign Policy Analysis* 8, 1 (January 2012): 71–91.

13. Evan S. Medeiros, *China's International Behavior: Activism, Opportunism, and Diversification* (Santa Monica: Rand, 2009), 49–50.

14. See Jonathan Adelman and Chih-yu Shih, *Symbolic War: The Chinese Use of Force, 1840–1980* (Taipei: Institute of International Relations, 1993).

15. See, for example, Wang Yiwei, "Why Is Pax-Americana Impossible? Comparing Chinese Ancient World Order with Today's American World Order," presented at the International Symposium on Civilizations and World Orders, Istanbul, Turkey, May 13, 2006.

16. M. Taylor Fravel, *Strong Borders, Secure Nation: Cooperation and Conflict in China's Territorial Disputes* (Princeton: Princeton University Press, 2008).

17. For the China threat as a self-fulfilling prophecy, see Khalid R. Al-Rodhan, "A Critique of the China Threat Theory: A Systematic Analysis," *Asian Perspective*

31, 3 (2007): 64; Drew Thompson, "Think Again: China's Military," *Foreign Policy* (March/April 2010): http://www.foreignpolicy.com/articles/2010/02/22/think_again_chinas_military?page=full accessed on April 26, 2012; Joseph Nye, "The Challenge of China," in Stephen Van Evera (ed.), *How to Make America Safe: New Policies for National Security* (Cambridge, MA: Tobin Project, 2006), 74.

18. Hence Chinese self-centrism, Tang Shiping and Dapeng Ji, "zhongguo waijiao taolun zhong de zhongguo zhongxinzhuyi yu meiguo zhongxinzhuyi" (China-Centrism and US-Centrism in China's Diplomatic Narratives), *Shijie Jingjie yu zhengzhi* (World Economy and Politics) 12 (2008): 62–70.

19. Muthiah Alagappa, "Managing Asian Security: Competition, Cooperation and Evolutionary Change," in Muthiah Alagappa (ed.), *Asian Security Order: Instrumental and Normative Features* (Stanford: Stanford University Press), 585–586.

20. William A. Callahan, *China: Pessoptimist Nation* (Oxford: Oxford University Press, 2009).

21. The White Paper on China's National Defense of 2002 set out for the first time the official position on China's national interests. They included "safeguarding state sovereignty, unity, territorial integrity and security; upholding economic development as the central task and unremittingly enhancing the overall national strength; adhering to and improving the socialist system; maintaining and promoting social stability and harmony; and striving for an international environment of lasting peace and a favorable climate in China's periphery." See http://news.xinhuanet.com/english/2002-12/10/content_654851.htm accessed on December 20, 2011.

22. http://english.gov.cn/official/2011-09/06/content_1941354_4.htm accessed on September 8, 2011.

23. See, for example, Daniel Gomà, "The Chinese-Korean Border Issue: An Analysis of a Contested Frontier," *Asian Survey* 46, 6 (November–December, 2006): 867–880; Zhao Hongwei, "zhong mian bianjie weni de jiejue: guocheng yu yingxiang" (The Settlement of the China-Burma Border Dispute: Course and Impact), *Nanyang wenti yanjiu* (Southeast Asian Affairs) General Serial 143 or No. 3 (2010): 37–40.

24. Zhao Quansheng, "Achieving Maximum Advantage: Rigidity and Flexibility in Chinese Foreign Policy," *American Asian Review* 13, 1 (Spring 1995): 61–93.

25. Yang Jiechi explained to Hillary Clinton why there has never been disharmony in the South China Sea in "Yang Jiechi chanshu qi dian zhuzhang bo xilali nan hai lun" (Yang Jiechi's Expounds Seven-Point Position to Rebut Hillary's Note on South China Sea). See http://dailynews.sina.com/bg/news/usa/uspolitics/chinapress/20100726/03191684304.html accessed on August 1, 2010.

26. The same principle was initially applied to the maritime dispute with Japan. Deng suggested the principle to the Philippine vice president in June 1986, and reiterated it to the Philippine president in April 1988. See also *Deng Xiaoping nianpu: 1975–1997* (The Chronicles of Deng Xiaoping: 1975–1997) 2 (Beijing: The CCP Research Department on Literature, 2004), 1122, 1227.

27. Amitav Acharya, "Seeking Security in the Dragon's Shadow: China and Southeast Asia in the Emerging Asian Order," *Working Paper Series* 44, Institute of Defense and Strategic Studies (March 2003), 5.

28. For more discussion, see Yin Jinwu, "*wenhua yu guoji xinren—jiyu dong ya xinren xingcheng de bijiao fenxi*" (Culture and International Trust: A Comparative Analysis of Trust Formation in East Asia), *Waijiao pinglun* (Diplomatic Review) 4, 2011: 21–39.

29. Duong Danh Huy, " 'Setting Aside Dispute, Pursuing Joint Development' the Chinese Way," *Vietnamnet Bridge* (November 7, 2011) http://english.vietnamnet.vn/en/politics/10482/-setting-aside-dispute—pursuing-joint-development—the-chinese-way.html accessed on November 12, 2011.

30. Beijing always protests on the ground of DoC, which however never acknowledges anyone's sovereignty.

31. Rao Aimin, "Hu, Aquino Agree to Downplay Maritime Disputes," *Xinhua* (September 1, 2011), http://www.china.org.cn/world/2011-09/01/content_23328684.htm.

32. This a quote from Deng Xiaoping that appears everywhere on Chinese blogs. For the complete text, see, for example, http://www.chinareviewnews.com/doc/1015/6/2/9/101562905_3.html?coluid=6&kindid=26&docid=101562905&mdate=0107094837 accessed on April 20, 2012.

33. Note as well that the Beijing authorities may allow a certain level of social protest as well as implicit warning/bluffing. For example, see Editorial, "ba Feilyubin dang chutouniao chengfa" (Punishing the Philippines as the head sticking out), *Huanqiu shibao* (Global Times) (January 30, 2012), http://opinion.huanqiu.com/roll/2012-01/2385629.html accessed on January 25, 2012.

34. While Vietnam, the Philippines, and China took action, Beijing signed a five-year trade and economic cooperation plan on October 11, 2011, with Hanoi and another with the Philippines on August 30.

35. Bernstein and Monroe, *The Coming Conflict with China.* Denny Roy, "Rising China and U.S. Interests: Inevitable vs. Contingent Hazards," *Orbis* 47, 1 (2003): 125–137.

36. Allen S. Whiting, "China's Use of Force, 1950–96, and Taiwan," in *International Security* 26, 2 (Autumn, 2001): 103–131.

37. For more discussion, see Zhang Qingmin, *Meiguo dui Tai jun shou zhengce yanjiu: juece de shijiao* (A Study of US Policy on Arms Sales to Taiwan: The Perspective of Decision Making) (Beijing: World Knowledge Press, 2006).

38. Yinghong Cheng, "From Campus Racism to Cyber Racism: Discourse of Race and Chinese Nationalism," *The China Quarterly* 207 (2011): 561–579.

39. Dan Haglund, "In It for the Long Term? Governance and Learning among Chinese Investors in Zambia's Copper Sector," *The China Quarterly* 199 (September 2009): 643.

40. Hongying Wang and James N. Rosenau, "China and Global Governance," *Asian Perspective* 33, 3 (2009): 17–22.

41. For case studies of private involvement, see Wang Yizhou, *Chuangzaoxing jieru: Zhongguo waijiao xin quxiang* (Creative Involvement: New Orientations in Chinese Diplomacy) (Beijing: Peking University Press, 2011).

42. See white papers of the Information Office of the State Council of the People's Republic of China, *Zhongguo de minzu zhengce yu ge minzu de gongtong fanrong fazhan* (China's Ethnic Policy and Common Prosperity and Development of All Ethnic Groups) (Beijing: Foreign Language Press, 2009).

43. Sharad Soni and Reena Marwah, "Tibet as a Factor Impacting China Studies in India," *Asian Ethnicity* 12, 3 (October 2011): 285–299.

44. A series of white papers on Tibet and nationality policy specifically take this position. The most recent was *Xizang heping jiefang liushi zhounian* (The 60th Anniversary of Peaceful Liberation of Tibet) (Beijing: State Council, 2011).

45. Douglas H. Paal, "China: Hu's State Visit an Opportunity," *Asia Pacific Brief* (January 3, 2011), http://carnegietsinghua.org/publications/?fa=42219

Chapter 2

1. According to one Chinese rebuttal, "The charge of neocolonialism is in large part the West's anxiety over China's rising presence and influence in Africa rather than just a humanitarian concern." See He Wenping, "The Balancing Act of China's Africa Policy," *China Security* 3, 3 (2007): 29.

2. Khadija Sharife, "China's New Colonialism," *Foreign Policy* (September 25, 2009), http://www.foreignpolicy.com/articles/2009/09/25/chinas_new_colonialism?page=0,0, accessed February 2, 2012; Stephen Marks, "China in Africa–The New Imperialism?," *Pambazuka News,* 244 (March 2, 2006) http://www.pambazuka.org/en/category/features/32432, accessed February 2, 2012.

3. See, for example, William Bauer, "China: Africa's New Colonial Power" http://www.policymic.com/articles/1657/china-africa-s-new-colonial-power, accessed February 1, 2012; Ali Askouri, "China's Investment in Sudan: Displacing Villages and Destroying Communities," in Firoze Manji and Stephen Marksi (eds.), *African Perspectives on China in Africa* (Cape Town: Fahamu, 2007), pp. 73–74.

4. Anabela A. Lemos and Daniel Ribeiro, "Taking Ownership or Just Changing Owners?" in Manji and Marks, pp. 64, 69.

5. Martha Saavedra, "Representations of Africa in a Hong Kong Soap Opera: The Limits of Enlightened Humanitarianism in *The Last Breakthrough,*" *The China Quarterly* 199 (September 2009): 744.

6. According to Peter Katzenstein, Anglicization is an intrinsic component of Sinicization. For more discussion, see Peter Katzenstein (ed.), *Sinicization and the Rise of China: Civilizational Processes beyond East and West* (London: Routledge, 2012).

7. For more discussion, see Yinghong Cheng, "From Campus Racism to Cyber Racism: Discourse of Race and Chinese Nationalism," *The China Quarterly* 207 (2011): 561–579.

8. Chris Alden, Daniel Large, and Ricardo Soares de Oliveira, *China Returns to Africa: A Rising Power and a Continent Embrace* (New York: Columbia University Press, 2008).

9. An overall policy statement was issued at the beginning of 2006 by the Ministry of Foreign Affairs, welcoming the Year of Africa, "China's African Policy," http://www.fmprc.gov.cn/eng/zxxx/t230615.htm accessed February 3, 2012.

10. He Wenping, "China and Africa: Cooperation in Fifty Stormy Years," *Asia and Africa Today* (Russian Academy of Sciences) 12 (2002).

11. For example, see John Rocha, "A New Frontier in the Exploitation of Africa's Natural Resources: The Emergence of China," in Manji and Marks, p. 26.

12. Hence there is a call for sophisticated analyses. Daniel Large, "Beyond 'Dragon in the Bush': The Study of China-Africa Relations," *African Affairs*, 107/426 (2008): 60.

13. The "Records of Jeune Afrique's Interview with Director-General Lu Shaye," http://www.focac.org/eng/zxxx/t885029.htm accessed on February 1, 2011.

14. This bias is well-noted by Bates Gill and James Reilly, "The Tenuous Hold of China Inc. in Africa," *The Washington Quarterly* (2007): 37.

15. This is also apparent in Chinese medicine. For how belief in socialism and anti-imperialist feeling may lead to trust, see Elisabeth Hsu, "The Medicine from China Has Rapid Effects: Patients of Traditional Chinese Medicine in Tanzania," in Elisabeth Hsu and Erling Høg (eds.), "Countervailing Creativity: Patient Agency in the Globalisation of Asian Medicines," special issue, *Anthropology and Medicine* 9, 3 (2002): 205–363.

16. For the Chinese cultural preference for diversity and the appropriation of this by Chinese foreign policy, see Liu Shan and Xue Jundu (ed.), *New Analysis of Chinese Foreign Affairs* (Beijing: World Affairs Press, 1998).

17. Pak K. Lee, Gerald Chan, and Lai-ha Chan, "China's 'Realpolitik' Engagement with Myanmar," *China Security* 13, http://www.chinasecurity.us/index.php?option=com_content&view=article&id=224&Itemid=8#lcc8 accessed on March 12, 2012.

18. Barry Sautman and Yan Hairong, "Friends and Interests: China's Distinctive Links with Africa," *African Studies Review* 50, 3 (2007): 75–114.

19. "Confrontation Over Darfur 'Will Lead Us Nowhere'," *China Daily* (July 27, 2007), http://www.chinadaily.com.cn/2008/2007-07/27/content_5445062.htm accessed on January 29, 2012.

20. Called "the genocide games," see Andrew Higgins, "Oil Interests Push China into Sudanese Mire," *The Washington Post* (December 24, 2011), http://www.washingtonpost.com/world/asia_pacific/oil-interests-push-china-into-sudanese-mire/2011/12/19/gIQANkzGGP_story.html accessed on March 10, 2012.

21. The "Records of Jeune Afrique's Interview with Director-General Lu Shaye."

22. Chinese analysts largely abide by this understanding of soft power, though, and American-style soft power as regards Africa is lauded by Chinese writers. For example, see He Wenping, "The Balancing Act of China's Africa Policy," *China Security* 3, 3 (2007): 28.

23. Lucien Pye, "China: Erratic State, Frustrated Society," *Foreign Affairs* 69, 4 (Fall): 56–74; *The Mandarin and the Cadre: China's Political Culture* (Ann Arbor, MI: The Center for Chinese Studies, University of Michigan, 1988).

24. For more discussion, see Chih-yu Shih, "Assigning Role Characteristics to China: The Role State Versus The Ego State," *Foreign Policy Analysis* 8, 1 *(2012): 71–91.*

25. "We just tell them the good practices that we believe. Whether they will adopt them or not and how will they adopt them, it's up to them to decide. We have never asked African countries to follow China's model." The "Records of Jeune Afrique's Interview with Director-General Lu Shaye."

26. In one survey, almost 70 percent of respondents ranked Africans lowest in social status, Min Zhou, "Meeting Strangers in a Globalized City: Chinese Attitudes toward Black Africans in Guangzhou China," presented at Wah Ching Centre of Research on Education in China, Hong Kong (June 15, 2011).

27. Dismas Nyamwana, "Cross-cultural Adaptation African Students in China," *Ife PsychologIA* 12, 2 (2004): 10.

28. Ibid.

29. Leu Siew Ying, "Guangzhou Residents at Odds with Increase in Foreigners," *South China Morning Post* (February 22, 2007), http://archive.scmp.com/showarticles.php accessed on February 3, 2012.

30. Heidi Østbø Haugen and Jørgen Carling, "On the Edge of the Chinese Diaspora: The Surge of Baihuo Business in an African City," *Ethnic and Racial Studies* 28, 4 (2005): 647.

31. Dan Haglund, "In It for the Long Term? Governance and Learning among Chinese Investors in Zambia's Copper Sector," *The China Quarterly* 199 (September 2009): 643.

32. See Martin Jacques, "The Middle Kingdom Mentality," *Guardian* (April 16, 2005), http://www.guardian.co.uk/world/2005/apr/16/china.usa accessed on March 6, 2012.

33. Barry Bearak, "Zambia Uneasily Balances Chinese Investment and Workers' Resentment," *The New York Times* (November 21, 2010): A8.

34. Julia C. Strauss, "The Past in the Present: Historical and Rhetorical Lineages in China's Relations with Africa," *The China Quarterly* 199 (September 2009): 777–795.

Chapter 3

1. Sandra Harding, *Is Science Multicultural? Postcolonialisms, Feminisms, and Epistemologies* (Bloomington: Indiana University Press, 1998); Paul Diesing and Richard Hartwig, *Science and Ideology in the Policy Sciences* (Piscataway, NJ: Aldine Transaction, 2005); Nico Stehr and Volker Meja (eds.), *Society and Knowledge: Contemporary Perspectives in the Sociology of Knowledge and Science* (Piscataway, NJ: Transaction Publishers, 2005).

2. Gary D. Phye, *Handbook of Academic Learning: Construction of Knowledge* (St. Louis, MO: Academic Press 1997), 52, 110; Jason Stanley, *Knowledge and*

Practical Interests (Oxford: Oxford University Press, 2008); Robert C. Stalnaker, *Our Knowledge of the Internal World* (Oxford: Oxford University Press, 2010).

3. These interviews are taken from the Oral History of China Studies Project, carried out by the Research and Educational Center for Mainland Chinese Affairs and Cross-Strait Relations, Department of Political Science, National Taiwan University. The project has been supported since 2007 by Taiwan's National Science Council, along with a number of small grants.

4. Paul Diesing, *How Does Social Science Work? Reflections on Practice* (Pittsburgh: University of Pittsburgh Press, 1992); Michael E. Latham, *Modernization as Ideology: American Social Science and "Nation Building" in the Kennedy Era* (Chapel Hill: University of North Carolina Press, 2000).

5. Baogang He, "The Dilemmas of China's Political Science in the Context of the Rise of China," *Journal of Chinese Political Science* 16, 2 (2011): 257–277; Wu Guoguang, "Politics against Science: Reflections on the Study of Chinese Politics in Contemporary China," *Journal of Chinese Political Science* 16, 3 (2011): 279–297.

6. Chih-yu Shih, "China Studies That Defend Chineseness: The Im/possibility of China-centrism in the Divided Sino-phone World," in Reena Marwah and Swaran Singh (eds.), *Emerging China* (New Delhi: Routledge, 2011).

7. Bruce Cummings, "Boundary Displacement: Area Studies and International Studies during and after the Cold War," *Bulletin of Concerned Asian Scholars* 29, 1 (Jan-Mar, 1997): 6–27.

8. For further discussion of Taiwan's political and economic history, social cleavage, and hybrid identities, see Gunter Schubert and Jens Damm (eds.), *Taiwanese Identity in the 21st Century. Domestic, Regional and Global Perspective* (London and New York: Routledge, 2011); Stephane Corcuff (ed.), *Memories of the Future: National Identity Issues and the Search for a New Taiwan* (Armonk, NY: M. E. Sharpe 2002); Alan Wachman, *Taiwan: National Identity and Democratization* (Armonk, NY: M. E. Sharpe, 1994).

9. Shih Ming, unpublished interview with Yeh Hong-lin., cited in Chih-yu Shih and Chun-liang Pao, "Studying Mainland/China in Taiwan: Politics of Knowledge and Knowledge of Politics," presented at the Conference on Political Science: Retrospect and Prospect, the Institute of Political Science of Academia Sinica, August 7, 2012 (Taipei).

10. Rwei-ren Wu, "The Dialectics of the Motherland: A Note on Wen-kui Liao's Thought on Taiwan Nationalism," *Si yu yan* (Thought and Word) 37, 3 (Fall 1999): 47–100. Electoral fraud perpetrated against his family reinforced Liao's alienation from KMT rule.

11. One notable example is Tsai Pei-huo. See Chih-yu Shih, "Taiwan as East Asia in Formation: Subaltern Appropriation of the Colonial Narratives," in Gunter Schubert and Jens Damm (eds.), *Taiwanese Identity in the 21st Century: Domestic, Regional and Global Perspective* (London and New York: Routledge, 2010).

12. Chen Li-sheng, unpublished interview with Wen Chia-yi., cited in Shih and Pao, "Studying Mainland/China in Taiwan: Politics of Knowledge and Knowledge of Politics."

13. Interview with Yu Tzong-Shian, conducted by Chi-nien Wang, January 17, March 17, and May 30, 2009. See http://politics.ntu.edu.tw/RAEC/act/tw-13.doc, accessed on August 23, 2011.

14. Interview with Li Kuo-chi, conducted by Chih-chieh Chou and Pi-chun Chang, August 26, 2010. See http://politics.ntu.edu.tw/RAEC/comm2/LiGuoQi.doc, accessed on August 29, 2011.

15. Interview with Chang Huan-ching, conducted by Chi-nien Wang, October 14, October 22, November 19, and December 17, 2008. See http://politics.ntu.edu.tw/RAEC/act/tw-9.doc, accessed on April 20, 2012.

16. Unpublished interview with Yeh Chih-cheng, conducted by Yuan-kui Chu, November 11, November 18, and December 23, 2009, and December 30, 2010, cited in Shih and Pao, "Studying Mainland/China in Taiwan: Politics of Knowledge and Knowledge of Politics."

17. Interview with Chen Peng-jen, conducted by Hsuan-lei Shao and Li-ben Wang, January 21, 2011, cited in Shih and Pao, "Studying Mainland/China in Taiwan: Politics of Knowledge and Knowledge of Politics."

18. Interview with Parris Chang, conducted by Hong-lin Yeh, August 12, 18, and 26, 2010, cited in Shih and Pao, "Studying Mainland/China in Taiwan: Politics of Knowledge and Knowledge of Politics."

19. Chen Peng-jen; also, interview with Hsu Chieh-lin, conducted by Li-ch'en Chen, April 24, June 10, and July 13, 2009. See http://politics.ntu.edu.tw/RAEC/act/tw-7.doc, accessed on August 19, 2011.

20. Interview with Shih Chian-sheng, conducted by Yuan-kui Chu on various days in March 2011. See http://politics.ntu.edu.tw/RAEC/act/tw-16.doc, accessed on August 21, 2011.

21. Interview with Peter Li Nan-hsiong, conducted by Chun-liang Pao, September 5, 2008. See http://politics.ntu.edu.tw/RAEC/act/tw-3.doc, accessed on August 19, 2011.

22. For example, see Tse-Kang Leng and Yun-Han Chu (eds.), *Dynamics of Local Governance in China During the Reform Era* (Lanham, MD: Lexington Books, 2010); Chih-Jou Jay Chen, *Transforming Rural China: How Local Institutions Shape Property Rights in China* (London and New York: Routledge, 2004); Philip S. C. Hsu, "In Search of Public Accountability: The 'Wenling Model' in China," *Australian Journal of Public Administration* 68, 1 (March 2009): 40–50; Bi-huei Tsai, "Rights Issues in China as Evidence for the Existence of Two Types of Agency Problems," *Issues & Studies* 44, 3 (2008): 43–70.

23. Yang Kuo-shu, "Indigenising Westernised Chinese Psychology," in M. H. Bond (ed.), *Working at the Interface of Cultures: Eighteen Lives in Social Science* (London: Routledge, 1997), 62–76; M. Shams and Kwang-kuo Hwang, "Special Issue on Responses to the Epistemological Challenges to Indigenous Psychologies," *Asian Journal of Social Psychology* 8, 1 (2005): 3–4.

24. Yeh Chi-cheng.

25. Interview with Lucie Cheng, conducted by Chia-yi Wen, March 28, 2008. See http://politics.ntu.edu.tw/RAEC/act/tw-2.doc, accessed on August 28, 2011.

26. Interview with Hsieh Jiann, conducted by Hsin-wei Tang, August 11, 13, and 26, 2009. See http://politics.ntu.edu.tw/RAEC/act/tw-121.doc, accessed on August 21, 2011.

27. Yu Tzong-Hsian.

28. Interview with Rui He-chen, conducted by Hsin-hsien Wang on various days in October 2008. See http://politics.ntu.edu.tw/RAEC/act/tw-15.doc, accessed on August 29, 2011.

29. Interview with Wang Chang-ling, conducted by Chia-yi Wen, Summer 2009. See http://politics.ntu.edu.tw/RAEC/comm2/InterviewTWang.doc, accessed on April 26, 2012.

30. Chang Huan-ching.

31. Li Kuo-chi.

32. Chang Huan-ching.

33. Chen Li-sheng.

34. Interview with Hsiao Hsing-yi, conducted by Chung-ben Bai and Hsuan-lei Shao, March 29, April 5, April 10, and April 19, 2008. See http://politics.ntu.edu.tw/RAEC/comm2/HisaoHsinI.doc, accessed on August 20, 2011.

35. Interview with Chiang Hsin-li, conducted by Hsin-wei Tang, September 16, November 18, and December 23, 2008. See http://politics.ntu.edu.tw/RAEC/act/tw-6.doc, accessed on August 28, 2011.

36. Interview with Philip Chen Ming, conducted by Lu-fan Yeh on various days in October and November 2008. See http://politics.ntu.edu.tw/RAEC/comm2/ChenMing.doc, accessed on August 22, 2011.

37. Interview with Chang King-yuh, conducted by Yuan-ming Yao on various days in July 2008. See http://politics.ntu.edu.tw/RAEC/act/tw-1.doc, accessed on August 29, 2011.

38. Interview with Lee (Leo) Ou-fan, conducted by Te-hsing Shan, Hsiao-yan Peng, Chia-yi Wen, and Albert Tseng, May 18 and 19, 2008. See http://politics.ntu.edu.tw/RAEC/act/interviewU李歐梵.doc, accessed on August 22, 2011.

39. Interview with Weng (Byron) Sung-jan, conducted by Chun-liang Pao, October 3, 2008, and February 23, 2009. See http://politics.ntu.edu.tw/RAEC/act/tw-8.doc, accessed on August 28, 2011.

40. Interview with Huang (Mab) Mou, conducted by Chih-chieh Chou and Pi-chun Chang, February 26 and May 7, 2010.

41. Interview with James Hsiung Chieh, conducted by Chung-ben Bai and Hsuan-lei Shao, March 16, 2009. See http://politics.ntu.edu.tw/RAEC/act/interviewU熊玠.doc, accessed August 29, 2011.

42. See, for example, Li You-tan and Chien-ming Chao, "Transition in a Party-State System—Taiwan's Democratization as a Model for China," presented at the international conference, "The Chinese Communist Party in a New Era: Renewal and Reform," Singapore.

43. See, for example, Huang Chun-chieh, "On the Interaction between Confucian Knowledge and Political Power in Traditional China and Korea: A Historical Overview," *Taiwan Journal of East Asian Studies* 8, 1(Issue 15 June 2011): 1–19.

44. Interview with Liu Shu-hsien, conducted by Yuan-kui Chu, September 2, 2009. See http://politics.ntu.edu.tw/RAEC/act/tw-14.doc, accessed on August 28, 2011.

Chapter 4

1. Chun-chieh Huang, "Lun Zhongguo jingdian zhong 'Zhongguo' gainian de hanyi ji qi zai jinshi Riben yu xiandai Taiwan de zhuanhua" (The idea of "Zhongguo" and its transformation in early modern Japan and contemporary Taiwan), *Taiwan Journal of East Asian Studies* (*Taiwan dongya wenming yanjiu xuekan*) 3, 2 (2006): 91–100.

2. Paul A. Cohen, *Discovering History in China: American Historical Writing on the Recent Chinese Past.* (New York: Columbia University Press, 1984); Harry Harding, "The Study of Chinese Politics: Toward a Third Generation of Scholarship," *World Politics* 36, 2 (January 1984): 284–307; Mizoguchi Yuzo, *Hoho to shite no Chugoku* (China as Method) (Tokyo: The University of Tokyo Press, 1989).

3. For example, Yang Kuo-shu and his group have endeavored to develop an indigenous psychological agenda that may eventually lead to a truly universal discipline of psychology. See Yang Kuo-shu, "women weisheme yao jianli Zhongguoren de bentu xinlixue?" (Why do we want to establish Chinese indigenous psychology?) *Bentu xinlixue* (Indigenous Psychology) 1 (June 1993): 6–88.

4. Chinese are those who consider themselves to be Chinese or who are designated by Western scholars as such, willingly or unwillingly. Sinophone scholars usually belong to the category of "Chinese."

5. This ended when Deng Xiaoping decided to call a halt to ideological debate in order to clear the ground for reform. Instead, pragmatism, together with trial-and-error methods, was the new spirit of socialism with "Chinese characteristics."

6. One notable attempt is Liang Shoude, "Maixiang 21 shiji de shijie yu Zhongguoren duiwai jiaowang yuanze de tantao" (Stepping into the 21st century and exploring the principles of Chinese external relations), presented at the conference on the Chinese Stepping into the 21st Century, Taipei (June 6, 1996).

7. Chih-yu Shih, "A Postcolonial Approach to the State Question in China," *The Journal of Contemporary China* 17, 7 (1998): 125–139.

8. Ge Sun, *Zhunei hao de beilun* (The Dilemma of Takeuchi Yoshimi) (Beijing: Beijing University Press, 2005).

9. For notable exceptions, see Guo-Ming Chen and W. J. Starosta, "On Theorizing Difference: Culture as Centrism," *International and Intercultural Communication Annual* 26 (2003), 277–287; Kwang-kuo Hwang, "Reification of Culture in Indigenous Psychology: Merit or Mistake?" *Social Epistemology* 25, 2 (2011): 125–131.

10. Harry Harding, "The Study of Chinese Politics: Toward a Third Generation of Scholarship," *World Politics* 36, 2 (January 1984): 284–307.

11. "Symposium on Chinese Studies and the Discipline," *Journal of Asian Studies* 23, 4 (August 1964): 505–38.

12. Andrew G. Walder, "The Transformation of Contemporary China Studies, 1977–2002," in David L. Szanton (ed.), *The Politics of Knowledge: Area Studies and the Disciplines* (University of California Press/University of California International and Area Studies Digital Collection, Edited Volume #3, 2002. http://repositories.cdlib.org/uciaspubs/editedvolumes/3/8)

13. New Haven: Yale University Press, 1982.

14. Armonk, NY: M. E. Sharpe, 1988.

15. Ibid., 1999.

16. Hsiang-jui Meng, *Dao xifang xie Zhongguo da lishi: Huang Renyu de weiguan jingyan yu ta de Zhongguo xue shequn* (Writing Chinese macro-history for the "west": Ray Huang's micro-career and his China studies community) (Taipei: The Research and Educational Center for China Studies and Cross Taiwan-Strait Relations, Department of Political Science, National Taiwan University, 2009).

17. Ray Huang, *Taxation and Governmental Finance in Sixteenth-Century Ming China* (Cambridge: Cambridge University Press, 1975).

18. Ray Huang, *Dibei tiannan xu gujin* (Narrating the past and the contemporary between the earth in the north and the heaven in the south) (Taipei: Lien Ching, 1991), 81.

19. This criticism is in *Shiliu shiji Zhongguo Mingdai de caizheng yu shuishou* (Chinese version of *Taxation and Governmental Finance in Sixteenth-Century Ming China*) (Taipei: Lien Ching, 2001), 572.

20. Ibid., 285–286, 307–311, 499–506, 563–571.

21. Ray Huang, *Da lishi buhui weisuo* (The Grand History Will Not Atrophy) (Taipei: Lian Ching, 2004).

22. For Samuel Kim's recollections of his scholarship, see http://politics.soc.ntu.edu.tw/RAEC/act02.php (interviewed on June 6–10, 2006); Kim's synthetic scholarship is best exemplified by his edited volumes; see, for example, Samuel S. Kim (ed.), *China and the World: Chinese Foreign Policy in the Post-Mao Era* (Boulder: Westview Press, 1984); Samuel S. Kim (ed.), *China and the World: New Directions in Chinese Foreign Relations* (Boulder: Westview Press, 1989); Samuel S. Kim (ed.), *China and the World: Chinese Foreign Relations in the Post-Cold War Era* (Boulder: Westview Press, 1994); Samuel S. Kim (ed.), *China and the World: Chinese Foreign Policy Faces the New Millennium* (Boulder: Westview Press, 1998).

23. Samuel Kim's authors derided their own writing by saying that those who do not produce theories are only writing literature reviews. See Davis B. Babrow and Steven Chan, "On a Slow Boat to Where? Analyzing Chinese Foreign Policy," in Samuel Kim (ed.), *China and the World: Chinese Foreign Policy in the Post-Mao Era* (Boulder: Westview, 1984), 32.

24. The end result of this meeting was a collective volume that came out five years later, in traditional Chinese characters and printed in Taiwan. See Shaoguang Wang, Yun-han Chu, and Quansheng Zhao (eds.), *Huaren shehui zhengzhi xue bentu yanjiu de lilun yu shijian* (Theory and practice of indigenous political science in Chinese societies) (Taipei: Laurel Press, 2002).

25. Zhao was presenting a paper entitled "Achieving Maximum Advantage: Rigidity and Flexibility in Chinese Foreign Policy," at the American Political Science Association Annual Meeting, September 1, 1990, San Francisco.

26. Yongnian Zheng, "Political Incrementalism: Political Lessons from Chinas Twenty Years of Reform," presented at the Conference on PRC Reform at 20: Retrospect and Prospects (Taipei, April 8–9, 1999).

27. Hsu was the discussant of Zheng's paper. Later, Hsu touched upon his criticism again in his "Zhongguo dalu zhengzhi gaige de zhengyi: yige wenxian de huigu" (Debate on China's Reform: A Literature Review), *Zhongguo dalu yanjiu* (Mainland China Studies) 47, 1 (2004).

28. Yongnian Zheng, *Discovering Chinese Nationalism in China: Modernization and International Relations* (New York: Cambridge University Press, 1999).

29. In the Maryland workshop, Wang was among the most ardent defenders of social science universalism. See his defense of Chinese nationalism in Fei-ling Wang, "Self-Image and Strategic Intentions: National Confidence and Political Insecurity" in Yong Deng and Fei-ling Wang (eds.), *In the Eyes of the Dragon: China Views the World* (Lanham, Boulder, New York & London: Rowman & Littlefield, 1999), 21–46.

30. For example, Suisheng Zhao, *A Nation-State by Construction: Dynamics of Modern Chinese Nationalism* (Stanford, CA: Stanford University Press, 2004); *Debating Political Reform in China: Rule of Law vs. Democratization* (Armonk, NY: M. E. Sharpe, 2006).

31. In reply to an invitation for interview on August 27, 2006, Zhao indicated that he had no specific theoretical preference. Chia-chia Kuo, *Lisanzhe de Zhongguo minzuzhuyi: hua yi xuezhe Zhao Suisheng, Zheng Yongnian miandui Zhongguo de shenfen celyue* (Diasporic Chinese nationalism: Identity strategies of overseas Chinese scholars Zhao Suisheng and Zheng Yongnian facing China) (Taipei: The Research and Educational Center for China Studies and Cross Taiwan-Strait Relations, Department of Political Science, National Taiwan University, 2008).

32. Tingyang Zhao, *Tianxia tixi* (The all-under-heaven system) (Nanjing: Jiangsu Education Press, 2005).

33. Hu Jintao first mentioned the notion of the "harmonious world" in April 2005 at an Asian-African summit meeting in Jakarta. The term was specifically included in a joint statement issued by Beijing and Moscow in July the same year. Two months later, Hu gave a speech at the United Nations in which he elaborated on the idea. See http://big5.xinhuanet.com/gate/big5/news.xinhuanet.com/ziliao/2006-08/24/content_5000866.htm, accessed on March 13, 2008.

34. Lucian Pye, *The Spirit of Chinese Political Culture* (Cambridge, MA: MIT Press, 1968); Richard Solomon, *Mao's Revolution and the Chinese Political Culture* (Berkeley: University of California Press, 1971).

35. Michael Ng-quinn, *China and International Systems: History, Structures and Processes*, PhD dissertation, Harvard University, 1978; Victoria Tin-bor Hui, *War*

and State Formation in Ancient China and Early Modern Europe (Cambridge: Cambridge University Press, 2005).

36. Alastair Iain Johnston, Cultural Realism (Princeton: Princeton University Press, 1995).

37. Stefan Tanaka, Japan's Orient: Rendering Pasts into History (Berkeley: University of California Press, 1993).

38. These disciplines include anthropology, political economy, national defense, political culture, comparative politics, and international relations. See, for example, Chih-yu Shih, Collective Democracy: Political and Legal Reform in China (Hong Kong: The Chinese University of Hong Kong Press, 1999); State and Society in China's Political Economy: The Cultural Dynamics of China's Socialist Reform (Boulder: Lynne Rienner, 1995); Autonomy, Ethnicity and Poverty in Southwestern China: The State Turned Upside Down (London: Palgrave, 2007).

39. William A. Callahan, "Chinese Visions of World Order: Tianxia, Empire and World Order," International Studies Association (ISA) Annual Conference paper, 2007, Chicago.

40. Yang Chung-fang, "Zhongguoren zhenshi jiti zhuyi ma?" (Are Chinese really collectivistic?) in Kuo-shu Yang and An-bang Yu (eds.), Zhongguoren de jiazhi guan 2 (Values of Chinese Societies II) (Taipei: Laureate Press, 1994), 321–434.

41. For a typical example, see Thomas Gottlieb, Chinese Foreign Policy Factionalism and the Origins of the Strategic Triangle, Rand Report R-1902-NA (Santa Monica: Rand Corporation, 1977).

42. See Yu-shan Wu, Wen-cheng Lin, and Shui-ping Chiang, Hou Deng shiqi dui dalu ji Taiwan de zhengdang (The Impact of the Post-Deng Period on Mainland China and Taiwan) (Taipei, Tung-ta).

43. Tai-chun Kuo and Ramon H. Myers, Understanding Communist China: Communist China Studies in the United States and the Republic of China, 1949–1978 (Stanford: The Hoover Institution Press, 1986).

44. Bruce Cummings, "Boundary Displacement: Area Studies and International Studies during and after the Cold War." Bulletin of Concerned Asian Scholars 29, 1 (1997): 6–27.

45. Tsai Cheng-wen, "Shan yong quanli pingheng gainian, tiaozheng wo guo duiwai celue" (Properly using the concept of balance of power, adjusting the foreign policy of our nation), United Daily (August 25, 1992): 2.

46. Aron's legacy is quoted everywhere in Tsai's first book, Hezi shidai guoji guanxi de tezhi: tixi, heping, zhanzheng (The characteristics of international relations in the nuclear age: system, peace, and war) (no publisher, 1977).

47. You Ying-long, the initiator of the reform, later joined the proindependence cabinet as vice chairman of the Mainland Affairs Council.

48. Culture would be an inappropriate point of analysis since it obscures the difference between Taiwan and China. See, for example, Shiow-duan Hwang's book review in Taiwan minzhu jikan (Taiwan Democracy Quarterly) 5, 2 (June 2008): 181–186.

49. For examples available in English, see Takeshi Hamashita, The Tribute Trade System and Modern Asia (Memoirs of the Research Department of the Toyo

Bunko, 1988); Yoshimi Takeuchi, *What Is Modernity? Writings of Takeuchi Yohimi* (ed.) (trans.), Richard F. Calichman (New York: Columbia University Press, 2005); Yuzo Mizoguchi, "A Search for the Perspective on the Studies of East Asia: Centering on Chinese Studies," *Sungkyun Journal of East Asian Studies* 1 (2001): 7–15.

50. William Callahan, "Tianxia, Empire and the World: Soft Power and China's Foreign Policy Discourse in the 21st Century," in W. Callahan and E. Barabantseva (eds.), *China Orders the World? Soft Power, Norms and Foreign Policy* (Washington, D.C.: Woodrow Wilson Center Press, 2009).

Chapter 5

1. For an epistemological discussion on causal mechanisms, see Ron Herré, *The Philosophies of Science: An Introductory Survey* (New York: Oxford University Press, 1972), p. 65; James Mahoney, "Beyond Correlational Analysis: Recent Innovations in Theory and Method," *Sociological Forum* 16, 3 (2001): 575–593. For case studies that adopt mechanism analysis, see Alastair Iain Johnston, *Social States: China in International Institutions, 1980–2000* (Princeton: Princeton University Press, 2007); Peter Katzenstein, *Sinicization and the Rise of China: Civilizational Processes beyond East and West* (London: Routledge, 2012).

2. For more discussions on these dyadic identities, see Vivienne Shue, *The Reach of the State: Sketches of the Chinese Body Politic* (Stanford: Stanford University Press, 1990); Richard Madsen, *Morality and Power in a Chinese Village* (Berkeley: University of California Press, 1986); Lucien Pye, *The Mandarin and the Cadre: China's Political Cultures* (Ann Arbor: The Center for Chinese Studies, University of Michigan, 1988).

3. For illustrations of revolving, see Shaoguang Wang, *Failure of Charisma: The Cultural Revolution in Wuhan* (Oxford: Oxford University Press, 1995); Honglin Yeh, *Following the Footsteps of the Empire: Tokutomi Soho's Perspectives on China* (Taipei: Research and Educational Center of Mainland China Studies and Cross-strait Relations, 2009).

4. Structures can be global or regional, economic or cultural, political or social, and so on. See, for example, Gordon White, *Riding the Tiger: The Politics of Economic Reform in Post-Mao China* (Stanford: Stanford University Press, 1993); Richard Bernstein and Ross H. Munro, *The Coming Conflict with China* (New York: Vintage, 1998); Geremé Barmé, *The Forbidden City* (Cambridge: Harvard University Press, 2008); Dali L. Yang, *Calamity and Reform in China: State, Rural Society, and Institutional Change Since the Great Leap Famine* (Stanford: Stanford University, 1998); David Kang, *China Rising: Peace, Power, and Order in East Asia* (New York: Columbia University Press, 2007).

5. The project "Folk Perspectives on State-Society Relations on the Chinese Mainland" is sponsored by the NTU Political Science Academic Cultural Foundation. The diaries are filed under the first street address of residence in China of each researcher: Report B (April–June 2011), Report D

(December 2010–February 2011); Report J (March–June 2011); Report Q (March–May 2011); Report Y (March–June 2011); Report Z (September–December 2011).

6. For rationales of multisited research, refer to George E. Marcus, "Ethnography in/of the World System: The Emergence of Multi-Sited Ethnography," *Annual Review of Anthropology* 24 (1995): 95–117.

7. For the China that has no shared identity among its users, see Ann Anagnost, *National Past-Times: Narrative, Representation, and Power in Modern China (Body, Commodity, Text)* (Durham: Duke University Press, 1997); David Goodman and Gerald Segal, *China Deconstructs: Politics, Trade and Regionalism* (London: Routledge, 1995); Chih-yu Shih, *Negotiating Ethnicity in China: Citizenship as a Response to the State* (London: Routledge, 2002); Leo Suryadinata, *Understanding the Ethnic Chinese in Southeast Asia* (Singapore: Institute of Southeast Asian Studies, 2007).

8. Hu Jintao, "Zai qingzhu Zhongguo gongchandang chengli jiushi zhounian dahui shang de jianghua" (Speech at the ceremony to celebrate the 90th anniversary of the Chinese Communist Party), *Xinhua Net* (July 1, 2011), http://big5.xinhuanet.com/gate/big5/news.xinhuanet.com/politics/2011-07/01/c_1216 12030.htm, accessed on March 10, 2012.

9. *Zhong gong zhongyang guanyu jiaqiang dang tong renmin qunzhong lianxi de jueding* (The CCP Central Committee's decision on strengthening the party's ties with the masses of the people) (Shanghai: New China Bookstore, 1990).

10. Commentary Department, *Renmin Ribao,* "Cadre Style Is the Lifeline of Their Public Credibility" (March 17, 2011), http://theory.people.com.cn/GB/14163183.html, accessed on March 12, 2012.

11. Commentary Department, *Renmin Ribao,* "Bie rang gan qun guanxi chuxian minyi chizi" (Do not allow a public opinion deficit to emerge) (January 6, 2011), http://opinion.people.com.cn/GB/13664139.html, accessed on March 12, 2012.

12. Commentary Department, *Renmin Ribao,* "Yi baorong xin duidai yizhi siwei" (Treat heterogeneous thinking with a tolerant attitude) (April 28, 2011), http://opinion.people.com.cn/GB/14505701.html, accessed on March 12, 2012.

13. Commentary Department, Renmin Ribao, "Rang liyi ganggan qiaojie shehui maodun" (Apply the lever of interest to opening up social contradictions) (April 14, 2011), originally available http://opinion.people.com.cn/GB/40604/14221209.html, accessed on March 12, 2012, but later deleted from the people.com webpage.

14. Report B.

15. Report Q.

16. Report J.

17. Report Q.

18. Reports Y and D record the rumor that the government deliberately indulges them.

19. Report Z.

20. Report Z.
21. Report D.
22. "Three-Self" refers to self-governing, self-sustaining, and self-preaching.
23. Report Z.
24. Report J.
25. Tianbiao Zhu, "Compressed Development, Flexible Politics, Informal Practices, and Multiple Traditions in China's Economic Ascent," in Katzenstein, *Sinicization and the Rise of China.* For criticism of state-society analysis, see Chih-yu Shih, *State and Society in China's Political Economy* (Boulder: Lynne Rienner, 1995); Martin Evenden and Gregory Sandstrom, "Calling for Scientific Revolution in Psychology: K. K. Hwang on Indigenous Psychologies," *Social Epistemology* 25, 2 (April 2011): 153–166.
26. Report Z.
27. Report Z.
28. Reports Q, B, J, and D. Report Q tells of a bus driver carrying a long stick precisely for the purpose of hitting cars from the driver's window of the bus.
29. Especially Reports B and Y.
30. Report D.
31. The author of Report Y was seized round the neck from behind and robbed of her belongings, some of which were returned a month later after the police had arrested the robber in a neighboring province.
32. Mostly from Reports B and Y.
33. Reports Q and Y.
34. Report B.
35. Report Z.
36. Report Z.
37. Report Z.
38. Report Q.
39. Report Q.
40. Report Q.
41. Report D.
42. Reports J and Q. Report Q cites one such extreme remark on the tsunami: ". . .why did it not strike even harder? "
43. Report Z.
44. Report B.
45. Report Q.
46. Report Z.
47. Report Z.
48. Report Z.
49. Report Z.
50. Report D.
51. Reports Y and B.
52. Report B.
53. Report Y.

54. Reports B, Y, and Z.
55. Report Q.
56. Report Q.
57. Report B.
58. Report Q.
59. Report B.
60. Peasants also affect city dwellers' habits. For example, peasants, like city dwellers, do not look at traffic lights when crossing a main road. Report Q.

Chapter 6

1. The Washington consensus is about transforming socialism through immediate privatization and marketization. In contrast, the Beijing consensus refers to incremental development assured by political stability under the control of one-party rule. See Stefan Halper, *The Beijing Consensus: Legitimizing Authoritarianism in Our Time* (New York: Basic Books, 2012); Baogang Guo and He Li (eds.), *The Chinese Labyrinth: Exploring China's Model of Development* (Lanham, MD: Lexington Books, 2011); S. Philip Hsu, Yu-shan Wu, and Suisheng Zhao (eds.), *In Search of China's Development Model: Beyond the Beijing Consensus* (London: Routledge, 2011).

2. Whether or not China represented a distinctive model of transition to socialism was once a subject of heated debate among Marxist scholars. To trace this forgotten debate, please consult *Monthly Review* and *Modern China*. For a few examples, see Paul M. Sweezy and Charles Bettelheim, *On the Transition to Socialism* (New York: Monthly Review Press, 1971), 105, 119–122; Richard M. Pfeffer, "Mao and Marx in the Marxist-Leninist Tradition: A Critique of 'The China Field' and a Contribution to a Preliminary Reappraisal," *Modern China* 2, 4 (1976): 421–460; Maurice Meisner, "Mao and Marx in the Scholastic Tradition," *Modern China* 3, 4 (1977): 401–406. Note also the special issue on China's economic strategy, *Monthly Review* 27, 3 (1975) and on China since Mao, *Monthly Review* 30, 3 (1978).

3. For example, see Gordon White, *Riding the Tiger* (Stanford: Stanford University Press, 1993); Edward Friedman, *National Identity and Democratic Prospects in Socialist China* (Armonk: M. E. Sharpe, 1995); Suisheng Zhao (ed.), *Debating Political Reform in China: Rule of Law versus Democratization* (Armonk: M. E. Sharpe, 2006); Victor Nee and Yang Cao, "Market Transition and the Firm: Institutional Change and Income Inequality in Urban China," *Management and Organizations Review* 1,1 (2004): 23–56; Andrew Nathan, China's Transition (New York: Columbia University Press, 1997); Andrew Walder and Jean C. Oi (eds.), *Property Rights and Economic Reform in China* (Stanford: Stanford University Press, 1999); Peter Gries, *China's New Nationalism: Pride, Politics, and Diplomacy* (Berkeley: University of California Press, 2005); Chih-yu Shih, *Autonomy, Ethnicity and Poverty in Southwestern China: The State Turned Upside Down* (London: Palgrave, 2007).

4. For example, Mizoguchi Yuzo, *Zuowei fangfa de zhongguo* (China as method), trans. You-chong Lin (Taipei: National Institute for Compilation and Translation, 1999).

5. For example, Vasily V. Makeeve (ed.), *China: Threats, Risks, Challenges to Development* (in Russian) (Moscow: Carnegie Moscow Center, 2005).

6. For example, Takeshi Hamashita, "Tribute and Treaties: East Asian Treaty Ports Networks in the Era of Negotiation, 1834–1894," *European Journal of East Asian Studies* 1, 1 (2002): 59–87.

7. Kwang-kuo Hwang, *Easternization: Socio-cultural Impact on Productivity* (Tokyo: Asian Productivity Organization, 1995).

8. For example, Shaoguang Wang, "Money and Autonomy: Patterns of Civil Society Finance and Their Implications," *Studies in Comparative International Development* 40, 4 (Winter 2006): 3–29.

9. Kapyn Sanyl (ed.), *Rethinking Capitalist Development: Primitive Accumulation, Governmentality and Post-Colonial Capitalism* (New Delhi: Routledge, 2007).

10. Dipesh Chakrabarty, *Provincializing Europe: Postcolonial Thought and Historical Difference* (Princeton: Princeton University Press, 2007).

11. Henry Yuhuai He, *Dictionary of the Political Thought of the People's Republic of China* (Armonk: M. E. Sharpe, 2001), 26.

12. See, for example, Franz Schurmann, *Ideology and Organization in Communist China* (Berkeley: University of California Press, 1965).

13. Note, for example, the founding of the journal *Post-communist and Transition Studies* in 1984.

14. Lowell Dittmer and Yu-shan Wu, "Leadership Coalitions and Economic Transformation in Reform China: Revisiting the Political Business," in Lowell Dittmer and Guoli Liu (eds.), *China's Deep Reform: Domestic Politics in Transition* (Lanham, MD: Rowman & Littlefield, 2006).

15. This subject is equally popular among Sinophone authors; see, for example, Peter Ho, *Institutions in Transition: Land Ownership, Property Rights and Social Conflict in China* (Oxford: Oxford University Press, 2005); Chih-jou Jay Chen, *Transforming Rural China* (London: Taylor & Francis, 2007); Xiaobao Hu, *Problems in China's Transitional Economy: Property Rights and Transitional Models* (Singapore: World Scientific Pub. Co. Inc., 1998).

16. Lawrence E. Harrison and Samuel Huntington (eds.), *Culture Matters: How Values Shape Human Progress* (New York: Basic Books, 2001). The title of this book is ironic considering that the main theme of most of the chapter authors is that the existing culture should not matter in order for progressive transition to take place.

17. See Max Weber, *The Religion of China* (New York: Free Press, 1951).

18. Ontological individualism is implicitly ubiquitous in the leading scholarship of China under transition. See, for example, Nan Lin, Social Capital and the Labor Market: Transforming Urban China, (New York: Cambridge University Press, 2007); Neil. J. Diamant, Stanley B. Lubman, and Kevin J. O'Brien (eds.), *Engaging the Law in China: State, Society and Possibilities for Justice* (Stanford: Stanford

University Press, 2005); Joshua Kurlantizick, *Charm Offensive: How China's Soft Power Is Transforming the World* (New Haven: Yale University Press, 2008).

19. Homi Bhabha, "The World and the Home," *Social Text* 31–32 (1993): 141–153.

20. See the report in Chih-yu Shih, "Responding to Globalization: Taiwanese Professional Women's Role in the Construction of China" Paper presented at the International Conference on Gender and Development in Asia, Hong Kong, November 29, 1997.

21. See the field report in Chih-yu Shih, "Between the Mosque and State," *Religion, State and Society* 28, 2 (2000): 197–211.

22. For more discussion on this subject, see Sue Ellen M. Charlton, Jana Everett, and Kathleen Staudt (eds.), *Women, the State and Development* (Albany: State University of New York Press, 1989). Also see Karlin Jurczyk, "Time in Women's Everyday Lives: Between Self-determination and Conflicting Demands," *Time and Society* 7, 2 (1989): 283–308; Pamela Odih, "Gendered Time in the Age of Deconstruction," *Time and Society* 8, 1 (1999): 9–38.

23. See the field report in Chih-yu Shih, *Collective Democracy: Political and Legal Reform of China* (Hong Kong: Chinese University of Hong Kong Press, 1999). Also see the discussion in Jong Wong, Rong Ma, and Ma Yang (eds.), *China's Entrepreneurs* (Singapore: Times Academic Press, 1995); Kevin O'Brien, "Rightful Resistance," *World Politics* 49, 1 (1996): 31–55.

24. See the report in Chih-yu Shih, *Negotiating Ethnicity in China: Citizenship as a Response to the State* (London: Routledge, 2002); also see Mette Halskov Hansen, *Lessons in Being Chinese* (Seattle: University of Washington, 1999).

25. See the discussion in Shih, *Collective Democracy.*

26. See the report in Shih, *Negotiating Ethnicity,* and also the discussion in Chih-yu Shih, *Navigating Sovereignty: World Politics Lost in China* (London: Palgrave, 2003).

27. See my report on the western Hunan case in *Autonomy, Ethnicity and Poverty in Southwestern China.*

28. See my report in "How Ethnic Is Ethnic Education: The Issue of School Enrollment in Meigu's Yi Community," *Prospect Quarterly* 2, 3 (July 2001).

29. See my discussion in "The Eros of International Politics: Madame Chiang Kai-shek and the Question of State in China," *Comparative Civilizations Review* 46 (Spring 2002).

30. See my discussion in *Democracy Made in Taiwan: The "Success State" as a Political Theory* (Lanham: Lexington, 2007).

Chapter 7

1. For a brief history of the *Japan Times,* see Chan Li, *Shijie xinwen shi* (The world's history of news reporting) (Taipei: Sanmin Bookstore, 1992), 808, 867; http://tw.knowledge.yahoo.com/question/?qid=1205071801848, accessed on May 8, 2007.

2. For more information, see http://www.applyesl.com/zh/news/news_1010.asp? EvtMsg=Sel,0,4, accessed on February 6, 2007.

3. Keisuke Okada, director and managing editor, and Sayuri Daimon, director of the newspaper's news division, interviewed by Victoria Yang (in the reception room of the *Japan Times* headquarters, Tokyo, December 11, 2006).

4. For these reports and commentaries in the *New York Times,* see Victoria Yang, *Pingfan wuqi de 1997:Riben shibao dui Zhongguo de qu jingqi baodao* (A year of no significance: Desensitizing report on China in the *Japan Times* 1997), MA thesis, Institute of Political Science, National Sun Yat-sen University, July 2007.

5. For more about Friedrich Hegel as discussed by Koyasu Nobukumi, who considers Hegel's concept to be a major origin of the anxiety among modern Japanese thinkers on Asia and the meaning of being Japanese, see his *Dong ya lun: Riben xiandai sixiang pipan* (The thesis on East Asia: a critique on Japanese contemporary thought), trans., Jinghua Zhao (Changchun: Jilin People's Press, 2004), 27–28.

6. For examples of such narratives, see Akira Iriye, (ed.), *The Chinese and the Japanese: Essays in Political and Cultural Interactions* (Princeton, NJ: Princeton University Press, 1980); Joshua A. Fogel, *The Literature of Travel in the Japanese Rediscovery of China, 1862–1945* (Stanford, CA: Stanford University Press, 1996).

7. The original text of his assertion can be found at http://blechmusik.xrea.jp/d/hirayama/h03/2007.0.06, accessed on April 11, 2012.

8. Yukichi Fukuzawa, *Fuze Yuji zizhuan: yige yingxiang Riben jindaihua zhiju de wan tong* ([The autobiography of] Fukuzawa Yukichi: A disobedient child who greatly influenced Japan's modernization), trans., Yong-lian Yang (Taipei: Maitian, 2006); Ge Sun, *Yazhou yiwei zhe sheme—wenhua jian de "Riben"* (What could Asia imply?—"Japan" between cultures) (Taipei: Chyu-liu, 2001), 29–30.

9. Robert Bellah, *Dechuan zongjiao: xiandai Riben de wenhua yuanyuan* (Tokugawa Religion: The Cultural Roots of Modern Japan), trans., Xiaoshan Wang and Rong Dai, (Beijing: Sanlian, 1998), 100–103.

10. Incidentally, Max Weber saw the effective control of desire by the Puritan tradition as the psychological prerequisite of the capitalist accumulation that triggered progression to modernity in Europe.

11. Takeuchi Yoshimi, *Jindai de chaoke* (Overcoming of modernity), trans., Dongmu Li, Jinghua Zhao, and Ge Sun (Beijing: Sanlian, 2000).

12. For further comments on the study of world history, see David Williams, *Defending Japan's Pacific War: The Kyoto School Philosophers and Post-White Power* (London and New York: Routledge Curzon, 2004); Naoki Sakai, Translation & Subjectivity: On "Japan" and Cultural Nationalism (Minneapolis & London: University of Minnesota Press, 1997).

13. Stefan Tenaka, *Japan's Orient: Rendering Pasts into History* (Berkeley: California University Press, 1993), 122–41.

14. The book was published in English. Okakura Kakuzo, *The Ideals of the East with Special Reference to the Arts of Japan* (London: John Murray, 1903).

15. For a critical review of this search for universalism, see David Williams, "In Defense of the Kyoto School: Reflections on Philosophy, the Pacific War and the Making of a Post-White World," *Japan Forum* 12, 2 (September 2000): 143–156.

16. For the linkage between Nishida's thought and the Shinto underpinning of Fascism, see Graham Parkes, "The Putative Fascism of the Kyoto School," *Philosophy East and West* 47, 3 (1997).

17. Yoshimi Takeuchi, "Asia as Method," in *What Is Modernity? Writings of Takeuchi Yoshimi,* trans., Richard F. Calichman (New York: Columbia University Press, 2004), 164–165.

18. Mizoguchi Yuzo, *Zuowei fangfa de zhongguo* (China as a Method), trans., Youchong Lin (Taipei: National Institute for Compilation and Translation,1999), 106.

19. The Kyoto School of philosophers were the major participants of the notorious workshop, "Overcoming Modernity," that was held in support of Japan's war with the United States.

20. For related discussions, see Wei-fen Chen, "Riben guanyu 'dongya' de sikao" (Japanese Reflections on "East Asia"), *Sixiang* (Thoughts) 3, Taipei: Lian-ching, 2006.

21. For more discussion and the literature, see Ge Sun, *Zhuti misan de kongjian* (The Space with Pervasive Subjectivities) (Nanchang: Jiangxi Education Press, 2003).

22. Mizoguchi *Zuowei fangfa de zhongguo,* 19–22.

23. Ping Liu, *Jintian Zuoyouji yanjiu* (A Study of Tsuda Soukichi) (Beijing, Chunghua Bookstore, 2004), 170–181, 234–235, 283–287.

24. Mizoguchi, *Zuowei fangfa de zhongguo,* ch. 6; Wang Ping, "Lun Ribenren 'Zhongguo guan' de lishi bianqian" (On the historical evolution of Japanese "views on China"), *Riben Xuekan* (Journal of Japan Studies) 2 (2003): 44.

25. See Shaodang Yan, *Zhanhou liushi nian Ribenren de Zhongguo guan* (Japanese views on China in the sixty years since the war), *Riben yanjiu* (Japan Studies) 3 (2005); Kimihiko Baba, "Zhanhou Riben luntan Zhongguo guan de bianqian— cong 'shijie' zazhi de xiangguan baodao zhong suo kandaode" (Changing views on China in the postwar Japanese forum—as seen in related reports in World Magazine), *Kaifang shidai* (Open Epoch) 5 (2002): 66–79.

26. This is called "neo-withdrawal"; see Weijia Zhou, "Haiyang Riben lun de zhengzhihua si chao jiqi pingjia" (Sea power Japan theory and its impact on trends of Japan's development), *Riben xuekan* (The Journal of Japan Studies) 2 (2001): 35–49.

27. Ge Sun, *Zhunei Hao de bei lun* (The irony of Takeuchi Yoshimi's narratives) (Beijing: Peking University Press, 2005), 8.

28. Sun Ge, "Wanshan zhennan de liangnan zhi jing" (The condition of dilemma of Maruyama Mazao) in Mazao Maruyama, *Riben zhengzhi sixiang shi yanjiu* (A study of the history of Japanese political thought), trans., Sun and Wang (Beijing: Sanlian), 12–29.

29. Banghe Sheng, "Wanshan Zhennan: chuantong yanhua yu wenhua de xiandaihua" (Maruyama Mazao: Evolution of tradition and modernization of culture), *Riben xuekan* (The Journal of Japan Studies) 3 (2002): 113.

30. Koyasu, *Dong ya lun,* 7–8; Nobukumi Koyasu, "Zuowei shijian de Chulai xue: sixiang shi fangfa de zai cikao" (The scholarship of Ogyu Sorai as an event: Re-reflections on the method of thought history), *Taida lishi xuebao* (NTU History Journal) 29 (2002.06): 182.

31. Shuisheng Xu, "Wanshan Zhennan de Riben sixiang gu ceng lun chu tan" (Maruyama Mazao's preliminary thesis on the ancient layer of Japanese thought), *Wuhan daxue xuebao* (Wuhan University Journal) (Humanities and Social Science Section) 53 (2000.05): 327.

32. "Chinese Community Grieves Deng Xiaoping," and "Chinese Here Ponder Possible Turmoil," both appeared on February 20.

33. "Hong's Future Secure as China Set to Return, Exec Says," (March 21); "Ministry Strikes Deal to Protect Japan Interests in Hong Kong" (May 15); "Ikeda to Attend Controversial Investiture in Hong Kong" (June 25); "Hong Kong Execs Say City Is Still in Business" (July 17); "Tung Hears out Tokyo's Hopes for Hong Kong" (October 16). In comparison, the *New York Times* printed seven articles on the subject on July 1 alone.

34. "Japan to Offer Thailand $4 Billion in United Loans" (August 11, 1997).

35. "Overseas A-bomb Victims Seek Equality" (July 8); "Defense Agency Urges Crisis-response Legislation" (July 15); "Foreign Ministry Goes Through Post Reshuffle" (July 29); "Hashimoto to Visit War Museum during China Trip" (August 4); "Beijing Seeks 450 Billion Yen in Loans for Infrastructure" (August 4); "Youths Learn about Horror of Nuclear War" (August 4); "Japan, China Open Fisheries Negotiations" (August 6); "Fisheries Talks with China to Start" (August 18); "Damages Sought by Victims of Biological Warfare in China" (August 11); "Supreme Court Backs Ienaga in Textbook Suit" (August 29).

36. "Rain Fails to Dampen Turnout at Yasukuni" and "Seven Ministers Visit Yasukuni on Anniversary."

Chapter 8

1. Edwin O. Reischauer, "Sinic World in Perspective," *Foreign Affairs* 52 (1973/4): 341–348.

2. David Kang, "Civilization and State Formation in the Shadow of China," in Peter J. Katzenstein (ed.), *Civilizations in World Politics: Plural and Pluralist Perspectives* (London and New York: Routledge, 2010), 91–113; Yong Deng, *China's Struggle for Status: The Realignment of International Relations* (Cambridge: Cambridge University Press, 2008); Chih-yu Shih, *The Spirit of Chinese Foreign Policy: A Psychocultural View* (London: Macmillan, 1990); Mark Mancall, *China at the Center: 300 Years of Foreign Policy* (New York: Free Press, 1984).

3. Peter Katzenstein. "A World of Plural and Pluralist Civilizations: Multiple Actors, Traditions and Practices," in Peter J. Katzenstein (ed.), *Civilizational Politics in World Affairs: Plural and Pluralist Perspectives* (New York: Routledge,

2010), 1–40; William Callahan, *A Contingent State: Greater China and Transnational Relations* (Minneapolis: University of Minnesota, 2004); Chih-yu Shih, *Autonomy, Ethnicity and Poverty in Southwestern China: The State Turned Upside Down* (London: Palgrave, 2007).

4. Stefan Tanaka, *Japan's Orient: Rendering Pasts into History* (Berkeley: University of California Press, 1993); Joshua Fogel, *Politics and Sinology: The Case of Naito Konan, 1866–1934* (Cambridge, MA: Harvard University Press, 1984).

5. Susumu Nishibe, *Hanbei to iu sahō (The way to resist America)* (Tokyo: Shogakkan, 2002); Pierre Lavelle, "The Political Thought of Nishida Kitaro," *Monumenta Nipponica* 49, 2 (1994): 139–165; Granham Gerald Ong, "Building an IR theory with 'Japanese Characteristics': Nishida Kitaro and 'Emptiness'," *Millennium* 33, 1 (2004): 35–58; Agnieszka Kozyra, "Nishida Kitaro's Logic of Absolutely Contradictory Self-identity and the Problem of Orthodoxy in the Zen Tradition," *Japan Review* 20 (2007): 69–110.

6. Inoguchi Takashi, "Are There Any Theories of International Relations in Japan?" *International Relations of Asia Pacific* 7, 3 (2007): 369–390.

7. Christopher Goto-Jones, *Political Philosophy in Japan: Nishida, the Kyoto School, and Co-prosperity* (Leiden: Routledge Leiden Series in Modern East Asia, 2005).

8. David Williams, *Defending Japan's Pacific War: The Kyoto School Philosophers and Post-White Power* (London: RoutledgeCurzon, 2005).

9. Kimitada Miwa, "Fukuzawa Yukichi's 'Departure from Asia': A Prelude to the Sino-Japanese War," in E. Skrzypczak (ed.), *Japan's Modern Century* (Tokyo: Sophia University, 1968), 1–40.

10. Yoshimi Takeuchi, *What Is Modernity? Writings of Takeuchi Yoshimi*, trans. and ed. Richard F. Calichman (New York: Columbia University Press, 2005).

11. Masao Maruyama, *Thought and Behavior in Modern Japanese Politics* (New York: ACLS Humanities E-Book, 2008); Nobukuni Koyasu, *Dong ya lun: Riben xiandai sixiang pipan* (Theses on East Asia: A Critique on Japanese Modern Thought) trans. J. Zhao (Changchun: Jilin People's Press, 2004), 18.

12. Maruyama's painstakingly effort to trace modernist roots in ancient Japan was nonetheless a case of subscribing to the European identity disguised as Japan's own potential for liberalism. To that extent, Maruyama's agenda was externally prescribed rather than coming from Japan's own historical trajectory, as he claimed.

13. Jilin Xu, "Yi Zhongguo wei fangfa, yi shijie wei mudi" (China as Method, the World as Destiny), *Guowai shehui kexue* 1 (1988): 54–58; Zhaoguang Ge, "Jiulingniandai Riben Zhongguo xue de xin guannian: du Goukou Xiongsan de zuo wei fangfa de Zhongguo" (The New Approach to China in Japan in the 1990s: Reading Mizoguchi Yuzo's China as Method), in Zhaoguang Ge (ed.), *Yuwai Zhongguo xue shi lun* (Ten theses on China studies overseas) (Shanghai: Fudan University Press, 2002), 16–31; Ge Sun, "Japan as Method," *Dushu* 3 (1995): 103–9.

14. Mizoguchi Yuzo, *Hoho to shite no Chugok* (China as method) (Tokyo: Tōkyō Daigaku Shuppankai, 1989); *Zuowei fangfa de zhongguo* (China as method),

trans. Y. Lin (Taipei: National Institute for Compilation and Translation, 1999); "A Search for the Perspective on the Studies of East Asia: Centering on Chinese Studies," *Sungkyun Journal of East Asian Studies* 1, 1 (2005), http://sjeas.skku. edu/backissue/issue_article.jsp?RNUM=1&SEQ=6, accessed on August 23, 2011.

15. Yuzo Mizoguchi, *China as Method,* 119–120.

16. Soukichi Tsuda, *What Is the Oriental Culture,* trans. Yasotaro Morri (Tokyo: Hokuseido Press, 1955).

17. Yoshimi Takeuchi, *What Is Modernity? Writings of Takeuchi Yoshimi,* trans. and ed. Richard F. Calichman (New York: Columbia University Press, 2005).

18. Yuzo Mizoguchi, "Chuangzao Ri Zhong zhishi gongtong kongjian" (Creating Shared Intellectual Space for Japan and China), *Dushu* 5 (2001): 3–11.

19. Lily Ling, *Postcolonial International Relations: Conquest and Desire Between Asia and the West* (London: Palgrave Macmillan, 2002); Xiguang Li, "The Inside Story of the Demonization of China," *Contemporary Chinese Thought* 30, 2 (Winter 1998/9): 13–77; Rey Chow, *Woman and Chinese Modernity: The Politics of Reading between West and East* (Minneapolis: University of Minnesota, 1991).

20. Wei Pan and Ma Ya, *Renmin gongheguo liushi nian yu zhongguo moshi* (Sixty Years of the People's Republic and the Chinese Model) (Beijing: New Knowledge Sanlian, 2010).

21. Sun Yat-sen, *Guo fu quan ji* (Comprehensive Collection of the National Father's Literature), 2 (China Cultural Service, 1973), 156.

22. Fei Xiaotong, "Zhonghua minzu de duoyuan yiti geju" (The Structure of Pluralistic Integration of the Chinese Nation), *Beijing daxue xuebao* 4 (1989): 1–11.

23. John Fitzgerald, *Awakening China: Politics, Culture and Class in the Nationalist Revolution* (Stanford: Stanford University, 1998).

24. Lucian Pye, "China: Erratic State, Frustrated Society," *Foreign Affairs* 69, 4 (Fall 1990): 56–74.

25. Samuel Huntington, "The Clash of Civilizations," *Foreign Affairs* 72, 3 (Summer 1993): 22–49.

26. William Callahan, *China: The Pessoptimist Nation* (Oxford: Oxford University Press, 2009).

27. Wu Tsong-han, *Xizang wenti yanjiu shiye xia de Zhongguo renshi* (Views on China in Tibet Studies: Comparing the Indian and the Australian Literature) (Taipei: Research and Educational Center for China Studies and Cross Taiwan-Strait Relations, Department of Political Science, National Taiwan University, 2010).

28. Chih-yu Shih. "China Studies That Defend Chineseness: The Im/Possibility of China-Centrism in the Divided Sino-Phone World," in Reena Marwah and Swaran Singh (eds.), *Emerging China* (New Delhi: Routledge, 2011), 117–142.

29. Naito Torajiro, *Zhongguo shixue shi* (The History of Chinese Historiography) (Tokyo: Kobundo, 1949).

30. Jin Taeha, *The Oral History of Jin Taeha* (Taipei: The Research and Educational Center for China Studies and Cross Taiwan-Strait Relations, Department of Political Science, National Taiwan University, 2008), http://politics.ntu.edu.tw/RAEC/comm2/InterviewTaehaJin_C.doc, accessed on April 26, 2011.

31. John K. Fairbank (ed.), *The Chinese World Order: Traditional China's Foreign Relations* (Cambridge, MA: Harvard University Press, 1968).

32. Hae-jong Chun, "Sino Korean Tributary Relations in the Ch'ing Period," in John K. Fairbank (ed.), *The Chinese World Order: Traditional China's Foreign Relations* (Cambridge, MA: Harvard University Press, 1968).

33. Chun Hae-jong, "Han-Jung jogong gwangye go" (A Historical Survey of the Sino-Korean Tributary Relationship), *Dongyangsahak* 1 (1966): 10–41; "Hankook gwa Jungkook: Han-Jung gwangyesa doroneui ilcheok" (Some Notes on the History of the Sino-Korean Relationship), *Dongbanghakji* 9 (1968): 1–19; "Handaeeui Jogong jedoae daehan ilgochal" (A Study on the Tribute System in the Former Han Dynasty), *Dongyangsahakyeongu* 6 (1973): 1–15; "Donga godaemunwhaeui Joongsimgwa jubyeonae daehan shiron" (Civilization's Center and Peripheries in Premodern East Asian History), *Dongyangsahakyeongu* 8 (1975): 1–23.

34. Lee Choon-shik, "Jogongeui giwongwa geu euimi" (On a Tribute—Its Origin and Significance), *GukjeJoongkukhankyeongu* 10 (1969): 1–21.

35. Ibid., 1.

36. Chung Yong-hwa, "Chosuneui Jogong Cheje Inshikgwa hwalyong" (Chosun Dynasty's Perception and Utilization of the Tribute System), *Hankookjeongchioegyosanonchong* 27, 2 (2006): 5–31.

37. Noosgoi Altantsetseg, *Mongolchuud Manjiin esreg erkh chuluunii tuluuh hudulguuniig BNHAU herhen uzej bui ni* (China's View of the Mongolian Movement for Freedom Against the Manchus) (Ulaanbaatar, 1985); Noosgoi Altantsetseg, *Movement 1911 onii hudulguun BNHAU-iin uzleer* (China's view of 1911) (Ulaanbaatar, 2001).

38. Noosgoi Altantsetseg, *Movement 1911 onii hudulguun BNHAU-iin uzleer;* Noosgoi Altantsetseg, *Mongolchuud Manjiin esreg erkh chuluunii tuluuh hudulguuniig BNHAU herhen uzej bui ni.*

39. For example, Myagmar Erdene, "Comparative Cranial Nonmetric Study of Archaeological Populations from Inner Asia," *Mongolian Journal of Anthropology, Archaeology and Ethnology* 4, 1 (2010): 184–212.

40. Jamsran Khereid Bayasakh, *The Oral History of Bayasakh* (Taipei: The Research and Educational Center for China Studies and Cross Taiwan-Strait Relations, Department of Political Science, National Taiwan University, 2010), 1–2, http://politics.ntu.edu.tw/RAEC/act/InterviewM%20Jamsran%20Khereid%20Bayasakh.doc, accessed on April 2, 2012.

41. Nguyen Huy Quy, *The Oral History of Nguyen* (Taipei: The Research and Educational Center for China Studies and Cross Taiwan-Strait Relations, Department of Political Science, National Taiwan University, 2009), http://politics.ntu.edu.tw/RAEC/act/Vietnam_03C.doc, accessed on April 26, 2011.

42. Ruan (Nguyen) Huaiqiu, *Cong bianyuan kan daguo: Yuenan Zhongguo yanjiu qikan dui Yue Zhong guanxi de renshi* (Looking at the major power from the periphery: views on Vietnam-China relations in the Vietnamese *Journal of China Studies*) (Taipei: The Research and Educational Center for China Studies and Cross Taiwan-Strait Relations, Department of Political Science, National Taiwan University, 2009).

43. Phan Van Cac, *The Oral History of Phan* (Taipei: The Research and Educational Center for China Studies and Cross Taiwan-Strait Relations, Department of Political Science, National Taiwan University, 2009), http://politics.ntu.edu.tw/RAEC/act/Vietnam_04C.doc, accessed on November 22, 2011.

44. Suryadinata Leo, "Anti-Chinese Riots in Indonesia Perennial Problem But Major Disaster Unlikely," *Straits Times* (February 25, 1998): 36.

45. Wang Gungwu, *A Short History of Nanyang Chinese* (Singapore: Eastern Universities Press, 1959); *Community and Nation: Essays on Southeast Asia and the Chinese* (Singapore: Heinemann Education Books, 1981).

46. Steve Lee, *Malaixiya Guanghua Ribao de Zhongguo renshi: zai huaren yu huaqiao liang zhong shenfen zhi jian* (The Malaysian Kwong Wah Newspapers' View of China: Between the Chinese Overseas and Guest Chinese) (Taipei: The Research and Educational Center for China Studies and Cross Taiwan-Strait Relations, Department of Political Science, National Taiwan University, 2009).

47. Caroline S. Hau, *On the Subject of the Nation: Filipino Writings from the Margins, 1981–2004* (Quezon City: Ateneo De Manila University Press, 2004).

48. Caroline Hau, "Becoming 'Chinese' in China and Southeast Asia," Paper presented at the international workshop on Sinicization (Beijing, March 25–26, 2011).

49. Chih-yu Shih, *Negotiating Ethnicity in China: Citizenship as a Response to the State* (London: Routledge, 2002).

Chapter 9

1. Peter Katzenstein, "China's Rise: Return, Rupture or Recombination?"; also see Peter Katzenstein and Takashi Shiraishi (eds.), *Beyond Japan, The Dynamics of East Asian Regionalism* (Ithaca: Cornell University 2006). Incidentally, Prasenjit Duara argues that the rise of China is replacement of one configuration by the other that is characterized by transnational forces including religion and capitalism, "Periodizing the Cold War: The Imperialism of Nation States," a lecture at the Institute of Modern History, Academia Sinica, Taipei (June 22, 2009).

2. See Chia-chia Kuo, *Lisanzhe de zhongguo minzuzhuyi: huayi xue zhe zhao suisheng yu zheng yongnian miandui zhongguo de shenfen celue* (Chinese Diaspora's Nationalism: The Identity Strategies of Chinese Overseas Scholars Zhao Suisheng and Zheng Yongnian in Facing China) (Taipei: The Research and Educational Center for China Studies and Cross Taiwan-Strait Relations, Department of Political Science, National Taiwan University, 2008), 112–116.

3. For a vivid example, see Ray Huang's recollection of his position facing the charge of American imperialism in *Huanghe qingshan* (Yellow River and Blue Mountains) (Taipei: Lien Ching, 2001), 284, 521.

4. Sheng Ding, "Digital Diaspora and National Image Building: A New Perspective on Chinese Diaspora Study in the Age of China's Rise," *Pacific Affairs* 80, 4 (2008): 627–648; Ming-chin Tsai, *Huiyi wen ge: zai chaoyue yu zaixian jian de xuanze shiye* (Revisiting the Cultural Revolution: Taking a Position between Transcendence and Re-presentation) (Taipei: The Research and Educational Center for China Studies and Cross Taiwan-Strait Relations, Department of Political Science, National Taiwan University, 2009), 172–175.

5. Unless otherwise specified, the source is from the interview with Akira Iriye on October 17–18, 2007, at the Research and Educational Center for China Studies and Cross-Strait Relations of the Department of Political Science, National Taiwan University, see http://140.112.150.151/RAEC/act/interviewJ+iriye+1-2.doc, accessed on April 30, 2010.

6. Akira Iriye, "East Asia and the Emergence of Japan, 1900–1945," in Michael Howard and Wm. Roger Louis (eds.), *The Oxford History of the Twentieth Century* (New York: Oxford University Press, 1998), 139–141.

7. Akira Iriye, "Stepping Out: Japan Can Help Shape the Emerging Asia Pacific: Is It Ready?" *The Harvard Asia Pacific Review* 1, 1 (1997): 60.

8. Andrew Linklater and Hidemi Suganami, *The English School of International Relations: A Contemporary Reassessment* (Cambridge: Cambridge University Press, 2006), 192.

9. Himemi Suganami, *The Domestic Analogy and World Order Proposals* (Cambridge: Cambridge University Press, 1989), 156; Linklater and Suganami, 254.

10. Unless otherwise specified, the source is from the interview with Samuel Kim on June 5, 7, 12, 2007, at the Research and Educational Center for China Studies and Cross-Strait Relations of the Department of Political Science, National Taiwan University, see http://140.112.150.151/RAEC/act/Sam20%Kim20%Interviews.doc, accessed on April 30, 2010.

11. Samuel Soonki Kim, *Anson Burlingame: A Study in Personal Diplomacy*, PhD dissertation (Columbia University, 1966).

12. Samuel Kim, *China, the United Nations and World Order* (Princeton: Princeton University, 1979).

13. In the first of the four editions on the state of art in Chinese foreign policy, two of his authors deride that those who cannot analyze, write about the state of art. See Davis B. Babrow and Steven Chan, "On a Slow Boat to Where? Analyzing Chinese Foreign Policy," in Samuel Kim (ed.), *China and the World: Chinese Foreign Policy in the Post-Mao Era* (Boulder: Westview, 1984), 32.

14. David Kang, *China Rising: Peace, Power, and Order in East Asia* (New York: Columbia University Press 2007), 4.

15. Kang, 201.

16. Unless otherwise specified, the source is from the interview with John Wong on November 5–9, 2007, at the Research and Educational Center for China

Studies and Cross-Strait Relations of the Department of Political Science, National Taiwan University, see http://140.112.150.151/RAEC/act/Singapore-1.doc, accessed on April 30, 2010.

17. John Wong, "Southeast Asian Ethnic Chinese Investing in China," *EAI Working Paper* 15, (1999).

18. John Wong, "The Rise of China: Bane or Boon to Southeast Asia," *Harvard Asia Quarterly* (2003): 23–30; John Wong, "China's Economic Rise: Implications for East Asian Growth and Integration," *Bulletin on Asia-Pacific Perspective* (2004/5): 31–44.

19. Yongnian Zheng and John Wong (eds.), *The SARS Epidemic: Challenges to China's Crisis Management* (Singapore and London: World Scientific, 2004).

20. For example, see Yongnian Zheng, "Society Must Be Defended: Reform, Openness and Social Policy in China," *EAI working Papers*, 152, (2009); Yongnian Zheng, *Discovering Chinese Nationalism in China: Modernization, Identity, and International relations* (Cambridge: Cambridge University Press, 1999).

21. Unless otherwise specified, the source is from the interview with John Wong on May 18–20, 2008, at the Research and Educational Center for China Studies and Cross-Strait Relations of the Department of Political Science, National Taiwan University, see http://140.112.150.151/RAEC/act/Singapore-1.doc, accessed on April 30, 2010.

22. John King Fairbank, *Trade and Diplomacy on the China Coast: the Opening of the Treaty Ports* (Cambridge, MA: Harvard University Press, 1964); Samuel Huntington, *The Clash of Civilizations and the Remaking of World Order* (New York: Simon & Schuster, 1996).

23. Tan Chung and Patricia Uberoi (eds.), *The Rise of Asian Giants: The Dragon-Elephant Tango* (New Delhi: Anthem Press, 2009).

24. Tan Chung, "*caiyong diyuan wenming fangshi cujin zhong yin guanxi fazhan*" (Taking a Geo-civilizational Approach to Improving Sino-Indian Relations through), *Nan Ya Yanjiu Jikan* (South Asian Studies Quarterly) 2009, 2, 1–9.

25. Laurent Malvezin, "The Problems with (Chinese) Diaspora: An interview with Wang Gungwu," in Gregor Benton and Hong Liu (eds.), *Diasporic Chinese Ventures, The life and Work of Wang Gungwu* (London: RoutledgeCurzon, 2004), 49–57.

26. David Williams, *Defending Japan's Pacific War: The Kyoto School Philosophers and Post-White Power* (London: Routledge, 2005); Christopher Goto-Jones, *Political Philosophy in Japan: Nishida, the Kyoto School, and Co-Prosperity* (Leiden Series in Modern East Asia) (London: Routledge, 2005).

27. Takeuchi Yoshimi and Richard Calichman, *What Is Modernity? Writings of Takeuchi Yoshimi* (New York: Columbia University Press, 2005), 164–5.

28. Nobukuni Koyasu, "*Kindai no chōkoku" to wa nani ka* (What Is It about Overcoming Modernity) (Tokyo: Seidosha, 2008).

29. See Yuzo Mizoguchi, *Hoho to shite no Chugoku* (China as Method) (Tokyo: Tokyo Daigaku Shuppankai, 1989).

30. For example, Samuel Kim, *The Two Koreas and the Great Powers* (Cambridge: Cambridge University Press, 2006), in which he formally claims a synthetic approach, and *Korea's Democratization* (Cambridge: Cambridge University Press, 2003).

31. Samuel Kim, "China and Globalization: Confronting Myriad Challenges and Opportunities," *Asian Perspective* 33, 3 (2009): 36.

32. Leo Suryadinata, "Chinese Search for National Identity in Southeast Asia: The Last Half Century," in Suryadinata, *Chinese and Nation-Building in Southeast Asia* (Singapore: Singapore Society of Asian Studies, 1997), 15–22; Leo Suryadinata, "Ethnic Chinese in Southeast Asia: Overseas Chinese, Chinese Overseas or Southeast Asians?" in L. Suryadinata (ed.), *Ethnic Chinese as Southeast Asians* (Singapore: ISEAS, 1997), 2–4.

33. Chang-hung Chen and Yuan-ning Yang, *Huayi liqun renshi zhongguo de liangzhong tujing* (Two Diasporic Approaches to China among Chinese Overseas), *Dongnanya xuekan* (Southeast Asian Studies) 6, 2 (2009): 97–138.

34. Tan Chung, *China and Brave New World* (Durham, NC: Carolina Academic Press, 1978).

35. Tan Chung and Ravni Thakur, *Across the Himalayan Gap: An Indian Quest for Understanding China* (New Delhi: Indira Gandhi National Centre for the Arts, 1998).

36. Tan Chung, "*caiyong diyuan wenming fangshi cujin zhong yin guanxi fazhan*" (Taking a Geo-civilizational Approach to Improving Sino-Indian Relations through), *Nan Ya Yanjiu Jikan* (South Asian Studies Quarterly) 2009, 2, 1–9.

37. Among them, the two webs that are most popular with Chinese readers (www.zaobao.com and www.chinareviewniews.com) are probably based in Singapore and Hong Kong, respectively.

38. Liu, Bo and Ma, Juan, "wenming de jiaorong: rang women gengjia xiang hu yilai" (The Fusion of Civilizations: Let Us Depend More on Each Other), 21 *shiji jingji baodao* (The Twenty-First Century Economy on Report) (November 11, 2006), http://view.news.qq.com/a/20061212000023_1.htm, accessed January 20, 2009) Xuan Liu, "guoji wenhuazhuyizhe ru jianzhao: huyu chaoyue guojia de wenming jiaoliu" (International Culturalist Iriye Akira: Calling for Civilizational Exchanges to Transcend Nation-states), *PKU News* (November 6, 2006), http://pkunews.pku.edu.cn/xwzh/2006-11/06/content_110280.htm, accessed on January 6, 2011).

39. Akira Iriye "The Role of Philanthropy and Civil Society in U.S. Foreign Relations," in Yamamoto Tadashi, Akira Iriye, and Iokibe Makoto (eds.), *Philanthropy and Reconciliations: Rebuilding Postwar U.S.—Japan Relations* (Tokyo: Japanese Center for International Exchange, 2006), 38.

40. Samuel Kim, *Korea's Democratization* (Cambridge: Cambridge University Press, 2003), 57.

Conclusion: Serious Hypocrisy

1. Officially, both China's long-held principle of peaceful coexistence and its insistence on nonintervention in the age of globalization testify to resistance against actions taken in the name of liberalism. Intellectually, the Beijing consensus, the China model, the Chongqing model, and so on oppose liberalism by refusing to undertake radical economic reform or political democratization.

2. For a discussion of the politics of China studies in the Anglophone and Sinophone communities, see Geremie R. Barmé, "On New Sinology," http://rspas.anu.edu.au/pah/chinaheritageproject/newsinology/newsinology.php, accessed on April 20, 2010.

3. Alfred H. Bloom, *The Linguistic Shaping of Thought: A Study in the Impact of Language on Thinking in China and the West* (Hillsdale, NJ: Lawrence Erlbaum Associates, 1981), 31–32; E. G. Kim-Rivera, "English Language Education in Korea Under Japanese Colonial Rule," *Language Policy* 3, 1 (2002): 261–281; Elaine Chan, "Beyond Pedagogy: Language and Identity in Post-colonial Hong Kong," *British Journal of Sociology of Education* 23, 2 (2002): 271–285.

4. Boyu Chen, Ching-Chane Hwang, and L. H. M. Ling, 2009, "Lust/Caution in IR: Democratising World Politics with Culture as a Method," *Millennium* 37, 3: 749; Kuan-Hsing Chen, "Why Is 'Great Reconciliation' Impossible? De-Cold War/Decolonization, or Modernity and Its Tears (Parts I-II)," *Inter-Asia Cultural Studies* 3, 1–2 (2002): 79.

5. One version of the mix of these larger forces contains realism, idealism, Confucianism, and Islamism. See Yu-ching Wang, *Tongshi, buguo fenkai: Xifang pubianzhuyi lunshu xia de rujia yu yisilan* (Simultaneity and yet in Separation: Confucianism and Islam in the Western Universalist Narratives) (Taipei: The Research and Educational Center for China Studies and Cross Taiwan-Strait Relations, Department of Political Science, National Taiwan University, 2008). Another version is Korea in between China and Japan, Socialism and Capitalism, and East and West. See Myonsob Kim and Horace Jeffery Hodges, "Korea as a Clashpoint of Civilizations," *Korea Observer* 37, 3 (Autumn 2006): 513–545.

Bibliography

Acharya, Amitav. 2003. "Seeking Security in the Dragon's Shadow: China and Southeast Asia in the Emerging Asian Order," *Working Paper Series* 44, Institute for Defence and Strategic Analysis (March), 5.

Adelman, Jonathan and Chih-yu Shih. 1993. *Symbolic War: The Chinese Use of Force, 1840–1980* (Taipei: Institute of International Relations).

Alagappa, Muthiah. "Managing Asian Security: Competition, Cooperation and Evolutionary Change," in Muthiah Alagappa (ed.), *Asian Security Order: Instrumental and Normative Features* (Stanford, CA: Stanford University Press), 585–586.

Alden, Chris Daniel Large, and Ricardo Soares de Oliveira. 2008. *China Returns to Africa: A Rising Power and a Continent Embrace* (New York: Columbia University Press).

Al-Rodhan, Khalid R. 2007. "A Critique of the China Threat Theory: A Systematic Analysis," *Asian Perspective* 31, 3: 64.

Altantsetseg, Noosgoi. 1985. *Mongolchuud Manjiin esreg erkh chuluunii tuluuh hudulguuniig BNHAU herhen uzej bui ni* (Ulaanbaatar: publisher n.a.).

Altantsetseg, Noosgoi. 2001. *Movement 1911 onii hudulguun BNHAU-iin uzleer* (China's View of 1911) (Ulaanbaatar: publisher n.a.).

Anagnost, Ann. 1997. *National Past-Times: Narrative, Representation, and Power in Modern China (Body, Commodity, Text)* (Durham: Duke University Press).

Askouri, Ali. 2007. "China's Investment in Sudan: Displacing Villages and Destroying Communities," in Firoze Manji and Stephen Marksi (eds.), *African Perspectives on China in Africa* (Cape Town: Fahamu), 73–74.

Author, n.a., "Report B," The Project "Folk Perspectives on State-Society Relations on the Chinese Mainland," sponsored by the NTU Political Science Academic Cultural Foundation (Taipei, 2010–2011).

Author, n.a., "Report D," The Project "Folk Perspectives on State-Society Relations on the Chinese Mainland," sponsored by the NTU Political Science Academic Cultural Foundation (Taipei, 2010–2011).

Author, n.a., "Report J," The Project "Folk Perspectives on State-Society Relations on the Chinese Mainland," sponsored by the NTU Political Science Academic Cultural Foundation (Taipei, 2010–2011).

Author, n.a., "Report Q," The Project "Folk Perspectives on State-Society Relations on the Chinese Mainland," sponsored by the NTU Political Science Academic Cultural Foundation (Taipei, 2010–2011).

Author, n.a., "Report Y," The Project "Folk Perspectives on State-Society Relations on the Chinese Mainland," sponsored by the NTU Political Science Academic Cultural Foundation (Taipei, 2010–2011).

Author, n.a., "Report Z," The Project "Folk Perspectives on State-Society Relations on the Chinese Mainland," sponsored by the NTU Political Science Academic Cultural Foundation (Taipei, 2010–2011).

Baba, Kimihiko. 2002. "Zhanhou Riben luntan Zhongguo guan de bianqian—cong 'shijie' zazhi de xiangguan baodao zhong suo kandaode" (Changing Views on China in the Postwar Japanese Forum—as seen in Related Reports in World Magazine), *Kaifang shidai* (Open Epoch) 5, 66–79.

Babrow, Davis B. and Steven Chan. 1984. "On a Slow Boat to Where? Analyzing Chinese Foreign Policy," in Samuel Kim (ed.), *China and the World: Chinese Foreign Policy in the Post-Mao Era* (Boulder: Westview), 32–56.

Barmé, Geremé. 2008. *The Forbidden City* (Cambridge: Harvard University Press).

Bauer, William. 2012. China: Africa's New Colonial Power http://www.policymic.com/articles/1657/china-africa-s-new-colonial-power, accessed on February 1.

Bayasakh, Jamsran Khereid. 2010. *The Oral History of Bayasakh* (Taipei: The Research and Educational Center for China Studies and Cross Taiwan-Strait Relations, Department of Political Science, National Taiwan University), 1–2, http://politics.ntu.edu.tw/RAEC/act/InterviewM%20Jamsran%20Khereid%20Bayasakh.doc, accessed on April 2, 2012.

Bearak, Barry. 2010. "Zambia Uneasily Balances Chinese Investment and Workers' Resentment, *The New York Times* (November 21): A8.

Bellah, Robert. 1998. *Dechuan zongjiao: xiandai Riben de wenhua yuanyuan* (Tokugawa Religion: The Cultural Roots of Modern Japan), trans., Xiaoshan Wang and Rong Dai (Beijing: Sanlian), 100–103.

Bernstein, Richard and Ross H. Munro. 1998. *The Coming Conflict with China* (New York: Vintage).

Bernstein, Richard and Ross Monroe. 2000. *The Coming Conflict with China*. Denny Roy, "Rising China and U.S. Interests: Inevitable vs. Contingent Hazards," *Orbis* 47, 1: 125–137.

Bhabha, Homi.1993. "The World and the Home," *Social Text* 31–32: 141–153.

Callahan, William. 2004. *A Contingent State: Greater China and Transnational Relations* (Minneapolis: University of Minnesota).

Callahan, William. 2007. A. "Chinese Visions of World Order: Tianxia, Empire and World Order," *International Studies Association (ISA) Annual Conference* paper, Chicago.

Callahan, William. 2009. "Tianxia, Empire and the World: Soft Power and China's Foreign Policy Discourse in the 21st Century," in W. Callahan and E. Barabantseva (eds.), *China Orders the World? Soft Power, Norms and Foreign Policy* (Washington, D.C.: Woodrow Wilson Center Press).

Callahan, William A. 2009. *China: Pessoptimist Nation* (Oxford: Oxford University Press).

Chakrabarth, Dipesh. 2007. *Provincializing Europe: Postcolonial Thought and Historical Difference* (Princeton: Princeton University Press).

Chang, Huan-ching. 2008. Interview conducted by Chi-nien Wang, October 14, October 22, November 19, and December 17, 2008. See http://politics.ntu.edu.tw/RAEC/act/tw-9.doc, accessed on April 20, 2012.

Chang, King-yuh. 2011. Interview conducted by Yuan-ming Yao on various days in July 2008. See http://politics.ntu.edu.tw/RAEC/act/tw-1.doc, accessed on August 29, 2011.

Chang, Parris. 2010. Interview conducted by Hong-lin Yeh, August 12, 18, and 26, 2010, cited in Chih-yu Shih and Chun-liang Pao, "Studying Mainland/China in Taiwan: Politics of Knowledge and Knowledge of Politics," presented at the Conference on Political Science: Retrospect and Prospect, the Institute of Political Science of Academia Sinica, August 7, 2012 (Taipei).

Charlton, Sue Ellen M. Jana Everett and Kathleen Staudt, eds. 1989. *Women, the State and Development* (Albany: State University of New York Press).

Chen. 2008. Philip Ming. Interview conducted by Lu-fan Yeh on various days in October and November. See http://politics.ntu.edu.tw/RAEC/comm2/ChenMing.doc, accessed on August 22, 2011.

Chen, Chang-hung and Yuan-ning Yang. 2009. *Huayi liqun renshi zhongguo de liangzhong tujing* (Two Diasporic Approaches to China among Chinese Overseas), *Dongnanya xuekan* (Southeast Asian Studies) 6, 2: 97–138.

Chen, Chih-Jou Jay. 2004. *Transforming Rural China: How Local Institutions Shape Property Rights in China* (London and New York: Routledge).

Chen, Chih-Jou Jay. 2007. *Transforming Rural China* (London: Taylor & Francis).

Chen, Guo-Ming and W. J. Starosta. 2003. "On Theorizing Difference: Culture as Centrism," *International and Intercultural Communication Annual* 26, 277–287.

Chen, Peng-Jen. 2011. Interview conducted by Hsuan-lei Shao and Li-ben Wang, January 2, cited in Shih and Pao, "Studying Mainland/China in Taiwan: Politics of Knowledge and Knowledge of Politics," presented at the Conference on Political Science: Retrospect and Prospect, the Institute of Political Science of Academia Sinica, August 7, 2012 (Taipei).

Chen, Wei-fen. 2006. "Riben guanyu "dongya" de sikao" (Japanese reflections on "East Asia"), *Sixiang (Thoughts) 3*, (Taipei: Lian-ching).

Chen, Yu-wen. 2012. "Xinjiang 13 Revisited," *Asian Ethnicity* 13, 1: 111–113.

Cheng, Lucie. 2008. Interview conducted by Chia-yi Wen, March 28. See http://politics.ntu.edu.tw/RAEC/act/tw-2.doc, accessed on August 28, 2011.

Cheng, Yinghong. 2011. "From Campus Racism to Cyber Racism: Discourse of Race and Chinese Nationalism," *The China Quarterly* 207, 561–579.

Chiang, Hsin-li. Interview conducted by Hsin-wei Tang, September 16, November 18, and December 23, 2008. See http://politics.ntu.edu.tw/RAEC/act/tw-6.doc, accessed on August 28, 2011.

Chow, Rey. 1991. *Woman and Chinese Modernity: The Politics of Reading between West and East* (Minneapolis: University of Minnesota).

Chun, Hae-jong. 1966. "Han-Jung jogong gwangye go" (A Historical Survey of the Sino-Korean Tributary Relationship), *Dongyangsahak* 1, 10–41.

Chun, Hae-jong. 1968. "Hankook gwa Jungkook: Han-Jung gwangyesa doroneui ilcheok" (Some Notes on the History of the Sino-Korean Relationship), *Dongbanghakji* 9, 1–19.

Chun, Hae-jong. 1968. "Sino Korean Tributary Relations in the Ch'ing Period," in John K. Fairbank (ed.), *The Chinese World Order: Traditional China's Foreign Relations* (Cambridge, MA: Harvard University Press).

Chun, Hae-jong. 1973. "Handaeeui Jogong jedoae daehan ilgochal" (A Study on the Tribute System in the Former Han Dynasty), *Dongyangsahakyeongu* 6: 1–15.

Chun, Hae-jong. 1975. "Donga godaemunwhaeui Joongsimgwa jubyeonae daehan shiron" (Civilization's Center and Peripheries in Premodern East Asian History), *Dongyangsahakyeongu* 8: 1–23.

Chung Yong-hwa. 2006. "Chosuneui Jogong Cheje Inshikgwa hwalyong" (Chosun Dynasty's Perception and Utilization of the Tribute System), *Hankookjeongchioegyosanonchong* 27, 2: 5–31.

Cohen, Paul A. 1984. *Discovering History in China: American Historical Writing on the Recent Chinese Past* (New York: Columbia University Press).

Commentary Department. 2011. *Renmin Ribao*, "Bie rang gan qun guanxi chuxian minyi chizi" (Do not allow a public opinion deficit to emerge) (January 6), http://opinion.people.com.cn/GB/13664139.html, accessed on March 12, 2012.

Commentary Department. 2011. *Renmin Ribao*, "Cadre Style Is the Lifeline of Their Public Credibility" (March 17), http://theory.people.com.cn/GB/14163183.html, accessed on March 12, 2012.

Commentary Department. 2011. *Renmin Ribao*, "Rang liyi ganggan qiaojie she-hui maodun" (Apply the lever of interest to opening up social contradictions) (April 14), http://opinion.people.com.cn/GB/40604/14221209.html, accessed on March 12, 2012 (already deleted from the people.com webpage).

Commentary Department. 2011. *Renmin Ribao*, "Yi baorong xin duidai yizhi siwei" (Treat heterogeneous thinking with a tolerant attitude) (April 28), http://opinion.people.com.cn/GB/14505701.html, accessed on March 12, 2012.

Commentator. 1990. *Zhong gong zhongyang guanyu jiaqiang dang tong renmin qunzhong lianxi de jueding* (The CCP Central Committee's Decision on Strengthening the Party's Ties with the Masses of the People) (Shanghai: New China Bookstore).

Commentator. 1997. "Damages Sought by Victims of Biological Warfare in China" *The Japan Times* (August 11).

Commentator. 1997. "Defense Agency Urges Crisis-response Legislation" *The Japan Times* (July 15).

Commentator. 1997. "Fisheries Talks with China to Start" *The Japan Times* (August 18).

Commentator. 1997. "Foreign Ministry Goes Through Post Reshuffle" *The Japan Times* (July 29).

Commentator. 1997. "Hashimoto to Visit War Museum during China Trip" *The Japan Times* (August 4).

Commentator. 1997. "Japan, China Open Fisheries Negotiations" *The Japan Times* (August 6)

Commentator. 1997. "Overseas A-bomb Victims Seek Equality" *The Japan Times* (July 8).

Commentator. 1997. "Supreme Court Backs Ienaga in Textbook Suit" *The Japan Times* (August 29).

Commentator. 1997. "Youths Learn about Horror of Nuclear War" *The Japan Times* (August 4)

Commentator. 2007. "Beijing Seeks 450 Billion Yen in Loans for Infrastructure" (August 4).

Commentator. 2007. "Confrontation Over Darfur 'Will Lead Us Nowhere'," *China Daily* (July 27), http://www.chinadaily.com.cn/2008/2007-07/27/content_5445062.htm, accessed on January 29, 2012.

Corcuff, Stephane, ed. 2002. *Memories of the Future: National Identity Issues and the Search for a New Taiwan* (Armonk, NY: M. E. Sharpe).

Cummings, Bruce. 1997. "Boundary Displacement: Area Studies and International Studies During and After the Cold War," *Bulletin of Concerned Asian Scholars* 29, 1 (Jan – Mar): 6–27.

Deng, Xiaoping. 2004. *Deng Xiaoping nianpu: 1975–1997* (The Chronicles of Deng Xiaoping: 1975–1997) 2 (Beijing: The CCP Research Department on Literature), 1122, 1227.

Deng, Xiaoping. 2011. *Gezhi zhengyi gongtong kaifa qianti zhuquan zai wo* (Shelfing Disputes to jointly Develop Is Premised Upon Our Sovereign Rightshttp://www.chinareviewnews.com/doc/1015/6/2/9/101562905_3.html?coluid=6&kindid=26&docid=101562905&mdate=0107094837, accessed on April 20, 2012.

Deng, Yong. 2008. *China's Struggle for Status: The Realignment of International Relations* (Cambridge: Cambridge University Press).

Diamant, Neil. J. Stanley B. Lubman, and Kevin J. O'Brien, eds. 2005. *Engaging the Law in China: State, Society and Possibilities for Justice* (Stanford, CA: Stanford University Press).

Diesing, Paul. 1992. *How Does Social Science Work? Reflections on Practice* (Pittsburgh: University of Pittsburgh Press).

Diesing, Paul and Richard Hartwig. 2005. *Science and Ideology in the Policy Sciences* (Piscataway, NJ: Aldine Transaction).

Ding, Sheng. 2008. "Digital Diaspora and National Image Building: A New Perspective on Chinese Diaspora Study in the Age of China's Rise," *Pacific Affairs* 80, 4: 627–648.

Dittmer, Lowell and Yu-shan Wu. 2006. "Leadership Coalitions and Economic Transformation in Reform China: Revisiting the Political Business," in Lowell Dittmer and Guoli Liu (eds.), *China's Deep Reform: Domestic Politics in Transition* (Lanham, MD: Rowman & Littlefield).

Duara, Prasenjit. 2009. *Periodizing the Cold War: The Imperialism of Nation States* (Taipei: A Lecture at the Institute of Modern History, Academia Sinica) (June 22).

Duong, Danh Huy. 2011. " 'Setting Aside Dispute, Pursuing Joint Development' the Chinese Way," *Vietnamnet Bridge* (November 7) http://english.vietnamnet.

vn/en/politics/10482/-setting-aside-dispute—pursuing-joint-development—the-chinese-way.html, accessed on November 12, 2011.

Editor. 1964. "Symposium on Chinese Studies and the Discipline," *Journal of Asian Studies* 23, 4 (August): 505–538.

Editor. 1975. "The Special Issue on China's Economic Strategy," *Monthly Review* 27, 3

Editor. 1978. "The Special Issue on China Since Mao," *Monthly Review* 30, 3.

Editor. 2011. "Records of Jeune Afrique's Interview with Director-General Lu Shaye," http://www.focac.org/eng/zxxx/t885029.htm, accessed on February 1.

Editorial. 2012. "ba Feilubin dang chutouniao chengfa" (Punishing the Philippines as the Head Sticking Out), *Huanqiu shibao* (Global Times) (January 30), http://opinion.huanqiu.com/roll/2012-01/2385629.html, accessed on January 25, 2012.

Erdene, Myagmar. 2010. "Comparative Cranial Nonmetric Study of Archaeological Populations from Inner Asia," *Mongolian Journal of Anthropology, Archaeology and Ethnology* 4, 1: 184–212.

Evenden, Martin and Gregory Sandstrom. 2011. "Calling for Scientific Revolution in Psychology: K. K. Hwang on Indigenous Psychologies," *Social Epistemology* 25, 2 (April): 153–166.

Fairbank, John K., ed. 1968. *The Chinese World Order: Traditional China's Foreign Relations* (Cambridge, MA: Harvard University Press).

Fairbank, John King. 1964. *Trade and Diplomacy on the China Coast: the Opening of the Treaty Ports* (Cambridge, MA: Harvard University Press).

Fei, Xiaotong. 1998. "Zhonghua minzu de duoyuan yiti geju" (The Structure of Pluralistic Integration of the Chinese Nation), *Beijing daxue xuebao* 4 (1989): 1–11.

Fitzgerald, John. *Awakening China: Politics, Culture and Class in the Nationalist Revolution* (Stanford, CA: Stanford University Press).

Fogel, Joshua. 1984. *Politics and Sinology: The Case of Naito Konan, 1866–1934* (Cambridge, MA: Harvard University Press).

Fogel, Joshua A. 1996. *The Literature of Travel in the Japanese Rediscovery of China, 1862–1945* (Stanford, CA: Stanford University Press).

Fravel, M. Taylor. 2008. *Strong Borders, Secure Nation: Cooperation and Conflict in China's Territorial Disputes* (Princeton: Princeton University Press).

Friedman, Edward. 1995. *National Identity and Democratic Prospects in Socialist China* (Armonk: M. E. Sharpe).

Fukuzawa, Yukichi. 2006. *Fuze Yuji zizhuan: yige yingxiang Riben jindaihua zhiju de wan tong* ([The Autobiography of] Fukuzawa Yukichi: a Disobedient Child who Greatly Influenced Japan's Modernization), trans. Yong-lian Yang (Taipei: Maitian).

Ge, Zhaoguang. 2002. "Jiulingniandai Riben Zhongguo xue de xin guannian: du Goukou Xiongsan de zuo wei fangfa de Zhongguo" (The New Approach to China in Japan in the 1990: Reading Mizoguchi Yuzo's China as Method), in Zhaoguang Ge (eds.), *Yuwai Zhongguo xue shi lun* (Ten Theses on China Studies Overseas) (Shanghai: Fudan University Press), 16–31.

Gill, Bates and James Reilly. 2007. "The Tenuous Hold of China Inc. in Africa," *The Washington Quarterly* 37.

Goldman, Merle. 2007. *From Comrade to Citizen: The Struggle for Political Rights in China* (Cambridge, MA: Harvard University Press).

Gomà, Daniel. 2006. "The Chinese-Korean Border Issue: An Analysis of a Contested Frontier," *Asian Survey* 46, 6 (Nov – Dec): 867–880.

Goodman, David and Gerald Segal. 1995. *China Deconstructs: Politics, Trade and Regionalism* (London: Routledge).

Goto-Jones, Christopher. 2005. *Political Philosophy in Japan: Nishida, the Kyoto School, and Co-prosperity* (Leiden Series in Modern East Asia) (London: Routledge).

Gottlieb, Thomas. 1977. *Chinese Foreign Policy Factionalism and the Origins of the Strategic Triangle, Rand Report R-1902-NA* (Santa Monica: Rand Corporation).

Government Information Office. 2011. *China's Foreign Policies for Pursuing Peaceful Development*, http://english.gov.cn/official/2011-09/06/content_1941354_4.htm, accessed on September 8, 2011.

Gries, Peter. 2005. *China's New Nationalism: Pride, Politics, and Diplomacy* (Berkeley: University of California Press).

Guo, Baogang and He Li, eds. 2011. *The Chinese Labyrinth: Exploring China's Model of Development* (Lanham, MD: Lexington Books).

Haglund, Dan. 2009. "In It for the Long Term? Governance and Learning among Chinese Investors in Zambia's Copper Sector," *The China Quarterly* 199 (September): 643.

Halper, Stefan. 2009. *The Beijing Consensus: How China's Authoritarian Model Will Dominate the Twenty-First Century* (New York: Basic Books, 2010).

Halper, Stefan. 2012. *The Beijing Consensus: Legitimizing Authoritarianism in Our Time* (New York: Basic Books).

Hamashita, Takeshi. 1988. *The Tribute Trade System and Modern Asia* (Tokyo: Memoirs of the Research Department of the Toyo Bunko).

Hamashita, Takeshi. 2002. "Tribute and Treaties: East Asian Treaty Ports Networks in the Era of Negotiation, 1834–1894," *European Journal of East Asian Studies* 1, 1: 59–87.

Hansen, Mette Halskov. 1999. *Lessons in Being Chinese* (Seattle: University of Washington).

Harding, Harry. 1984. "The Study of Chinese Politics: Toward a Third Generation of Scholarship," *World Politics* 36, 2 (January): 284–307.

Harding, Sandra. 1998. *Is Science Multicultural? Postcolonialisms, Feminisms, and Epistemologies* (Bloomington: Indiana University Press).

Harrison, Lawrence E. and Samuel Huntington, eds. 2001. *Culture Matters: How Values Shape Human Progress* (New York: Basic Books).

Hau, Caroline S. 2004. *On the Subject of the Nation: Filipino Writings from the Margins, 1981–2004* (Quezon City: Ateneo De Manila University Press).

Hau, Caroline. 2011. *Becoming "Chinese" in China and Southeast Asia*, Paper Presented at the International Workshop on Sinicization, Beijing (March 25–26).

Haugen, Heidi Østbø and Jørgen Carling. 2005. "On the Edge of the Chinese Diaspora: The Surge of Baihuo Business in an African City," *Ethnic and Racial Studies* 28, 4: 647.

He, Baogang. 2011. "The Dilemmas of China's Political Science in the Context of the Rise of China," *Journal of Chinese Political Science* 16, 2: 257–277.

He, Henry Yuhuai. 2001. *Dictionary of the Political Thought of the People's Republic of China* (Armonk: M. E. Sharpe), 26.

He, Wenping. 2002. "China and Africa: Cooperation in Fifty Stormy Years," *Asia and Africa Today* (Russian Academy of Sciences) 12.

He, Wenping. 2007. "The Balancing Act of China's Africa Policy," *China Security* 3, 3: 29.

Herré, Ron. 1972. *The Philosophies of Science: An Introductory Survey* (New York: Oxford University Press), 65.

Higgins, Andrew. 2011. "Oil Interests Push China into Sudanese Mire," *The Washington Post* (December 24), http://www.washingtonpost.com/world/asia_pacific/oil-interests-push-china-into-sudanese-mire/2011/12/19/gIQANkzGGP_story.html, accessed on March 10, 2012.

Ho, Peter. 2005. *Institutions in Transition: Land Ownership, Property Rights and Social Conflict in China* (Oxford: Oxford University Press).

Hoare-Vance, Stephen. 2010. *The Confucius Institutes and China's Evolving Foreign Policy* (Saarbrücken: LAP Academic Publishing).

Hsiao, Hsing-yi. 2008. Interview conducted by Chung-ben Bai and Hsuan-lei Shao, March 29, April 5, April 10, and April 19. See http://politics.ntu.edu.tw/RAEC/comm2/HisaoHsinI.doc, accessed on August 20, 2011.

Hsieh, Jiann. 2009. Interview conducted by Hsin-wei Tang, August 11, 13, and 26. See http://politics.ntu.edu.tw/RAEC/act/tw-121.doc, accessed on August 21, 2011.

Hsiung, James Chieh. 2009. Interview conducted by Chung-ben Bai and Hsuan-lei Shao, March 16. See http://politics.ntu.edu.tw/RAEC/act/interviewU熊玠.doc, accessed on August 29, 2011.

Hsu, Chieh-lin. 2009. Interview conducted by Li-ch'en Chen, April 24, June 10, and July 13. See http://politics.ntu.edu.tw/RAEC/act/tw-7.doc, accessed on August 19, 2011.

Hsu, Elisabeth. 2002. "The Medicine from China Has Rapid Effects: Patients of Traditional Chinese Medicine in Tanzania," in Elisabeth Hsu and Erling Høg, "Countervailing Creativity: Patient Agency in the Globalisation of Asian Medicines," special issue, *Anthropology and Medicine* 9, 3: 205–363.

Hsu, S. Philip, Yu-shan Wu, and Suisheng Zhao, eds. 2011. *In Search of China's Development Model: Beyond the Beijing Consensus* (London: Routledge).

Hsu, Sichian. 2004. "Zhongguo dalu zhengzhi gaige de zhengyi: yige wenxian de huigu" (Debate on China's Reform: A Literature Review), *Zhongguo dalu yanjiu* (Mainland China Studies) 47, 1.

Hsu, Philip S.C. 2009. "In Search of Public Accountability: The 'Wenling Model' in China," *Australian Journal of Public Administration* 68, 1 (March): 40–50.

Hu, Jintao. 2005. "Build Towards a Harmonious World of Lasting Peace and Common Prosperity," Statement by President of the People's Republic of China At the United Nations Summit, New York (September 15).

Hu, Jintao. 2008. See http://big5.xinhuanet.com/gate/big5/news.xinhuanet.com/ziliao/2006-08/24/content_5000866.htm, accessed on March 13.

Hu, Jintao. 2011. "Zai qingzhu Zhongguo gongchandang chengli jiushi zhounian dahui shang de jianghua" (Speech at the ceremony to celebrate the 90th anniversary of the Chinese Communist Party), *Xinhua Net* (July 1) http://big5.xinhuanet.com/gate/big5/news.xinhuanet.com/politics/2011-07/01/c_121612030.htm, accessed on March 10, 2012.

Hu, Xiaobao. 1998. *Problems in China's Transitional Economy: Property Rights and Transitional Models* (Singapore: World Scientific Pub. Co. Inc.).

Huang, Chun-chieh. 2006. "Lun Zhongguo jingdian zhong 'Zhongguo' gainian de hanyi ji qi zai jinshi Riben yu xiandai Taiwan de zhuanhua" (The Idea of "Zhongguo" and its Transformation in Early Modern Japan and Contemporary Taiwan), *Taiwan Journal of East Asian Studies* (*Taiwan dongya wenming yanjiu xuekan*) 3, 2: 91–100.

Huang, (Mab) Mo. 2010. Interview conducted by Chih-chieh Chou and Pi-chun Chang, February 26 and May 7.

Huang, Chun-chieh. 2011. "On the Interaction between Confucian Knowledge and Political Power in Traditional China and Korea: A Historical Overview," *Taiwan Journal of East Asian Studies* 8, 1 (Issue 15 June): 1–19.

Huang, Ray. 1975. *Taxation and Governmental Finance in Sixteenth-century Ming China* (Cambridge: Cambridge University Press).

Huang, Ray. 1991. *Dibei tiannan xu gujin* (Narrating the Past and the Contemporary between the Earth in the North and the Heaven in the South) (Taipei: Lien Ching), 81.

Huang, Ray. 2001. *Shiliu shiji Zhongguo Mingdai de caizheng yu shuishou* (Chinese version of *Taxation and Governmental Finance in Sixteenth-century Ming China*) (Taipei: Lien Ching), 572.

Huang, Ray. 2004. *Da lishi buhui weisuo* (The Grand History Will Not Atrophy) (Taipei: Lian Ching).

Hui, Victoria Tin-bor. 2005. *War and State Formation in Ancient China and Early Modern Europe* (Cambridge: Cambridge University Press).

Huntington, Samuel. 1993. "The Clash of Civilizations," *Foreign Affairs* 72, 3 (Summer): 22–49.

Huntington, Samuel. 1996. *The Clash of Civilizations and the Remaking of World Order* (New York: Simon& Schuster).

Hwang, Kwang-kuo. 1995. *Easternization: Socio-cultural Impact on Productivity* (Tokyo: Asian Productivity Organization).

Hwang, Kwang-kuo. 2011. "Reification of Culture in Indigenous Psychology: Merit or Mistake?" *Social Epistemology* 25, 2: 125–131.

Hwang, Shiow-duan. 2008. "Book Review," *Taiwan minzhu jikan* (Taiwan Democracy Quarterly) 5, 2 (June): 181–186.

Information Office of the State Council of the People's Republic of China. 2009. White papers of, *Zhongguo de minzu zhengce yu ge minzu de gongtong fanrong fazhan* (China's Ethnic Policy and Common Prosperity and Development of All Ethnic Groups) (Beijing: Foreign Language Press).

Information Office of the State Council. 2011. *China's Peaceful Development*, Information Office of the State Council (September 6).

Iriye, Akira, ed. 1980. *The Chinese and the Japanese: Essays in Political and Cultural Interactions* (Princeton, NJ: Princeton University Press).

Iriye, Akira. 1997. "Stepping Out: Japan can help Shape the Emerging Asia Pacific: Is it Ready?" *The Harvard Asia Pacific Review* 1, 1: 60.

Iriye, Akira. 1998. "East Asia and the Emergence of Japan, 1900–1945," in Michael Howard and Wm. Roger Louis (eds.), *The Oxford History of the Twentieth Century* (New York: Oxford University Press), 139–141.

Iriye, Akira. 2006. "The Role of Philanthropy and Civil Society in U.S. Foreign Relations," in Yamamoto Tadashi, Akira Iriye, and Iokibe Makoto (eds.), *Philanthropy and Reconciliations: Rebuilding Postwar U.S.–Japan Relations* (Tokyo: Japanese Center for International Exchange), 38.

Iriye, Akira. 2007. Interview with on October 17–18, at the Research and Educational Center for China Studies and Cross-Strait Relations of the Department of Political Science, National Taiwan University, See http://140.112.150.151/RAEC/act/interviewJ+iriye+1-2.doc, accessed on April 30, 2010.

Jacques, Martin. 2005. "The Middle Kingdom Mentality," *Guardian* (April 16), http://www.guardian.co.uk/world/2005/apr/16/china.usa, accessed on March 6, 2012.

Jacques, Martin. 2009. *When China Rules the World: The End of the Western World and the Birth of a New Global Order* (New York: The Penguin Press).

Jin, Taeha. 2008. *The Oral History of Jin Taeha* (Taipei: The Research and Educational Center for China Studies and Cross Taiwan-Strait Relations, Department of Political Science, National Taiwan University), http://politics.ntu.edu.tw/RAEC/comm2/InterviewTaehaJin_C.doc, accessed on April 26, 2011.

Johnston, Alastair Iain. 1995. *Cultural Realism* (Princeton: Princeton University Press).

Johnston, Alastair Iain. 2007. *Social States: China in International Institutions, 1980–2000* (Princeton: Princeton University Press).

Jurczyk, Karlin. 1989. "Time in Women's Everyday Lives: Between Self-determination and Conflicting Demands," *Time and Society* 7, 2: 283–308.

Kakuzo, Okakura. 1903. *The Ideals of the East with Special Reference to the Arts of Japan* (London: John Murray).

Kang, David. 2007. *China Rising: Peace, Power, and Order in East Asia* (New York: Columbia University Press), 4.

Kang, David. 2010. "Civilization and State Formation in the Shadow of China," in Peter J. Katzenstein (ed.), *Civilizations in World Politics: Plural and Pluralist Perspectives* (London and New York: Routledge).

Katzenstein, Peter. 2006. "China's Rise: Return, Rupture or Recombination?" in Peter Katzenstein and Takashi Shiraishi (eds.), *Beyond Japan, the Dynamics of East Asian Regionalism* (Ithaca: Cornell University).

Katzenstein, Peter. 2010. "A World of Plural and Pluralist Civilizations: Multiple Actors, Traditions and Practices," in Peter J. Katzenstein (ed.), *Civilizational Politics in World Affairs: Plural and Pluralist Perspectives* (New York: Routledge), 1–40.

Katzenstein, Peter, ed. 2012 *Sinicization and the Rise of China: Civilizational Processes beyond East and West* (London: Routledge).

Kim, Samuel Soonki. 1966. *Anson Burlingame: A Study in Personal Diplomacy*, Ph.D. dissertation, Columbia University, New York.

Kim, Samuel. 1979. *China, the United Nations and World Order* (Princeton: Princeton University)

Kim, Samuel S., ed. 1984. *China and the World: Chinese Foreign Policy in the Post-Mao Era* (Boulder: Westview Press).

Kim, Samuel S., ed. 1989. *China and the World: New Directions in Chinese Foreign Relations* (Boulder: Westview Press).

Kim, Samuel S., ed. 1994. *China and the World: Chinese Foreign Relations in the Post-Cold War Era* (Boulder: Westview Press).

Kim, Samuel. 2003. *Korea's Democratization* (Cambridge: Cambridge University Press), 57.

Kim, Samuel. 2006. *The Two Koreas and the Great Powers* (Cambridge: Cambridge University Press).

Kim, Samuel. 2009. "China and Globalization: Confronting Myriad Challenges and Opportunities," *Asian Perspective* 33, 3: 36.

Kim, Samuel. Interview with Samuel Kim on June 5, 7, 12, 2007 at the Research and Educational Center for China Studies and Cross-Strait Relations of the Department of Political Science, National Taiwan University, See http://140.112.150.151/RAEC/act/Sam20%Kim20%Interviews.doc, accessed on April 30, 2010.

Kim, Samuel S., ed. 1998 *China and the World: Chinese Foreign Policy Faces the New Millennium* (Boulder: Westview Press).

Koyasu, Nobukumi. 2004. *Dong ya lun: Riben xiandai sixiang pipan* (The Thesis on East Asia: a Critique on Japanese Contemporary Thought), trans. Jinghua Zhao (Changchun: Jilin People's Press), 27–28.

Koyasu, Nobukuni. 2004. *Dong ya lun: Riben xiandai sixiang pipan* (Theses on East Asia: a Critique on Japanese Modern Thought) trans. J. Zhao (Changchun: Jilin People's Press), 18.

Koyasu, Nobukuni. 2008. *"Kindai no chōkoku" to wa nani ka* (What Is It about Overcoming Modernity) (Tokyo: Seidosha).

Koyasu, Nomukumi. 2002. "Zuowei shijian de Chulai xue: sixiang shi fangfa de zai cikao" (The Scholarship of Ogyu Sorai as an Event: Re-reflections on the Method of Thought History), *Taida lishi xuebao* (NTU History Journal) 29 (June): 182.

Kozyra, Agnieszka. 2007. "Nishida Kitaro's Logic of Absolutely Contradictory Self-identity and the Problem of Orthodoxy in the Zen Tradition." *Japan Review* 20: 69–110.

Kuo, Chia-chia. 2001. *Lisanzhe de zhongguo minzuzhuyi: huayi xue zhe zhao Suisheng yu zheng yongnian miandui zhongguo de shenfen celue* (Chinese Diaspora's Nationalism: The Identity Strategies of Chinese Overseas Scholars Zhao Suisheng and Ray Huang's Recollection of his Position Facing the Charge of American Imperialism). in *Huanghe qingshan* (Yellow River and Blue Mountains) (Taipei: Lien Ching), 284, 521.

Kuo, Chia-chia. 2008. *Lisanzhe de Zhongguo minzuzhuyi: hua yi xuezhe Zhao Suisheng, Zheng Yongnian miandui Zhongguo de shenfen celue* (Diasporic Chinese Nationalism: Identity Strategies of Overseas Chinese Scholars Zhao Suisheng and Zheng Yongnian Facing China) (Taipei: The Research and Educational Center for China Studies and Cross Taiwan-Strait Relations, Department of Political Science, National Taiwan University).

Kuo, Tai-chun and Ramon H. Myers. 1986. *Understanding Communist China: Communist China Studies in the United States and the Republic of China, 1949–1978* (Stanford: The Hoover Institution Press).

Kurlantizick, Joshua. 2008. *Charm Offensive: How China's Soft Power Is Transforming the World* (New Haven: Yale University Press).

Large, Daniel. 2008. "Beyond 'Dragon in the Bush': The Study of China-Africa Relations," *African Affairs* 107/426: 60.

Latham, Michael E. 2000. *Modernization as Ideology: American Social Science and "Nation Building" in the Kennedy Era* (Chapel Hill: University of North Carolina Press).

Lavelle, Pierre. 1994. "The Political Thought of Nishida Kitaro," *Monumenta Nipponica* 49: 2: 139–165.

Lee, Choon-shik. 1969. "Jogongeui giwongwa geu euimi" (On a tribute—its origin and significance), *GukjeJoongkukhankyeongu* 10: 1–21.

Lee, (Leo) Ou-fan. 2008. Interview conducted by Te-hsing Shan, Hsiao-yan Peng, Chia-yi Wen, and Albert Tseng, May 18 and 19. See http://politics.ntu.edu.tw/RAEC/act/interviewU李歐梵.doc, accessed on August 22, 2011.

Lee, Pak K. Gerald Chan, and Lai-ha Chan. 2008. "China's 'Realpolitik' Engagement with Myanmar," *China Security* 13, http://www.chinasecurity.us/index.php?option=com_content&view=article&id=224&Itemid=8#lcc8, accessed on March 12, 2012.

Lee, Steve. 2009. *Malaixiya Guanghua Ribao de Zhongguo renshi: zai huaren yu huaqiao liang zhong shenfen zhi jian* (The Malaysian Kwong Wah Newspapers' View of China: Between the Chinese Overseas and Guest Chinese) (Taipei: The Research and Educational Center for China Studies and Cross Taiwan-Strait Relations, Department of Political Science, National Taiwan University).

Lemos, Anabela A. and Daniel Ribeiro. "Taking Ownership or Just Changing Owners?" in Manji and Marks, 64, 69.

Leng, Tse-Kang and Yun-Han Chu, eds. 2010. *Dynamics of Local Governance in China During the Reform Era* (Lanham, MD: Lexington Books, 2010).

Leo, Suryadinata. 1997. "Chinese Search for National Identity in Southeast Asia: The Last Half Century," in L. Suryadinata (ed.), *Chinese and Nation-building in Southeast Asia* (Singapore: Singapore Society of Asian Studies, 1997), 15–22.

Leo, Suryadinata. 1997. "Ethnic Chinese in Southeast Asia: Overseas Chinese, Chinese Overseas or Southeast Asians?" in L. Suryadinata (ed.), *Ethnic Chinese as Southeast Asians* (Singapore: ISEAS, 1997), 2–4.

Leo, Suryadinata. 1998. "Anti-Chinese Riots in Indonesia Perennial Problem But Major Disaster Unlikely." *Straits Times* (February 25): 36.

Leo, Suryadinata. 2007. *Understanding the Ethnic Chinese in Southeast Asia* (Singapore: Institute of Southeast Asian Studies).

Leu, Siew Ying. 2007. "Guangzhou Residents at Odds with Increase in Foreigners," *South China Morning Post* (February 22), http://archive.scmp.com/showarticles. php, accessed on February 3, 2012.

Li, Chan. 1992. *Shijie xinwen shi* (The world's history of news reporting) (Taipei: Sanmin Bookstore), 808, 867; http://tw.knowledge.yahoo.com/question/ ?qid=1205071801848, accessed on May 8, 2007.

Li, Kuo-chi. 2010. Interview conducted by Chih-chieh Chou and Pi-chun Chang, August 26. See http://politics.ntu.edu.tw/RAEC/comm2/LiGuoQi.doc, accessed on August 29, 2011.

Li, Peter Nan-hsiong. 2008. Interview conducted by Chun-liang Pao, September 5. See http://politics.ntu.edu.tw/RAEC/act/tw-3.doc, accessed on August 19, 2011.

Li, Xiguang. 1998/9. "The Inside Story of the Demonization of China," *Contemporary Chinese Thought* 30, 2 (Winter): 13–77.

Li, You-tan and Chien-ming Chao. 2003. "Transition in a Party-State System— Taiwan's Democratization as a Model for China," presented at the international conference, "The Chinese Communist Party in a New Era: Renewal and Reform," Singapore (December 9–10).

Liang, Shoude. 1996. "Maixiang 21 shiji de shijie yu Zhongguoren duiwai jiaowang yuanze de tantao" (Stepping into the 21st century and exploring the principles of Chinese external relations), presented at the conference on the Chinese Stepping into the 21st Century, Taipei (June 6).

Lin, Nan. 2007. *Social Capital and the Labor Market: Transforming Urban China* (New York: Cambridge University Press).

Ling, Lily. 2002. *Postcolonial International Relations: Conquest and Desire Between Asia and the West* (London: Palgrave Macmillan).

Ling, Zhijun and Licheng Ma. 1998. *Jiao feng: Dangdai zhongguo san ci sixiang jiefang shilu* (Cross Fire: The Three Thought Liberations of Contemporary China on the Record) (Beijing: China Today).

Linklater, Andrew and Hidemi Suganami. 2006. *The English School of International Relations: A Contemporary Reassmessment* (Cambridge: Cambridge University Press), 192.

Liu, Bo and Juan Ma. 2006. "wenming de jiaorong: rang women gengjia xiang hu yilai" (The Fusion of Civilizations: Let Us Depend More on Each Other), 21 *shiji jingji baodao* (The 21st Century Economy on Report) (11 November), http://view. news.qq.com/a/20061212000023_1.htm, accessed on January 20, 2009).

Liu, Ping. 2004. *Jintian Zuoyouji yanjiu* (A study of Tsuda Soukichi) (Beijing: Chunghua Bookstore).

Liu, Shan and Jundu Xue, eds. 1998. *New Analysis of Chinese Foreign Affairs* (Beijing: World Affairs Press).

Liu, Shu-hsien. 2009. Interview conducted by Yuan-kui Chu, September 2. See http://politics.ntu.edu.tw/RAEC/act/tw-14.doc, accessed on August 28, 2011.

Liu, Xuan. 2006. "guoji wenhuazhuyizhe ru jianzhao: huyu chaoyue guojia de wenming jiaoliu" (International Culturalist Iriye Akira: Calling for Civilizational Exchanges to Transcend Nation-states), *PKU News* (November 6), http://pkunews. pku.edu.cn/xwzh/2006-11/06/content_110280.htm, accessed on January 6, 2011).

Liu, Yawei and Justin R. Zheng. 2011. "The Rise of China and Its Consequences," *The 9th Annual APSA Pre-conference on Political Communication* (August 31).

Madsen, Richard. 1986. *Morality and Power in a Chinese Village* (Berkeley: University of California Press).

Mahoney, James. 2001. "Beyond Correlational Analysis: Recent Innovations in Theory and Method," *Sociological Forum* 16, 3: 575–593.

Makeeve, Vasily V., ed. 2005. *China: Threats, Risks, Challenges to Development* (in Russian) (Moscow: Carnegie Moscow Center).

Malvezin, Laurent. 2004. "The Problems with (Chinese) Diaspora: An interview with Wang Gungwu," in Gregor Benton and Hong Liu (eds.), *Diasporic Chinese Ventures, The life and work of Wang Gungwu* (London: RoutledgeCurzon), 49–57.

Mancall, Mark. 1984. *China at the Center: 300 Years of Foreign Policy* (New York: Free Press).

Marcus, George E. 1995. "Ethnography in/of the World System: The Emergence of Multi-Sited Ethnography," *Annual Review of Anthropology* 24: 95–117.

Marks, Stephen. 2006. "China in Africa – The New Imperialism?", *Pambazuka News* 244 (March 2) http://www.pambazuka.org/en/category/features/32432, accessed on February 2, 2012.

Maruyama, Masao. 2008. *Thought and Behavior in Modern Japanese Politics* (New York: ACLS Humanities E-Book).

Mearsheimer, John. 2010. "The Gathering Storm: China's Challenge to US Power in Asia," *The Chinese Journal of International Politics* 3: 381–96.

Medeiros, Evan S. 2009. *China's International Behavior: Activism, Opportunism, and Diversification* (Santa Monica: Rand), 49–50.

Meisner, Maurice. 1977. "Mao and Marx in the Scholastic Tradition," *Modern China* 3, 4: 401–06.

Meng, Hsiang-jui. 2009. *Dao xifang xie Zhongguo da lishi: Huang Renyu de weiguan jingyan yu ta de Zhongguo xue shequn* (Writing Chinese Macro-History for the "west": Ray Huang's Micro-Career and his China Studies Community) (Taipei: The Research and Educational Center for China Studies and Cross Taiwan-Strait Relations, Department of Political Science, National Taiwan University).

Ministry of Foreign Affairs. 2006. "China's African Policy," (January 12) http://www. fmprc.gov.cn/eng/zxxx/t230615.htm, accessed on February 3, 2012.

Miwa, Kimitada. 1968. "Fukuzawa Yukichi's 'Departure from Asia': A Prelude to the Sino-Japanese War," in E. Skrzypczak (ed.), *Japan's Modern Century* (Tokyo: Sophia University), 1–40.

Mizoguchi, Yuzo. 1989. *Hoho to shite no Chugok* (China as method) (Tokyo: Tokyō Daigaku Shuppankai).

Mizoguchi, Yuzo. 1999. *Zuowei fangfa de zhongguo* (China as Method), trans. Y. Lin (Taipei: National Institute for Compilation and Translation).

Mizoguchi, Yuzo. 2001. "A Search for the Perspective on the Studies of East Asia: Centering on Chinese Studies," *Sungkyun Journal of East Asian Studies* 1: 7–15.

Mizoguchi, Yuzo. 2001. "Chuangzao Ri Zhong zhishi gongtong kongjian" (Creating Shared Intellectual Space for Japan and China), *Dushu* 5: 3–11.

Mizoguchi, Yuzo. 2005. "A Search for the Perspective on the Studies of East Asia: Centering on Chinese Studies," *Sungkyun Journal of East Asian Studies* 1: 1 http://sjeas.skku.edu/backissue/issue_article.jsp?RNUM=1&SEQ=6, accessed on August 23, 2011.

Munro, Ross H. 1998. *The Coming Conflict with China* (New York: Vintage).

Nathan, Andrew. 1997. China's Transition (New York: Columbia University Press).

Ng-quinn, Michael. 1978. *China and International Systems: History, Structures and Processes*, Ph.D. dissertation, Harvard University.

Nguyen, Huy Quy. 2009. *The Oral History of Nguyen* (Taipei: The Research and Educational Center for China Studies and Cross Taiwan-Strait Relations, Department of Political Science, National Taiwan University) http://politics.ntu.edu.tw/RAEC/act/Vietnam_03C.doc, accessed on April 26, 2011.

Nishibe, Susumu. 2002. *Hanbei to iu sahō* (The Way to Resist America) (Tokyo: Shogakkan).

Noosgoi, Altantsetseg. 1985. *Mongolchuud Manjiin esreg erkh chuluunii tuluuh hudulguuniig BNHAU herhen uzej bui ni* (China's View of the Mongolian Movement for Freedom Against the Manchus) (Ulaanbaatar: Publisher, n.a.).

Nyamwana, Dismas. 2004. "Cross-cultural Adaptation African Students in China," *Ife PsychologIA* 12, 2: 10.

Nye, Joseph. 2006. "The Challenge of China," in Stephen Van Evera (ed.), *How to Make America Safe: New Policies for National Security* (Cambridge, MA: Tobin Project), 74.

O'Brien, Kevin. 1996. "Rightful Resistance," *World Politics* 49, 1: 31–55.

Odih, Pamela. 1999. "Gendered Time in the Age of Deconstruction," *Time and Society* 8, 1: 9–38.

Okada, Keisuke. 2006. Director and Managing Editor, and Sayuri Daimon, Director of the Paper's News Division, Interviewed by Victoria Yang (In the Reception Room of the *Japan Times*) (Tokyo: headquarters, December 11).

Ong, Granham Gerald. 2004. "Building an IR theory with 'Japanese Characteristics': Nishida Kitaro and 'Emptiness'," *Millennium* 33, 1: 35–58.

Paal, Douglas H. 2011. "China: Hu's State Visit an Opportunity," *Asia Pacific Brief* (January 3), http://carnegietsinghua.org/publications/?fa=42219, accessed on September 19, 2012.

Paltiel, Jeremy. 2011. "Constructing Global Order with Chinese Characteristics: Yan Xuetong and the Pre-Qin Response to International Anarchy," *Chinese Journal of International Politics* 4, 4: 375–403.

Pan, Wei and Ya Ma. 2010. *Renmin gongheguo liushi nian yu zhongguo moshi* (Sixty Years of the People's Republic and the Chinese Model) (Beijing: New Knowledge Sanlian).

Parkes, Graham. 1997. "The Putative Fascism of the Kyoto School," *Philosophy East and West* 47, 3.

Pfeffer, Richard M. 1976. "Mao and Marx in the Marxist-Leninist Tradition: A Critique of 'The China Field' and a Contribution to a Preliminary Reappraisal," *Modern China* 2, 4: 421–460.

Phan, Van Cac. 2009. *The Oral History of Phan* (Taipei: The Research and Educational Center for China Studies and Cross Taiwan-Strait Relations, Department of Political Science, National Taiwan University) http://politics.ntu.edu.tw/RAEC/act/Vietnam_04C.doc, accessed on November 22, 2011.

Phye, Gary D. 1997. *Handbook of Academic Learning: Construction of Knowledge* (Maryland Heights, MO: Academic Press).

Pye, Lucian. 1968. *The Spirit of Chinese Political Culture* (Cambridge, MA: MIT Press).

Pye, Lucian. 1990. "China: Erratic State, Frustrated Society," *Foreign Affairs* 69, 4 (Fall): 56–74.

Pye, Lucien. 1988. *The Mandarin and the Cadre: China's Political Culture* (Ann Arbor: The Center for Chinese Studies, University of Michigan).

Pye, Lucien. 1990. "China: Erratic State, Frustrated Society," *Foreign Affairs* 69, 4 (Fall): 56–74.

Rao, Aimin. 2011. "Hu, Aquino Agree to Downplay Maritime Disputes," *Xinhua* (September 1). http://www.china.org.cn/world/2011-09/01/content_23328684.htm, accessed on September 20, 2012

Reischauer, Edwin O. 1973/4. "Sinic World in Perspective," *Foreign Affairs* 52, 341–348.

Rocha, John. 2007. "A New Frontier in the Exploitation of Africa's Natural Resources: The Emergence of China," in Firoze Manji and Stephen Marks (eds.), *African Perspectives on China in Africa* (Oxford/Nairobi: Fahamu), 15–34.

Ruan (Nguyen) Huaiqiu. 2009. *Cong bianyuan kan daguo: Yuenan* Zhongguo yanjiu qikan *dui Yue Zhong guanxi de renshi* (Looking at the Major Power from the Periphery: Views on Vietnam-China Relations in the Vietnamese *Journal of China Studies*) (Taipei: The Research and Educational Center for China Studies and Cross Taiwan-Strait Relations, Department of Political Science, National Taiwan University).

Rui, He-chen. 2008. Interview conducted by Hsin-hsien Wang on various days in October. See http://politics.ntu.edu.tw/RAEC/act/tw-15.doc, accessed on August 29, 2011.

Saavedra, Martha. 2009. "Representations of Africa in a Hong Kong Soap Opera: The Limits of Enlightened Humanitarianism in *The Last Breakthrough*," *The China Quarterly* 199 (September): 744.

Sakai, Naoki. 1997. *Translation & Subjectivity: On "Japan" and Cultural Nationalism* (Minneapolis & London: University of Minnesota Press).

Sanyl, Kapyn, ed. 2007. *Rethinking Capitalist Development: Primitive Accumulation, Governmentality and Post-Colonial Capitalism* (New Delhi: Routledge).

Sautman, Barry and Yan Hairong. 2007. "Friends and Interests: China's Distinctive Links with Africa," *African Studies Review* 50, 3: 75–114.

Schubert, Gunter and Jens Damm, eds. 2011. *Taiwanese Identity in the 21st Century. Domestic, Regional and Global Perspective* (London and New York: Routledge).

Schurmann, Franz. 1965. *Ideology and Organization in Communist China* (Berkeley: University of California Press).

Shambaugh, David, Robert F. Ash, and Seiichirō Takagi, eds. 2007. *China Watching: Perspectives from Europe, Japan and the United States* (New York: Routledge).

Shams, M. and Kwang-kuo Hwang. 2005. "Special Issue on Responses to the Epistemological Challenges to Indigenous Psychologies," *Asian Journal of Social Psychology* 8, 1: 3–4.

Sharife, Khadija. 2009. "China's New Colonialism," *Foreign Policy* (September 25), http://www.foreignpolicy.com/articles/2009/09/25/chinas_new_colonialism?page=0,0, accessed on February 2, 2012.

Sheng, Banghe. 2002. "Wanshan Zhennan: chuantong yanhua yu wenhua de xiandaihua" (Maruyama Mazao: Evolution of Tradition and Modernization of Culture), *Riben xuekan* (The Journal of Japan Studies) 3, 113.

Shih, Chian-sheng. 2011. Interview conducted by Yuan-kui Chu on various days in March. See http://politics.ntu.edu.tw/RAEC/act/tw-16.doc, accessed on August 21, 2011.

Shih, Chih-yu. 1990. *The Spirit of Chinese Foreign Policy: A Psychocultural View* (London: Macmillan).

Shih, Chih-yu. 1995. *State and Society in China's Political Economy: The Cultural Dynamics of China's Socialist Reform* (Boulder: Lynne Rienner).

Shih, Chih-yu. 1997. "Responding to Globalization: Taiwanese Professional Women's Role in the Construction of China," Paper presented at the International Conference on Gender and Development in Asia, Hong Kong (November 29).

Shih, Chih-yu. 1998. "A Postcolonial Approach to the State Question in China," *The Journal of Contemporary China* 17, 7: 125–139.

Shih, Chih-yu. 1999. *Collective Democracy: Political and Legal Reform in China* (Hong Kong: The Chinese University of Hong Kong Press).

Shih, Chih-yu. 2000. "Between the Mosque and State," *Religion, State and Society* 28, 2: 197–211.

Shih, Chih-yu. 2001. "How Ethnic Is Ethnic Education: The Issue of School Enrollment in Meigu's Yi Community," *Prospect Quarterly* 2, 3 (July).

Shih, Chih-yu. 2002. "The Eros of International Politics: Madame Chiang Kai-shek and the Question of State in China," *Comparative Civilizations Review* 46 (Spring).

Shih, Chih-yu. 2002. *Negotiating Ethnicity in China: Citizenship as a Response to the State* (London: Routledge).

Shih, Chih-yu. 2003. *Navigating Sovereignty: World Politics Lost in China* (London: Palgrave).

Shih, Chih-yu. 2007. *Autonomy, Ethnicity and Poverty in Southwestern China: The State Turned Upside Down* (London: Palgrave).

Shih, Chih-yu. 2007. *Democracy Made in Taiwan: The "Success State" as a Political Theory* (Lanham: Lexington).

Shih, Chih-yu. 2010. "Taiwan as East Asia in Formation: Subaltern Appropriation of the Colonial Narratives," in Gunter Schubert and Jens Damm (eds.), *Taiwanese Identity in the 21st Century: Domestic, Regional and Global Perspective* (London and New York: Routledge).

Shih, Chih-yu. 2011. "China Studies That Defend Chineseness: The Im/possibility of China-centrism in the Divided Sino-phone World," in Reena Marwah and Swaran Singh (eds.), *Emerging China* (New Delhi: Routledge), 117–142.

Shih, Chih-yu. 2012. "Assigning Role Characteristics to China: The Role State Versus the Ego State," *Foreign Policy Analysis* 8, 1 (January): 71–91.

Shih, Chih-yu and Chun-liang Pao. 2012. "Studying Mainland/China in Taiwan: Politics of Knowledge and Knowledge of Politics," Paper presented at the Conference on Political Science: Retrospect and Prospect, the Institute of Political Science of Academia Sinica, Taipei (August 7).

Shih, Chih-yu and Yu-wen Chen, eds. 2012. *Tibetan Studies in Comparative Perspective* (London: Routledge).

Shih, Ming, unpublished interview with Yeh Hong-lin., cited in Chih-yu Shih and Chun-liang Pao, "Studying Mainland/China in Taiwan: Politics of Knowledge and Knowledge of Politics," presented at the Conference on Political Science: Retrospect and Prospect, the Institute of Political Science of Academia Sinica, August 7, 2012 (Taipei).

Shue, Vivienne. 1990. *The Reach of the State: Sketches of the Chinese Body Politic* (Stanford, CA: Stanford University Press).

Solomon, Richard. 1971. *Mao's Revolution and the Chinese Political Culture* (Berkeley: University of California Press).

Soni, Sharad and Reena Marwah. 2011. "Tibet as a Factor Impacting China Studies in India," *Asian Ethnicity* 12, 3 (October): 285–299.

Stalnaker, Robert C. 2010. *Our Knowledge of the Internal World* (Oxford: Oxford University Press).

Stanley, Jason. 2008. *Knowledge and Practical Interests* (Oxford: Oxford University Press).

State Council. 2011. *Xizang heping jiefang liushi zhounian* (The 60th Anniversary of Peaceful Liberation of Tibet) (Beijing: State Council).

Stehr, Nico and Volker Meja, eds. 2005. *Society and Knowledge: Contemporary Perspectives in the Sociology of Knowledge and Science* (Piscataway: Transaction Publishers).

Strauss, Julia C. 2009. "The Past in the Present: Historical and Rhetorical Lineages in China's Relations with Africa," *The China Quarterly* 199 (September): 777–795.

Suganimi, Himemi. 1989. *The Domestic Analogy and World Order Proposals* (Cambridge: Cambridge University Press).

Sun, Yat-sen. 1973. *Guo fu quan ji* (Comprehensive Collection of the National Father's Literature) 2. (China Cultural Service).

Sun, Ge. 1995. "Japan as Method," *Dushu* 3: 103–109.

Sun, Ge. 2001. "Wanshan zhennan de liangnan zhi jing" (The Condition of Dilemma of Maruyama Mazao) in Mazao Maruyama (ed.), *Riben zhengzhi sixiang shi yanjiu* (A Study of the History of Japanese Political Thought), trans. Sun and Wang (Beijing: Sanlian), 12–29.

Sun, Ge. 2001. *Yazhou yiwei zhe sheme—wenhua jian de "Riben"* (What could Asia imply?—"Japan" between cultures) (Taipei: Chyu-liu), 29–30.

Sun, Ge. 2003. *Zhuti misan de kongjian* (*The Space with Pervasive Subjectivities*) (Nanchang: Jiangxi Education Press).

Sun, Ge. 2005. *Zhunei Hao de bei lun* (The Irony of Takeuchi Yoshimi's Narratives) (Beijing: Peking University Press).

Sun,Ge. 2005. *Zhunei hao de beilun.* (The Dilemma of Takeuchi Yoshimi) (Beijing: Beijing University Press).

Sweezy, Paul M. and Charles Bettelheim. 1971. *On the Transition to Socialism* (New York: Monthly Review Press).

Takashi, Inoguchi. 2007. "Are there any Theories of International Relations in Japan?" *International Relations of Asia Pacific* 7, 3: 369–390.

Takeuchi, Yoshimi and Richard Calichman. 2005. *What Is Modernity? Writings of Takeuchi Yoshimi* (New York: Columbia University Press).

Tan, Chung. 1978. *China and Brave New World* (Durham, NC: Carolina Academic Press, North Carolina).

Tan, Chung. 2009. "caiyong diyuan wenming fangshi cujin zhong yin guanxi fazhan" (Taking a Geo-civilizational Approach to Improving Sino-Indian Relations Through), *Nan Ya Yanjiu Jikan* (South Asian Studies Quarterly) 2 (October 18): 1–9.

Tan, Chung and Patricia Uberoi, eds. 2009. *The Rise of Asian Giants: The Dragon-Elephant Tango* (New Delhi: Anthem Press).

Tan, Chung and Ravni Thakur. 1998. *Across the Himalayan Gap: An Indian Quest for Understanding China* (New Delhi: Indira Gandhi National Centre for the Arts).

Tanaka, Stefan. 1993. *Japan's Orient: Rendering Pasts into History* (Berkeley: University of California Press).

Tang, Shiping and Dapeng Ji. 2008. "zhongguo waijiao taolun zhong de zhongguo zhongxinzhuyi yu meiguo zhongxinzhuyi" (China-centrism and US-centrism in China's Diplomatic Narratives), *Shijie Jingjie yu zhengzhi* (World Economy and Politics) 12: 62–70.

Terrill, Ross. 2004. *The New Chinese Empire: And What It Means for the United States* (New York: Basic Books).

The White Paper on China's National Defense of. 2002. See http://news.xinhuanet.com/english/2002-12/10/content_654851.htm, accessed on December 20, 2011.

Thompson, Drew. 2010. "Think Again: China's Military," *Foreign Policy* (March/April), http://www.foreignpolicy.com/articles/2010/02/22/think_again_chinas_military?page=full, accessed on April 26, 2012.

Torajiro, Naito. 1949. *Zhongguo shixue shi* (The History of Chinese Historiography) (Tokyo: Kobundo).

Tsai, Bi-huei. 2008. "Rights Issues in China as Evidence for the Existence of Two Types of Agency Problems," *Issues & Studies* 44, 3: 43–70.

Tsai, Cheng-wen. "*Shan yong quanli pingheng gainian, tiaozheng wo guo duiwai celyue*" (Properly Using the Concept of Balance of Power, Adjusting the Foreign Policy of our Nation), *United Daily* (August 25): 2.

Tsai, Cheng-wen. 1977. *Hezi shidai guoji guanxi de tezhi: tixi, heping, zhanzheng* (The Characteristics of International Relations in the Nuclear Age: System, Peace, and War) (Taipei: no publisher).

Tsai, Ming-chin. 2009. *Huiyi wen ge: zai chaoyue yu zaixian jian de xuanze shiye* (Revisiting the Cultural Revolution: Taking a Position Between Transcendence and Re-presentation) (Taipei: The Research and Educational Center for China Studies and Cross Taiwan-Strait Relations, Department of Political Science, National Taiwan University), 172–175.

Tsuda, Soukichi. 1955. *What Is the Oriental Culture,* trans. Yasotaro Morri (Tokyo: Hokuseido Press).

Victor, Nee and Yang Cao. 2004. "Market Transition and the Firm: Institutional Change and Income Inequality in Urban China," *Management and Organizations Review* 1, 1: 23–56.

Vukovich, Daniel. 2011. *China and Orientalism: Western Knowledge Production and the PRC* (London: Routledge).

Wachman, Alan. 1994. *Taiwan: National Identity and Democratization* (Armonk, NY: M. E. Sharpe).

Walder, Andrew and Jean C. Oi, eds. 1999. *Property Rights and Economic Reform in China* (Stanford, CA: Stanford University Press).

Walder, Andrew G. 2002. "The Transformation of Contemporary China Studies, 1977–2002," in David L. Szanton (ed.), *The Politics of Knowledge: Area Studies and the Disciplines* (University of California Press/University of California International and Area Studies Digital Collection, Edited Volume #3, http://repositories.cdlib.org/uciaspubs/editedvolumes/3/8)

Wang, Chang-ling. 2009. Interview conducted by Chia-yi Wen, Summer. See http://politics.ntu.edu.tw/RAEC/comm2/InterviewTWang.doc, accessed on April 26, 2012.

Wang, Fei-ling. 1999. "Self-Image and Strategic Intentions: National Confidence and Political Insecurity" in Yong Deng and Fei-ling Wang (eds.), *In the Eyes of the Dragon: China Views the World* (Lanham, Boulder, New York & London: Rowman & Littlefield), 21–46.

Wang, Gungwu. 1959. *A Short History of Nanyang Chinese* (Singapore: Eastern Universities Press).

Wang, Gungwu. 1981. *Community and Nation: Essays on Southeast Asia and the Chinese* (Singapore: Heinemann Education Books).

Wang, Hongying and James N. Rosenau. 2009. "China and Global Governance," *Asian Perspective* 33, 3: 17–22.

Wang Ping, "Lun Ribenren 'Zhongguo guan' de lishi bianqian" (On the Historical Evolution of Japanese "Views on China"), *Riben Xuekan* (Journal of Japan Studies) 2: 33–47.

Wang, Shaoguang Yun-han Chu and Quansheng Zhao, eds. 2002. *Huaren shehui zhengzhi xue bentu yanjiu de lilun yu shijian* (Theory and Practice of Indigenous Political Science in Chinese Societies) (Taipei: Laurel Press).

Wang, Shaoguang. 2006. "Money and Autonomy: Patterns of Civil Society Finance and Their Implications," *Studies in Comparative International Development* 40, 4 (Winter): 3–29.

Wang, Shaoguang. *Failure of Charisma: The Cultural Revolution in Wuhan* (Oxford: Oxford University Press, 1995).

Wang, Yiwei. 2006. "Why Is Pax-Americana Impossible? Comparing Chinese Ancient World Order with Today's American World Order," Paper presented at the International Symposium on Civilizations and World Orders, Istanbul, Turkey (May 13).

Wang, Yizhou. 2011. *Chuangzaoxing jieru: Zhongguo waijiao xin quxiang* (Creative Involvement: New Orientations in Chinese Diplomacy) (Beijing: Peking University Press).

Weber, Max. 1951. *The Religion of China* (New York: Free Press).

Weng, (Byron) Sung-jan. 2009. Interview conducted by Chun-liang Pao, October 3, 2008, and February 23, http://politics.ntu.edu.tw/RAEC/act/tw-8.doc, accessed on August 28, 2011.

White, Gordon. 1993. *Riding the Tiger: The Politics of Economic Reform in Post-Mao China* (Stanford, CA: Stanford University Press).

Whiting, Allen S. 2001. "China's Use of Force, 1950–96, and Taiwan," *International Security*, 26, 2 (Autumn): 103–131.

Williams, David. 2000. "In Defense of the Kyoto School: Reflections on Philosophy, the Pacific War and the Making of a Post-White World," *Japan Forum*, 12, 2 (September): 143–156.

Williams, David. 2004. *Defending Japan's Pacific War: The Kyoto School Philosophers and Post-White Power* (London and New York: Routledge Curzon).

Williams, David. 2005. *Defending Japan's Pacific War: The Kyoto School Philosophers and Post-White Power* (London: RoutledgeCurzon).

Wong, John. 1999. "Southeast Asian Ethnic Chinese Investing in China," *EAI Working Paper* 15, East Asian Institute, Singapore.

Wong, John. 2003. The Rise of China: Bane or Boon to Southeast Asia," *Harvard Asia Quarterly* 7: 23–30.

Wong, John. 2004. "China's Economic Rise: Implications for East Asian Growth and Integration," *Bulletin on Asia-Pacific Perspective* 5: 31–44.

Wong, John. 2007. Interview with John Wong on November 5–9, at the Research and Educational Center for China Studies and Cross-Strait Relations of the Department of Political Science, National Taiwan University, See http://140.112.150.151/RAEC/act/Singapore-1.doc, accessed on April 30, 2010.

Wong, Jong, Rong Ma, and Ma Yang, eds. 1995. *China's Entrepreneurs* (Singapore: Times Academic Press).

Wu, Guoguang. 2011. "Politics against Science: Reflections on the Study of Chinese Politics in Contemporary China," *Journal of Chinese Political Science* 16, 3: 279–297.

Wu, Rwei-ren. 1999. "The Dialectics of the Motherland: A Note on Wen-kui Liao's Thought on Taiwan Nationalism," *Si yu yan* (Thought and Word) 37, 3 (Fall): 47–100.

Wu, Tsong-han. 2010. *Xizang wenti yanjiu shiye xia de Zhongguo renshi* (Views on China in Tibet Studies: Comparing the Indian and the Australian Literature) (Taipei: Research and Educational Center for China Studies and

Cross Taiwan-Strait Relations, Department of Political Science, National Taiwan University).

Wu, Yu-shan, Wen-cheng Lin, and Shui-ping Chiang. 1995. *Hou Deng shiqi dui dalu ji Taiwan de zhengdang* (The Impact of the Post-Deng Period on Mainland China and Taiwan) (Taipei: Tung-ta).

Xu, Jilin. 1988. "Yi Zhongguo wei fangfa, yi shijie wei mudi" (China as Method, the World as Destiny). *Guowai shehui kexue* 1: 54–58.

Xu, Shuisheng. 2000. "Wanshan Zhennan de Riben sixiang gu ceng lun chu tan" (Maruyama Mazao's Preliminary Thesis on the Ancient Layer of Japanese Thought), *Wuhan daxue xuebao* (Wuhan University Journal) (Humanities and Social Science Section) 53 (May): 327.

Yan, Shaodang. 2005. *Zhanhou liushi nian Ribenren de Zhongguo guan* (Japanese Views on China in the Sixty Years Since the War), *Riben yanjiu* (Japan Studies) 3: 1–11.

Yan, Xuetong. 2011. *Ancient Chinese Thought and Modern Chinese Power,* ed. Daniel Bell and Zhe Sun, trans. Edmund Ryden (Princeton: Princeton University Press).

Yang, Chung-fang. 1994. "Zhongguoren zhenshi jiti zhuyi ma?" (Are Chinese Really Collectivistic?), in Kuo-shu Yang and An-bang Yu (eds.), *Zhongguoren de jiazhi guan* 2 (Values of Chinese Societies II) (Taipei: Laureate Press), 321–434.

Yang, Dali L. 1998. *Calamity and Reform in China: State, Rural Society, and Institutional Change Since the Great Leap Famine* (Stanford, CA: Stanford University Press).

Yang, Jiechi. 2010. "Yang Jiechi chanshu qi dian zhuzhang bo xilali nan hai lun" (Yang Jiechi's Expounds Seven-Point Position to Rebut Hillary's Note on South China Sea). See http://dailynews.sina.com/bg/news/usa/uspolitics/chinapress/20100726/03191684304.html, accessed on August 1, 2010.

Yang, Kuo-shu. 1993. "women weisheme yao jianli Zhongguoren de bentu xinlixue?" (Why do we want to Establish Chinese Indigenous Psychology?) *Bentu xinlixue* (Indigenous Psychology) 1 (June): 6–88.

Yang, Kuo-shu. 1997. "Indigenising Westernised Chinese Psychology," in M. H. Bond (ed.), *Working at the Interface of Cultures: Eighteen Lives in Social Science* (London: Routledge), 62–76.

Yang, Victoria. 2007. *Pingfan wuqi de 1997: Riben shibao dui Zhongguo de qu jingqi baodao* (A Year of No Significance: Desensitizing Report on China in the *Japan Times* 1997), M.A. thesis, Institute of Political Science, National Sun Yat-sen University, July.

Yeh, Chih-cheng. 2009. Interview conducted by Yuan-kui Chu, November 11, November 18, and December 23, and December 30, 2010, cited in Shih and Pao, "Studying Mainland/China in Taiwan: Politics of Knowledge and Knowledge of Politics," presented at the Conference on Political Science: Retrospect and Prospect, the Institute of Political Science of Academia Sinica, August 7, 2012 (Taipei).

Yeh, Hong-lin. 2009. *Following the Footsteps of the Empire: Tokutomi Soho's Perspectives on China* (Taipei: Research and Educational Center of Mainland China Studies and Cross-strait Relations).

Yin, Jinwu. 2011. "*wenhua yu guoji xinren—jiyu dong ya xinren xingcheng de bijiao fenxi*" (Culture and International Trust: A Comparative Analysis of Trust Formation in East Asia) *Waijiao pinglun* (Diplomatic Review) 4: 21–39.

Yoshimi, Takeuchi. 2000. *Jindai de chaoke* (Overcoming of Modernity), trans., Dongmu Li, Jinghua Zhao, and Ge Sun (Beijing: Sanlian).

Yu, Tzong-Shian. 2009. Interview conducted by Chi-nien Wang, January 17, March 17, and May 30. See http://politics.ntu.edu.tw/RAEC/act/tw-13.doc, accessed on August 23, 2011.

Zhang, Qingmin. 2006. *Meiguo dui Tai jun shou zhengce yanjiu: juece de shijiao* (A Study of U.S. Policy on Arms Sales to Taiwan: The Perspective of Decision Making) (Beijing: World Knowledge Press).

Zhang, Weiwei. 2012. *The China Wave: Rise of a Civilizational State* (Singapore: World Scientific).

Zhao, Hongwei. 2010. "*zhong mian bianjie weni de jiejue: guocheng yu yingxiang*" (The Settlement of the China-Burma Border Dispute: Course and Impact), *Nanyang wenti yanjiu* (Southeast Asian Affairs) General Serial 143 or No. 3: 37–40.

Zhao, Quansheng. 1990. "Achieving Maximum Advantage: Rigidity and Flexibility in Chinese Foreign Policy," Paper presented at the American Political Science Association Annual Meeting, San Francisco (September 1).

Zhao, Quansheng. 1995. "Achieving Maximum Advantage: Rigidity and Flexibility in Chinese Foreign Policy," *American Asian Review* 13, 1 (Spring), 61–93.

Zhao, Suisheng. 2004. *A Nation-State by Construction: Dynamics of Modern Chinese Nationalism* (Stanford, CA: Stanford University Press).

Zhao, Suisheng, ed. 2006. *Debating Political Reform in China: Rule of Law Versus Democratization* (Armonk, N.Y: M. E. Sharpe).

Zhao, Tingyang. 2006. "Rethinking Empire from a Chinese Concept 'All-under-Heaven' (Tian-xia)," *Social Identities* 12, 1 (January): 29–41.

Zhao, Tingyang. 2009. "A Political World Philosophy in Terms of All-Under-Heaven (Tian-xia)," *Diogenes* 56, 1: 5–18.

Zheng, Yongnian. 1999. *Discovering Chinese Nationalism in China: Modernization and International Relations* (New York: Cambridge University Press).

Zheng, Yongnian. 1999. "Political Incrementalism: Political Lessons from Chinas Twenty Years of Reform," presented at the Conference on PRC Reform at 20: Retrospect and Prospects, Taipei (April 8–9).

Zheng, Yongnian. 2009. "Society Must Be Defended: Reform, Openness and Social Policy in China," *EAI Working Papers* 152.

Zheng, Yongnian. 1999. *Discovering Chinese Nationalism in China: Modernization, Identity, and International Relations* (Cambridge: Cambridge University Press).

Zheng, Yongnian and John Wong, eds. 2004. *The SARS Epidemic: Challenges to China's Crisis Management* (Singapore and London: World Scientific).

Zhou, Min. 2011. "Meeting Strangers in a Globalized City: Chinese Attitudes toward Black Africans in Guangzhou China," presented at Wah Ching Centre of Research on Education in China, Hong Kong (June 15).

Zhou, Weijia. 2001. "Haiyang Riben lun de zhengzhihua si chao jiqi pingjia" (Sea Power Japan Theory and its Impact on Trends of Japan's Development), *Riben xuekan* (The Journal of Japan Studies) 2: 35–49.

Zhu, Tianbiao. 2012. "Compressed Development, Flexible Politics, Informal Practices, and Multiple Traditions in China's Economic Ascent," in K. Katzenstein (ed.), *Sinicization and the Rise of China* (Routledge: London).

Index